# The
# Lost
# Land

# THE
# LOST
# LAND

## THE CHICANO IMAGE
## OF THE SOUTHWEST

*John R. Chávez*

University of New Mexico Press
*Albuquerque*

To My Father,
*who first informed me that*
*California had once belonged to Mexico*

Library of Congress Cataloging in Publication Data

Chavez, John R., 1949–
    The lost land.

Bibliography: p.
    Includes index.
    1. Mexican Americans—Southwest, New—Attitudes.
    2. Mexican Americans—Southwest, New—History.
    3. Mexican Americans—Southwest, New—Ethnic identity.
    4. Southwest, New—History. 5. Southwest, New—Ethnic
    relations. I. Title.
    F790.M5C49    1984        979'.0046872        84-11950

Manufactured in the United States of America.
International Standard Book Number (clothbound) 0-8263-0749-3.
International Standard Book Number (paperbound) 0-8263-0750-7.
*First edition*

# Contents

# Acknowledgments

For their assistance I would like to thank the staffs of the libraries at the University of Michigan, the University of Southern California, and California State University, Los Angeles. Also, I am especially grateful to the personnel and for the collections at the Henry E. Huntington Library, the Chicano Resource Center of the East Los Angeles Public Library, and the Chicano Research Library of the University of California, Los Angeles.

I am, of course, indebted to Charles Gibson, David J. Weber, Thomas H. Flory, John O. King, James McIntosh, and Carlos H. Arce, all of whom offered invaluable suggestions for the improvement of the manuscript. Needless to say, the members of my family also deserve my thanks for their help: Linda and Manny for the initial typing, Carmela for the reading, and my mother and father for everything. Finally, I appreciate the kindness of everyone else who in one way or another contributed to the completion of my work.

# Introduction

## *The Chicano Homeland*

To the Anglo-American majority of the United States, the Southwest is vaguely identified as that group of states located at the corner of the country toward Mexico. Whether laymen or scholars, few Anglo-Americans agree on exactly which states the region comprises or what its characteristics are.[1] Chicanos, however, the region's Spanish-surnamed population, have a clearer image of the Southwest: to them, the Southwest is home, a land including California, Arizona, New Mexico, Texas, and Colorado, the states where 85 percent of U.S. citizens of Mexican descent reside.[2] But to Chicanos the Southwest is more than just their place of residence; it is their homeland, their lost homeland to be more precise, the conquered northern half of the Mexican nation.

Before the war between the United States and Mexico, which ended in 1848, present-day California, Texas, Nevada, Utah, Arizona, New Mexico, more than half of Colorado (the southern and western portions of the state), the Oklahoma Panhandle, and the southwestern corners of Wyoming and Kansas were all parts of Mexico's national territory. In the mind of the Chicanos, this immense territory remains their patrimony although they inhabit in significant numbers only five of the states mentioned.[3] Because of Mexico's prior possession of the Southwest, Chicanos consider themselves indigenous to the region. Their claims are supported by the fact that their ancestors not only explored and settled parts of the Southwest as early as the sixteenth century, but thousands of years earlier permanently occupied the region or migrated through it on their way south. The belief that the Southwest (especially the areas long settled by Mexicans) is the Chicano homeland and the belief that Mexicans are indigenous to and dispossessed of the region are beliefs that have had a formative and continuing influence on the collective Chicano mind.[4]

Within the individual Chicano mind the image of the Southwest is in the most literal sense a picture of a particular barrio street, of a specific rural adobe, of a particular brown child, or any number of other sensory percep-

1

tions that are peculiar to the Chicano's Southwest. This factual picture almost always possesses an emotional quality, a quality that often makes the perception to an extent fictitious. Thus, the picture of the child may include a smile that suggests happiness when in fact he may be sad. Every Chicano has at least such a perception of the Southwest. Of course, among the more experienced, the more traveled, the more educated, the image of the Southwest becomes more complex and abstract; it becomes a myth; yet its essence can always be translated into a picture, albeit of greater detail.[5] Thus a Chicano professor might picture a wall map of Mexico in the 1830s, a map suggesting Mexican control over territory dominated by Apaches. At its most sophisticated, the collective Chicano image of the Southwest and other ideas concerning such matters as race and culture together form a guiding myth that has affected Chicano history from earliest times to the present. Aspects of this myth can be traced from the chronicles of the Aztecs, through the Spanish-language newspapers of the 1850s, to the literature and social thought of Chicanos in the 1980s.

Because Chicanos have a distinct myth of the Southwest, many differences have arisen with Anglo-Americans (whites) concerning the character of the region. Anglos see the Southwest within a larger picture, the image of the American West or, as Henry Nash Smith has named it, the myth of the Virgin Land. "One of the most persistent generalizations," wrote Smith in 1950, "concerning American life and character is the notion that our society has been shaped by the pull of a vacant continent drawing population westward through the passes of the Alleghenies, across the Mississippi Valley, over the high plains and mountains of the Far West to the Pacific Coast."[6] Clearly this myth contradicts the Chicano view of the Southwest in several respects. First, of course, is the Anglos' image of the West as vacant before their arrival; Chicanos can hardly accept this since their predecessors had already founded such cities as San Antonio, Santa Fe, Tucson, and Los Angeles well before the appearance of Anglo-Americans. Second, such regional designations as "Far West," and, of course, "Southwest" itself, are applied from the perspective of the Anglo-American cultural centers on the Atlantic Seaboard. These designations certainly do not correspond to the Chicano picture since Chicanos view their region (despite their practical use of the term "Southwest") from the perspective of their cultural center in Mexico City. Furthermore, the current of their history has flowed south and north, not east to west.

As a result of this perspective, Chicanos view the Southwest as an extension of Mexico and Latin America, a Mexican region spreading beyond what is regarded as an artificial international boundary. Geographically, in fact, the Southwest does resemble the Mexican deserts and highlands more closely than it does the plains and woodlands of the eastern United States. To this familiar southwestern terrain the cultural influence of Mexico City has radiated for over three hundred years. Coastal California from San Diego to San Francisco, Arizona's Santa Cruz Valley from Tubac to Tucson, the Rio Grande Valley from El Paso to the New Mexico–Colorado state line, and South Texas including the lower Rio Grande and San Antonio—these four areas, formerly composing the far northern borderlands of New Spain, have been continuously Mexican in culture and population since before the United States imposed the present boundary on Mexico. And despite the invasion of the Anglos and their subsequent cultural dominance, Mexican culture today extends to other parts of the Southwest, wherever Chicanos have pushed out the margins of the old borderlands. In California, Chicanos have taken their culture into the Central and Imperial valleys; in Arizona, to Yuma and Phoenix; in Texas, to Houston and Dallas; and in Colorado many Chicanos have even settled in Denver beyond the lands of the Mexican Cession of 1848. Given this geography, it is small wonder that Chicanos and Anglos perceive the Southwest differently.[7]

The Chicano myth, however, does bear important similarities to the Native American image of the United States. Both Indians and Chicanos see themselves as indigenous to and dispossessed of their homelands, which in the Southwest means they claim the same territory. Nevertheless, in the twentieth century these overlapping claims have caused little conflict, for Anglos have simply possessed the land; instead these claims have led the two minorities to recognize that they have common backgrounds. In 1971 Armando Rendón, a Chicano journalist, acknowledged just that point:

> We maintain that there exist blood and cultural bonds to the land of the Southwest; we do not deny the Indian peoples' claims to the land. We believe we have had at least a share in its perpetuation through the hands of those who originally worked the land and who have historical claims to it. This issue of land and its relationship to the Chicano should be discussed with Indian tribesmen. . . . Chicanos have a blood relationship to our Indian forebears. Descendants of early Spanish colonists who reject such an alliance with the Indian natives of the Americas also reject the most obvious claim to the retribution for the misdeeds committed by the Anglos who stole the land.[8]

That knowledgeable Native Americans recognize such Chicano claims is evident from the following statement made in 1973 by Jack D. Forbes, a Native American scholar:

> The Aztecas del norte (an Azteca is a person of Aztlán or the "Southwest") com-
> pose the largest single tribe or nation of Anishinabeg (Indians) found in the
> United States today. . . . Some call themselves Chicanos and see themselves as
> people whose true homeland is Aztlán.

Since Chicanos are racially 70 to 80 percent Indian, they do indeed have much in common with Native Americans, a fact that must be considered in discussions of claims to the Southwest.[9]

Along with race, culture, and historical experience, the Chicanos' image of the Southwest is an important element in the overall self-image, the self-identity, of that people. Interacting with other elements of their self-identity, the Chicanos' regional myth not only distinguishes that minority from Anglos, but separates them from Mexicans south of the border. Unlike Mexican nationals, Chicanos see the Southwest more readily than Mexico as their homeland, and consequently picture themselves more readily as a people of that region than of Mexico. While they generally remain the same mestizo (racially mixed Indian and Spanish) people as Mexicans to the south, the Chicanos' view of themselves as distinct has merit because their residence in the Southwest has greatly modified their history and culture. Even though the boundary between the United States and Mexico is artificial in many respects, that boundary does make the Southwest a predominantly Anglo cultural region. This fact has led Chicanos to incorporate so many Anglo traits into their basic Mexican culture that a distinct way of life has emerged. While Mexico remains the homeland in the sense of a motherland—a cultural source and a nation of origin (be that the present republic or the republic at its greatest extent)—the Southwest is the present home of Chicanos, a home that since 1848 has helped make them what they are.

The Chicanos' present view of the Southwest had its beginning in 1848, as did their current self-image. In that year, on signing the Treaty of Guadalupe Hidalgo, Mexico surrendered the region and most of its inhabitants to the United States. Before that the Mexican view of the region, as far back as the sixteenth-century Aztec chronicles, had been focused on the feature of the homeland; the earliest Spanish conquistadores had, of course, seen the borderlands as foreign conquests, but their mestizo descendants came to call the region home. After the Anglo-American invasion, however, the Mexican image of the region incorporated the feature of the lost land, and Mexicans in the Southwest soon viewed themselves as a conquered people. Thus, though modified with time, the picture of the lost homeland came into being and was handed down to the present.

Over the last 130 years the myth of the lost land has served as a focus for

Mexican nationalism in the Southwest. Though sometimes evoking defeatism, the myth has more often roused the pride of Southwest Mexicans, reminding them of their long history in and prior rights to the region.[10] Indeed these rights have formed the foundation for claims of many kinds against U.S. society. Over the decades the region's Mexicans have defended their language, customs, property, freedom of movement, and their very dignity on the basis of their rights as a native people, as well as their rights as citizens. Those Mexicans living outside the region, both in the rest of the United States and Mexico, have also made legitimate claims against U.S. society based on the seizure of the Southwest from the Mexican nation as a whole. Yet the greatest significance of the myth of the lost land has been the recurring hope for the recovery of that territory in one form or another. In the late 1960s this deep wish reappeared in repeated Chicano allusions to the ancient Aztec homeland of Aztlán, traditionally located in the Southwest. Noting this phenomenon, Armando Rendón commented:

> The concept of Aztlán is undergirded by a desire for restitution of the land of Aztlán. The Chicano does not wish to have merely an empty dream. Just as for other displaced peoples in the world's history, the cry of the land is keen in our ears; we, too, have had title to the land which was violently taken from us. Geography and culture make the vision of a new state for the Chicano not quite so wild an idea; the direct roots we have sunk into the land can burgeon once more.[11]

The desire of Southwest Mexicans for recovery of the region has always been tied to their desire for cultural, political, and economic self-determination, a self-determination they believe can only be achieved through control of the space they occupy. The story of the struggle for that environment is central to Chicano history.[12]

# 1

## Aztlán, Cíbola,
## and Frontier New Spain

The distant ancestors of Chicanos and other indigenous American peoples arrived in the Western Hemisphere in small groups beginning from forty to seventy thousand years ago. Since by that time human beings had existed in the Old World for millions of years already, the discovery of the Americas was clearly the finding of a "New World," and the discoverers would certainly have been justified in viewing it as a "Virgin Land." Over the millennia the descendants of the first arrivals spread south from the point of entry, at what we now call the Bering Strait, to the tip of South America, where they arrived about 11,000 B.C.[1] During this migration, of course, countless groups broke off from the general movement south to establish themselves in local areas, which in time became their homelands. Despite the occurrence of these events in prehistoric times, this migration through and occupation of the Americas would later form an important part of the Chicanos' image of themselves as a native people of the Southwest, their ancient, as well as modern homeland. Because Chicanos would know their Native American ancestry by the color of their own skin, they could be sure that their forefathers had in the distant past crossed over from Siberia and moved south. And on their way south generations of these ancestors would necessarily have entered the Southwest, inhabited it permanently, or occupied it temporarily before moving on to Mexico proper.

These early ancestors probably had no conception of the Southwest on the scale visualized by their descendants. Southwestern cultures from earliest times until after the coming of the Europeans undoubtedly regarded their particular territories as sacred lands that provided sustenance as well as space,[2] but these homelands were always local areas corresponding to specific tribes. Since the Indian tribes of the Southwest were never united,[3] they most likely perceived the region as a whole about as much as modern man would perceive the world as a whole. The conception of the region as such began from a distant perspective, from central Mexico after the arrival of Cortés in 1519. Even though the history of Chicanos already lay deep in the Southwest itself,

7

their modern image of the region would develop from the perspective of Mexico City.

After taking Tenochtitlán (Mexico City) in 1521, the Spanish looked to the north for new lands to conquer and projected their own myths onto the unknown region that was to become the Southwest. They imagined that to the north there was a rich land of warrior women, that in that direction there were silver cities, or that at the very least the unexplored region touched on a waterway that would link Europe to the wealth of the Orient. All these myths manifested Edenic aspects which when viewed together formed the first general myth of the Southwest as a whole—the myth of the region as a land of golden promise. While this image was the invention of the foreign Spaniards, it soon influenced and was influenced by Indians both in the north and in central Mexico. The Indians on the northern frontier, probably to encourage the Spanish to move on to other areas, sometimes agreed with the invaders' conceptions of the region and elaborated on them. In this way the European legend of the Seven Cities of Silver, which led to Spain's exploration of the Southwest, became the native legends of the Seven Cities of Cíbola and the riches of Quivira.

In central Mexico the Spanish myth of the golden northern land aroused interest in the legend of Aztlán, the Edenic place of origin of the Mexica (the Aztecs). Aztlán, meaning either "land of the herons" or "land of whiteness," was an old name by Cortés' arrival. According to their own histories, the Aztecs had left that homeland, located somewhere in the north, in 1168 and journeyed to the lakes where in 1325 they founded Tenochtitlán.[4] After the Spanish conquest Indian, mestizo, and Spanish chroniclers, relying on native informants, recorded the legend of Aztlán along with the rest of the history of the Aztecs. However, in their histories the chroniclers, influenced by the myth of the golden north, placed Aztlán in the Southwest; in fact it was probably in Nayarit, only four hundred miles northwest of Mexico City. This error would later lead Chicanos to refer to the Southwest as Aztlán, an application of the name that would, nevertheless, be paradoxically appropriate.

By the middle of the seventeenth century the Edenic picture of the north had disappeared at least from the minds of the authorities in Mexico City. By then the region was seen as a series of frontier outposts established to defend central New Spain from northern intruders. On the other hand, Spanish missionaries still viewed the borderlands as golden areas of opportunity for spiritual conquest and agricultural development. But most significant for the future Chicano image of the Southwest was the increasingly popular belief among the settlers that the region was their homeland. To be more exact, the *descendants* of the first settlers apparently came to perceive the land in that way—

especially by the late eighteenth century. Since most of the settlers from the very beginning had been Indians and mestizos from central New Spain and had intermarried with the northern natives, it was not surprising that they eventually pictured the borderlands as home, much as their indigenous ancestors had perceived their own northern tribal lands.

The oldest evidence of these ancestors in the Southwest has been found in Texas and dates back to about 35,000 B.C. Some of the earliest evidence of a clearly distinguishable culture has been found in southern Arizona and dates back to about 8,000 B.C.[5] Significantly, according to anthropological studies of Indian languages, social organization, material culture, and origin myths, the Cochise culture of southern Arizona was the parent culture of peoples as far apart as the Ute of Colorado and the Aztec of the Valley of Mexico.[6] The ancestral Cochise people apparently spoke the language from which the Uto-Aztecan linguistic family derives. In addition to the Ute, the Gabrielino of California, the Pima of Arizona, some of the Pueblo peoples of New Mexico, the Comanche of Texas, and many other southwestern tribes have spoken Uto-Aztecan languages and probably descend from the Cochise people. In Mexico, besides the Aztec, Uto-Aztecan tribes include the Opata of Sonora, the Tarahumara of Sinaloa and Durango, the Huichol of Jalisco, and many others, forming an almost unbroken line from the Southwest to Mexico City. This together with other cultural evidence indicates that at about 1,000 B.C. descendants of the original Cochise people migrated south and became the direct ancestors of many of the Mexican people.[7] Thus, while Aztlán, the Aztecs' homeland of 1168, was relatively close to Mexico City, their more distant homeland in both time and space was in the Southwest.

Contact between the Southwest and the Valley of Mexico increased after 1,000 B.C. because just as Uto-Aztecan speakers were moving south, the technology of maize cultivation was moving north. The introduction of maize to the Southwest from Mexico led to the replacement of the hunting-and-gathering Cochise culture by the sedentary cultures of the Mogollon, Hohokam, Anasazi, and Pueblos. These cultures, which overlapped a great deal in time and space from about 300 B.C., existed largely in Arizona and New Mexico but also across the present border in Sonora and Chihuahua. As time passed, communication in the form of indirect trade became common throughout the Southwest and Mexico, and the cultural influence of the civilizations of central Mexico became dominant. After introducing squash, beans, and irrigation methods to the Southwest, the peoples of central Mexico—especially the Teotihuacanos, Toltecs, and Aztecs, from A.D. 200 to 1520—had an important impact on cloth making, pottery, architecture, and government in the region to the north.[8] Interestingly, the Indians of both the Southwest and Mexico reached their cultural high points at roughly the same time, between A.D. 900 and 1520. Clearly even in ancient times the Southwest was an extension of Mexico.

This interconnection became more pronounced with the capture of Tenochtitlán by the Spanish under Hernán Cortés in 1521. Though the Southwest had felt the effects of the rise and fall of Mexican cultures for two thousand years, the founding of New Spain would lead to closer ties than ever before between that northern region and the Valley of Mexico. While many of these new ties would be provided by a foreign European power, many others would be renewals of ties that had already existed for thousands of years. The most important of the renewed bonds would be racial, for as the Spanish expanded toward the north, they would be accompanied by central Mexican Indians more numerous than the conquerers themselves.

The importance of Spain's Indian allies for the expansion and unification of New Spain can hardly be exaggerated since it was as much they as the Spaniards who toppled the Aztecs. Anthropologist Eric Wolf has convincingly argued the importance of these allies to the capture of Tenochtitlán:

> [Cortés] enlisted on his side rulers and peoples who had suffered grievously at the hands of their Mexica enemies. . . . Spanish firepower and cavalry would have been impotent against the Mexica armies without the Tlaxcaltec, Texcocans and others who joined the Spanish cause. They furnished the bulk of the infantry and manned the canoes that covered the advance of the brigantines across the lagoon of Tenochtitlán. They provided, transported, and prepared the food supplies needed to sustain an army in the field. They maintained lines of communication between coast and highland, and they policed occupied and pacified areas. They supplied the raw materials and muscular energy for the construction of the ships that decided the seige of the Mexica capital. Spanish military equipment and tactics carried the day, but Indian assistance determined the outcome of the war.[9]

Just as the demolition of the Aztec state had been accomplished by an alliance of Spaniards and Indians, the creation of New Spain, racially and culturally, would be the accomplishment of these two groups and their descendants, the mestizos. This would be as true in the northern borderlands as in the center of the viceroyalty. Later this fact would lead to much uncertainty in the Chicanos' image of themselves in both Mexico and the Southwest, for being descendants of both conquered Indians and conquering Spaniards and Indians, Chicanos would vacillate between a self-identity as foreigners and a self-identity as natives.

The fall of Tenochtitlán was only the beginning of a series of explorations and conquests that was to expand New Spain. From the ruins of the Aztec capital, expeditions moved out in all directions, and interest in the distant north was soon aroused. Although the coast of present Texas had been sighted by Spaniards as early as 1519,[10] some of the more exciting news concerning territory that was probably within today's Southwest was heard in 1524. In *De Orbe Novo,* one of the earliest European histories of the New World, Peter Martyr wrote that when a group of Spanish explorers was

> wandering through the region that separates the great Panuco River from the Rio de las Palmas [along the Gulf Coast, two hundred miles south of Texas], they enquired of the natives what existed beyond the lofty mountains [the Sierra Madre Oriental] which bounded the horizon. . . . They answered that beyond those mountains existed vast plains and great cities ruled by warlike caciques [chiefs].[11]

To look beyond the mountains, the Spaniards had to look west or northwest; in both directions there were plains and deserts, and the only "cities" unknown to Spaniards in those directions were the Pueblo villages of New Mexico, a thousand miles to the northwest. While the coastal Indians may actually have heard of the Pueblos, it is possible they were giving the Spaniards a golden picture of distant lands just to get them to leave.

During the sixteenth century, especially after the conquest of the fabulously wealthy empire of the Aztecs, Spaniards were quite willing to believe any tale of golden lands, whether they heard these tales from Indians or read them in books. Consequently, in their minds the unknown north was filled with mythical peoples and cities surrounded by riches. A few years after his capture of Tenochtitlán, Cortés wrote, regarding the Mexican coast across from present Baja California,

> I am told that down the coast [meaning "to the north," since his expeditions went in that direction] . . . are many provinces . . . where, it is believed, are great riches and that in these parts of it there is one which is inhabited by women, without a single man, who have children in the way which the ancient histories ascribe to the Amazons.[12]

In a letter to Charles V, Cortés remarked that he was given this report by the Indian "lords of the province of Ciguatán [country of women]."[13] Since no such place existed, clearly the Spanish were projecting images derived from Greek mythology onto a real landscape, and most likely these images were simply being reflected by the Indians.

Interestingly, a novel involving Amazons, entitled *Las sergas de Esplandián* by Garcí Ordóñez de Montalvo, had been popular in Spain since 1510. This romance spoke of an island of gold called California ruled by an Amazon queen named Calafia, and located "on the right hand of the Indies . . . very near the Earthly Paradise. . . ." That the Spaniards took their reading literally is evident since one expedition after another went into the northwest seeking the realization of this fantasy. At first the explorers went by land up the western coast of the Mexican mainland, and then they went by sea. By 1535, Cortés himself had landed on the shore of present Baja California, and the peninsula received the name of Montalvo's imaginary island. Juan Rodríguez Cabrillo carried the name north when he led the first Spanish expedition to the coast of present California in 1542. Although Cabrillo encountered no Amazons in the northwest, the impact of those mythical women on the Spanish mind was such that in South America during the same decade, one Spaniard actually claimed to have seen a tribe of female warriors along what he named the Amazon River.[14]

Ever seeking golden lands, the Spaniards chased more than one dream into the distant north. They had barely entered Tenochtitlán in 1519 when they first heard mention of the Aztecs' wondrous land of origin, Aztlán. The description and legend of this place were preserved in the oral tradition and pictorial manuscripts of the Mexica during their rule; after the conquest Spanish chroniclers relied on these sources when they wrote histories of the Indians for the information of the king and church. In one such history, entitled *Historia de las Indias de Nueva España* (1579–81), Fray Diego Durán provided a vivid picture, derived from native informants, of this place called Aztlán:

> Our forebears dwelt in that blissful, happy place called Aztlan, which means "Whiteness." In that place there is a great hill in the midst of the waters, and it is called Colhuacan because its summit is twisted; this is the Twisted Hill. On its slopes were caves or grottos where our fathers and grandfathers lived for many years. There they lived in leisure, when they were called Mexitin and Azteca. There they had at their disposal great flocks of ducks of different kinds, herons, water fowl, and cranes. . . . They also possessed many kinds of large beautiful fish. They had the freshness of groves of trees along the edge of the waters. They had springs surrounded by willows, evergreens and alders, all of them tall and comely. Our ancestors went about in canoes and made floating gardens upon which they sowed maize, chilli, tomatoes, amaranth, beans and all kinds of seeds which we now eat and which were brought here from there.[15]

Such an Edenic description must certainly have excited the imaginations of the Spaniards, and after seeing the gold of Tenochtitlán, they must certainly have assumed the wealth of Aztlán to be in precious metals as well as in flora and fauna. The water imagery of this description indicates that Aztlán was in a semitropical location, and early sixteenth-century pictorial manuscripts place the Aztec homeland on an island.[16] Equipped with such descriptive details and having been told that Aztlán lay to the northwest, the Spanish sought that place where they sought the Amazons—along the Pacific coast of the Mexican mainland. In 1530, about four hundred miles northwest of Mexico City, the conquistador Nuño de Guzmán encountered a place called Aztatlán, whose name and environment resembled those of the legendary Aztlán. Though the evidence indicated (and still indicates) that Aztatlán and Aztlán were one and the same place, it must have seemed too mundane a location for a land that had been idealized to the point of a paradise on earth. Furthermore, storytellers had recounted that in Aztlán there were caves, specifically the Seven Caves, the totemic shrines of the Aztec clans. Since these caves had not been found in Aztatlán, the Spanish decided Aztlán must be farther to the north.[17]

As a consequence, in 1538 Juan de la Ascunción and Pedro Nadal, two Franciscan friars, set out in search of Chicomoztoc, another name for Aztlán meaning "place of the seven caves." Together with their Indian porters, these explorers marched west from Mexico City to the coast, then to the distant north, possibly as far as the Colorado River, which today forms the boundary between Arizona and California. If they actually went that far, they may have been the first formal expedition to reach the Southwest by land. In any case they were the first to seek Aztlán in that vicinity, and their search would lead to the centuries-old myth that Aztlán was in the Southwest. More than anything else, their expedition caused the image of the Aztec homeland to become the first known Native American image to be applied to the region as a whole. While the friars found no signs of the Seven Caves, on their return they reported hearing word from the Indians of great cities farther north—thus keeping alive the myth of the Southwest as a land of golden promise.[18]

Ascunción and Nadal had not been the first to hear of cities in the distant north. As we have seen, such news had been heard by Spaniards as early as 1524 on the coast south of Texas. Moreover, in 1536 Alvar Núñez Cabeza de Vaca had made similar reports from the same area the friars visited in 1538 (in fact his reports were partially responsible for their journey). In an almost unbelievable adventure, Cabeza de Vaca had set sail in 1528, had been marooned on the Florida shore, had sailed by raft along the Gulf of Mexico, and had landed on the Texas coast. From there he and a few companions had wandered across the width of what is now Texas, traveled along the present border between Mexico and New Mexico, and then turned south for six hundred miles before reaching a Spanish outpost on the Gulf of California. There they finally came back into contact with other Europeans. As a result of this journey, Cabeza de Vaca became the first European to explore extensively the territory of the Southwest, and his observations were eagerly noted in Mexico City. [19]

Somewhere near modern El Paso, Indians had presented Cabeza de Vaca with arrowheads and other gifts, some made of turquoise, a stone common in the present Santa Fe area of New Mexico. "These [arrowheads] looked quite valuable," Cabeza de Vaca later reported. "I asked where they came from. They said from lofty mountains to the north, where there were towns of great population and great houses." He had received the first definite information to reach the Spanish concerning the Pueblo Indians. Interestingly, Cabeza de Vaca's report was simple; he gave a straightforward account of what the Indians had said. Having seen a great deal of the Southwest and having encountered little that resembled civilization, Cabeza de Vaca was less likely than other Spaniards to cherish a fantasy of golden cities in the region. And having lived among Indians for years, he was also less likely to misunderstand or be misled by the stories they told. Cabeza de Vaca did indeed understand that the new land had potential for wealth, but that wealth would be in mines, rather than treasure rooms:

> The people who made it [a copper material] lived in fixed dwellings. We conceived the country they spoke of to be on the South Sea [the Pacific was thought to be quite close], which we had always understood was richer in mineral resources than that of the North [the Atlantic]. [20]

Naturally, Cabeza de Vaca's return from the wilderness caused excitement in Mexico City, and the less he said about the north, the more exaggerated became its image. People linked all sorts of fables with the north, the most common of which was the legend of the Seven Cities. According to the legend, sometime in the Middle Ages seven Portuguese bishops had fled the advancing Moors and founded the Seven Cities of Antilia or Silver in a land across the Atlantic. When the Spaniards arrived in the New World, they brought the legend, as can be seen in the name they gave the West Indian islands— the Antilles. As the West Indies failed to produce any cities, the locale of the tale was naturally assumed to be elsewhere, though still in the Americas. This locale was situated in northwest New Spain when the Spaniards began to associate the Seven Cities with the Seven Caves of the Aztecs. In fact when Nuño de Guzmán entered Aztatlán in 1530 he had probably been seeking both the caves and the cities. Since neither was found there, the location was shifted farther north. When Ascunción and Nadal sought the caves in the distant northwest and returned with news of cities matching Cabeca de Vaca's report, the myths of the Seven Caves and the Seven Cities merged.[21]

These superimposed images formed the guiding myth of the Spanish exploration of the Southwest. As fairness would have it, that myth was a combination of legends pertaining to the two peoples that would participate in the exploration and conquest—the Spanish and their central Mexican auxiliaries. The Indians of the north, not to be left out, would make their own distinct contribution to the myth during the 1539 expedition of Fray Marcos de Niza. Having taken Cabeca de Vaca's account seriously, the Spanish viceroy selected a friar to verify the report because friars, such as Ascunción and Nadal, had shown themselves to be good explorers and diplomats. Fray Marcos, moreover, had already served in Peru with Pizarro. Esteban, an African slave who had accompanied Cabeca de Vaca on his journey, was to guide the friar.[22]

Esteban moved ahead of the main expedition and sent reports and directions back to Fray Marcos. At one point Esteban reported that he had news from the Indians of "the greatest thing in the world." He reported that ahead of him was a city called "Cíbola" (bison)—the first of seven cities. Thus, a southwestern Indian conception of a local homeland was joined to the Spanish and Aztec image of the Seven Cities to form the broader regional myth of the Seven Cities of Cíbola. The nomadic and seminomadic Indians south of the Pueblo villages were probably being truthful when they described such towns to Esteban, but these nomads did not conceive of cities as did the Europeanized mind. In the process of translation, exaggeration was almost inevitable. The description of the Pueblo villages was fairly accurate; their houses were of stone and mortar and of multiple storeys. Yet it was a general description that gave rise to fantastic pictures in the minds of the explorers.[23]

All along the march north Fray Marcos continued to receive news from Esteban that further excited his imagination. Then, while in southern Arizona, Fray Marcos learned to his dismay that Esteban had been killed on reaching the first of the Seven Cities. Although his own life was now in danger, Fray Marcos claimed that he went ahead anyway until he came within sight of the first city itself, a city

which is seated on a plain at the bottom of a round hill. It has the appearance of a beautiful town, the best that I've seen in these parts; the houses are just as the Indians described them to me, all of stone with storeys and flat roofs, so it appeared to me from the height where I had placed myself to see. The population is greater than that of Mexico City; . . . in my opinion [Cíbola] is the largest and the best of all [the lands] discovered.

For one who had seen both Mexico and Peru to claim that a Pueblo village was larger and better than Mexico City is surprising. Probably Fray Marcos, frightened by the news of Esteban's death, turned around and fled toward home without seeing Cíbola at all. Too ashamed to admit his failure, he most likely wrote a description of the town based on Esteban's reports and his own memories of Mexico and Peru. In any case the authorities in Mexico City soon pictured the northwest as a "new" Mexico, and before long the famous Coronado expedition of 1540–42 was on its way.[24]

This expedition, which explored much of present-day Arizona, New Mexico, Texas, Oklahoma, and Kansas, did a good deal to make the Spanish conception of the distant north more realistic, at least for a time. With one of the largest expeditions in the history of Spanish exploration, Francisco Vázquez de Coronado marched north only to be disappointed. When the "Seven Cities" were seen to be small villages, Fray Marcos was severely criticized by everyone concerned. In a letter to the viceroy, Coronado put the matter bluntly: "To make a long story short, I can assure you he [Fray Marcos] has not told the truth in a single thing he has said, . . . except the name of the cities and the large stone houses."[25] Later, in a letter to the king, Coronado added,

> there wasn't a thing of those which Fray Marcos had mentioned, . . . the best that I have found is this river of Tiguex where I am and its settlements, which cannot be colonized because besides being four hundred leagues from the Sea of the North, and two hundred from the South Sea . . . the land is so cold, . . . that it seems impossible to be able to pass a winter in it.[26]

To his further embarrassment, after Coronado discovered the mundane reality of Cíbola, the local Indians convinced him that a far richer land called Quivira existed beyond the Pueblo villages in the plains to the northeast. Led on another futile search, Coronado trekked through vast sections of what we now know as Texas, Oklahoma, and Kansas, only to realize the Pueblo Indians had lied to him. A fabulously rich Quivira had probably never been part of the local Indian conception of the plains area, but had been invented purely for the imaginations of the Spaniards. Since the Spanish had conquered and brutally occupied the Pueblo villages, the Indians most likely fabricated the urban wealth of Quivira in order to lure Coronado into a wilderness from which they hoped he would never return. They must have realized he would believe the tale because they doubtless understood only too well that the Spanish image of the region was of a land of great cities and valuable metals, a land the Spaniards expected to conquer and exploit. Following Coronado's disappointing experiences, Spain heeded his reports and left the region unsettled for another fifty years. The golden image of the north had tarnished.[27]

Even though the myth of the Seven Cities disappeared before the reality of the Pueblo villages, the accompanying myth of the Seven Caves of Aztlán lived on, at least in the collective mind of the Aztecs and their descendants in central Mexico. In fact, for some Aztecs and mestizos the Spanish discovery of the Pueblos confirmed the existence and location of Aztlán because, unlike the Spaniards, the Indians had seen Aztlán more as an Edenic land of the past than a golden land of the present. The Pueblo villages were, therefore, present evidence of past Aztec civilization in the distant north, evidence which was incorporated into the sixteenth- and early seventeenth-century chronicles of the Aztecs. The anonymous *Códice Ramírez* (1583–87), for example, recounted that the Aztecs had come "from another land toward the north, where recently has been discovered a kingdom which is called New Mexico." Furthermore, the ancestral Aztecs had been "a very civil people as can be readily seen from the ways of those [the Pueblos] of New Mexico from where they [the Aztecs] came." We can infer from this that if the contemporary Pueblos were civilized, the ancestral Aztecs must have been even more so. According to the *Códice Ramírez,* the Aztecs in their ancient homeland had had houses and farmland, an orderly government, a complex religion, and an elaborate social organization.[28] Such descriptions caused the myth of Aztlán to take on utopian qualities, in addition to its traditional Edenic features. It was such qualities that Chicanos would later see when they chose Aztlán to symbolize their own ideal society in the Southwest.

While the Pueblos came to be seen—with some justification according to modern anthropology—as distant relatives of the Aztecs, the utopian features that had been included in the myth of Aztlán made it difficult for the chroniclers and their informants to view the Pueblo villages and Aztlán as the same place. The villages indicated that Aztlán had been in the region, but they could not be *the* ancestral homeland. Just as Nuño de Guzmán's Aztatlán had earlier seemed too mundane to be the mythical homeland, the Pueblo villages now also seemed too ordinary. Since the north, even after the Coronado expedition, was largely unknown terrain, there were still many other possible locations in that region for the mysterious Aztec homeland.

Because accurate information about California, New Mexico, and Florida was poorly disseminated, the chroniclers and their informants frequently confused those places with one another; with the result that Aztlán, even after being linked to the Pueblo villages, could be placed anywhere as long as it was to the north. In his *Historia de las Indias* (1579–81) Durán's informants actually located Aztlán "toward the north and near the region of La Florida."[29]

More often in the chronicles, Aztlán would appear in New Mexico, but the site would only be indirectly associated with the Pueblo villages. In the *Crónica Mexicayotl* (1610), for instance, the mestizo chronicler Alvarado Tezozomoc said the homeland of his ancestors "was out there, where, today it perhaps lies very close to the extensive coasts, the extensive shores, which today the Spaniards call New Mexico."[30]

In 1652, after the Pueblo areas of New Mexico had been colonized by Spain, another chronicler took up the issue of Aztlán. In his *Crónica miscelánea* Fray Antonio Tello placed the original Aztec homeland "between the north and the west," but he meant territory beyond what we now call the Southwest, for the frontiers of the unknown had moved farther north by the mid-seventeenth century. Tello stated that the Aztecs on their journey to central Mexico had "passed the strait of Anián, and that the province of Aztatlán [Aztlán] lies on the other side of the strait." The Spaniards had long believed in the existence of a strait cutting across North America, a strait that could, if found, link Europe directly to the riches of the Orient. Given the constant interchange between Spanish and Indian myths, it is no surprise that Tello placed Aztlán beyond that mythical waterway, the last important image of the golden north to interest the Spanish. Ultimately, however, Tello admitted that he was merely speculating concerning the Aztec homeland; "even *now*," he wrote, "no one knows exactly where the province of Aztatlán is, nor have any of our Spaniards seen it; we only know we have heard of it and that it lies *toward* the north."[31]

While the Indians of central Mexico during and after the late sixteenth century conceived of the north as an old land to which they were somehow indigenous, by the 1580s the Spaniards once more viewed the region as a new land of riches, a "new" Mexico. By then the disappointment of the Coronado expedition had abated. The Spanish still remembered that New Mexico had been found "poor in provisions and minerals; but beyond, it was said, was a great salt river, and lakes where the people used gold and silver." Once again a major expedition moved north. The expedition of Juan de Oñate, which began in 1596, was especially significant because it established the first permanent colony in what is now the Southwest.[32] Moreover, the first literary work concerning this frontier region of New Spain resulted from the colonization; in 1610 Gaspar Pérez de Villagrá, a Spanish officer under Oñate, published an epic poem entitled *Historia de la Nueva México* in Spain.

This work dealt with the first stages of the conquest and colonization and discussed the preparations for the expedition at length. Emphasizing that the purpose of the expedition was settlement and not the acquisition of quick riches, the poet chastized those in the Coronado venture (1540–42) who he believed had earlier forced the abandonment of New Mexico "because they did not stumble over bars of gold and silver immediately upon commencing their march into these regions, and because the streams and lakes and springs they met flowed crystalline waters instead of liquid golden victuals."[33] Nevertheless, Oñate did search for riches beyond the Pueblo villages, but again to no avail. When the colonists realized that the chance of their leading the life of landed gentry was small, many fled, almost causing the colony to fail. Finally, the settlement was solidly established, and a new, much less glamorous image of the northern borderlands began to form in the Spanish mind.

Although explorers such as Juan Rodríguez Cabrillo had followed fables into other parts of the north, New Mexico was first conquered and settled because there was some truth to the myth of the Seven Cities. In California there were no Amazons and there was no strait of Anián, but in New Mexico there were sedentary Indians who, while not rich in precious metals, could provide an agricultural base for a colony. Above all they could provide the disciplined labor unobtainable from nomadic peoples in other areas. Once the Spanish colony became established in New Mexico, it settled into a frontier life based on subsistence farming, and the north gradually lost its glossy image. Life in the borderlands was by no means luxurious, for difficulties between the Indians and colonists were continual, and starvation and disease were always a threat. Nevertheless, except for a brief period in the late seventeenth century, the colony survived and finally prospered. Reflecting these changed conditions, later descriptions of the northern frontier spoke of the land and its produce, rather than of silver cities.

In 1773 a number of settlements on both sides of today's international boundary formed the environs of El Paso, which at that time was much more closely linked to New Mexico than Texas. In that year a resident of the area described the vicinity in words that embodied the later Spanish picture of the borderlands:

This settlement includes five Indian missions. . . . The Mansos were its first inhabitants, but they are totally extinguished, and on their lands our citizens are living with their farms and homesteads, some by purchase, and some by gift from their chiefs. In these places Indians and Spaniards live commingled.

By the late eighteenth century the authorities in Mexico City perceived the borderlands as a series of outposts designed to keep intruders far from the core of New Spain. Missions were part of this defensive system because they helped pacify uncivilized Indians on the frontier. In this respect El Paso fit

Mexico City's picture of the north, even as it fit the missionaries' conception of the borderlands as a territory ripe for spiritual conquest. Of course, the Spanish authorities also saw the north as a colonial acquisition, and the sad facts concerning El Paso's Mansos justified that view. The lands of those Indians had been turned over to the settlers for agriculture which, as the Spaniards now realized, would produce much of the real wealth of the distant north. But the most interesting aspect of the description of El Paso was the intermingling of Indians and Spaniards.[34]

"The number of its [El Paso's] inhabitants," continued the anonymous author of the town's description, "reached 9,363 [*sic*] adult persons and a little over 500 children, including all classes of people, Indians and whites. In the last group are included the few Spaniards that are there and about eight or nine Europeans." This comment revealed that while the Mansos may have been extinguished as an identifiable tribal group, many of them most likely intermarried with the Indians and mestizos who always accompanied the Spaniards north on their marches from central Mexico. Furthermore, the existence of five missions meant that a significant number of local Indians were still part of El Paso's population in 1773. Since few of the people were identified as Spaniards, hispanicized Indians and mestizos made up the majority of the population.[35] Thus, despite the "extinction" of the Mansos, the population could still claim to be indigenous to El Paso, in much the way Chicanos would later claim to be native to the Southwest. Since so many of the town's people were Indians and related to local Indians, it could not have been much of a conceptual transformation for them to see the area as home. Indeed by the late eighteenth century the "Spanish settlers" of El Paso and other localities throughout the borderlands undoubtedly saw the region as their homeland and were more at home than most people have since realized.

Although New Mexico and El Paso were colonized in the late sixteenth and early seventeenth centuries, efforts in other areas were delayed. Once the Spanish authorities realized that the riches of the north would take great effort to develop, their enthusiasm for the region waned. While missionaries had been anxious to push the frontier northward, only in the late seventeenth century did the secular authorities permit missions in eastern Texas and Arizona, and not until the late eighteenth century in California. The Spanish missionaries had a sincere interest in the conversion of the Indians and were willing to undertake the tremendous effort necessary to gather nomads into civilized, Christian communities. Since farming was a necessary base for such communities, the missionaries saw the north as a potential agricultural as well as spiritual conquest. If their plans were to succeed, the missionaries realized that they would need to grow crops and were therefore always grateful for any good soil they found in the borderlands.

Father Eusebio Kino, who founded the first missions in what is now Arizona, raved about the bountiful land his converts worked:

> The greater the means the greater our obligation to seek the salvation of so many souls in the very fertile and pleasant lands and valleys of these new conquests and conversions. There are already very rich and abundant fields, plantings and crops of wheat, maize, frijoles, chick-peas, beans, lentiles. . . .

Father Kino went on to list the fruit, stock, and climate that made the region a golden land for economic as well as spiritual conquest.[36] Father Junípero Serra, the first missionary to Upper California, also saw the intrinsic economic and social value of the borderlands. The Spanish secular authorities, however, were reluctant to invest much of their treasury in the region, an attitude that contributed to the later loss of the borderlands to the United States.

Ironically, California and Texas were ultimately colonized as defensive measures to ward off foreign threats against Spain's empire from the north: Texas was established as a buffer against the French in Louisiana, California as a barrier against the English and Russians on the northwest coast. California and Texas, therefore, were perceived by the secular authorities as outposts, as frontiers rather than as colonies having intrinsic value. During the late eighteenth century, for instance, Spain abandoned all its outposts northeast of San Antonio because they were seen as unnecessary after Louisiana had come under Spanish control. Despite this official view, the people of the northeastern settlements themselves were incensed at being forced to move south, and eventually many returned north—the residents had come to perceive this region as home.[37] Nevertheless, the indifferent attitude of Spanish officials had important consequences for the future of Chicanos. Seen as less valuable than areas farther south, the borderlands received less money, fewer colonists, and in general less attention from Mexico City. Consequently, their development as integral parts of New Spain and Mexico was retarded, a situation which eventually worked to the advantage of the United States.

Yet Spain's advance into the region left an indelible mark on the Southwest, a mark that, paradoxically, was as much Mexican Indian as Spanish. While Anglo-Americans would later imagine the period of Spanish rule in terms of conquistadores and Franciscans, Chicanos would revive the facts of Indian and mestizo participation in the settlement of the region. They would note that for every conquistador and missionary who went north, ten or twenty Indians and mestizos, carrying their own customs and languages, went along as porters, soldiers, servants, and small farmers. The important expedition of Marcos de Niza, for example, was led by that friar but was composed almost entirely of central Mexican Indians. And Juan de Oñate, conquerer and colonizer of New Mexico, was himself married to a mestiza, the great-granddaughter of Moctezuma (she was also the granddaughter of Cortés).[38]

Chicanos would also point out the bonds that were felt between the Indians from central Mexico and those of the borderlands. For instance, when Vázquez de Coronado left New Mexico, he left behind several Mexican Indians who apparently felt sufficient affinity for the Pueblos to choose voluntarily to live among them. In 1680 when the Pueblos carried out a temporarily successful revolt, they were joined by many central Mexican Indians who were also disenchanted with Spanish rule. And, of course, throughout the colonial period there was a constant intermarrying between the Indians of north and south, as well as between Indians and Spaniards. All these facts would link modern Chicanos to southwestern Native Americans and would lend credibility to the Chicanos' image of themselves as indigenous to the Southwest, their homeland, both ancient and modern.[39]

# 2

## The Mexican Far North

By 1800 the Spanish and mestizo predecessors of today's Chicanos were solidly established in New Mexico and California; Texas and what is now Arizona, on the other hand, were still scarcely settled provinces on New Spain's far northern frontier, provinces that would nevertheless develop into integral parts of the native homeland perceived by modern Chicanos. Spain continued to see the borderlands as defensive outposts, valuable only insofar as they protected the more populated and civilized areas in central and southern New Spain; the residents of the borderlands themselves, however, saw the region as home and constantly argued for greater development of the frontier provinces. In the late eighteenth century Spain had expanded its settled empire into Arizona and California, but by the beginning of the nineteenth century, it had stalled in the region and in 1821 was replaced by the young Mexican nation. The change of administration that followed Mexico's war for independence (1810–21) caused the borderlands to receive greater attention in Mexico City, though the consequences of that attention ultimately proved unfortunate for Mexicans. Mexico's attempts to develop its far northern frontier by increasing the population and expanding commerce, rather than helping the region become an integral part of the nation, ultimately led to Anglo-American control.[1] Mexicans on the frontier, who had wanted more attention from Mexico City, in 1848 saw themselves completely cut off from that capital, with both their land and themselves under the control of a foreign people. At that point began the modern Chicanos' image of the Southwest and themselves; from that point they saw the region as a home now lost, themselves as natives now dispossessed.

In 1849 José Agustín Escudero published a book, entitled *Noticias históricas y estadísticas de la antigua provincia del Nuevo-México,* in Mexico City. This book, which incorporated two earlier works on New Mexico, revealed important features of the image that Mexicans in the borderlands had of themselves and the frontier between 1800 and 1848. One of the earlier works incorporated into Escudero's book was written in 1812 by New Mexico's delegate to the

Cortes (the Spanish parliament).[2] The delegate, Pedro Bautista Pino, discussed many aspects of New Mexico life from environment and population to religion and political affairs. Pino's intent was to give the Spanish government a full picture of the remote province of which he was a native. Throughout his report, Pino emphasized that Spain's neglect of the distant colony harmed the empire as a whole because it hindered New Mexico's internal development and thus prevented the colony from being an effective defensive outpost.

In describing the environment and natural resources of New Mexico, Pino left a picture of a bountiful land of promise. The mountains were beautiful and had much valuable timber; the hunting and fishing were good, especially the hunting of buffalo, which could be very profitable if it were ever fully developed as an industry. The colorful soils and stones of the region could be useful as building products. In addition, medicinal herbs were abundant, as were mineral products:

> There are many mineral veins in the mountains, containing silver, gold, copper, lead. . . . If the province were even fairly well protected, those mines could be worked . . ., and the treasury would then receive many thousands in taxes which it fails to receive today because of this neglect.[3]

As a frontier outpost, New Mexico was constantly concerned with defense— defense against nomadic Indians, especially the Apaches, and defense against the incursions of the United States. Since domestic development was difficult while the colony existed under a state of siege, political affairs between the colony and the central government revolved around military spending, or rather the lack of it. Because of its inefficient colonial administration, its incessant European wars, and its antiquated economic policies, Spain often found it difficult to provide funds where they were needed. This was such a problem that in the borderlands soldiers often went without pay, forced thus to depend on the local citizenry for support. Since their homes were at stake, the citizens could ill afford to abandon the soldiers, yet the minimal security that resulted from such irregular support restricted the development of the far north.[4]

However, neglect was only one factor involved in the problems of the northern provinces; the vast distances that separated the north from the more populated areas of New Spain made effective government difficult. Moreover, the long distances from central Mexico to California stretched across rough seas and to Arizona and New Mexico crossed high mountains and deserts. Pino was aware of this situation; he himself had made the journey from New Mexico to Veracruz, New Spain's major port, and from there to Spain. "New Mexico," he explained, "has 40,000 inhabitants, all of them citizens; it is isolated among tribes of wild Indians; it is separated by a distance of 240 leagues from any other province. . . ." The problem of distance affected all phases of life in the borderlands. For instance, to appeal a judicial decision, a *nuevomexicano* had to travel to Guadalajara, six hundred leagues away; to receive a dispensation to marry a close relative, he had to visit the bishop in Durango, four hundred leagues away. Similar distances naturally had to be traveled in order to engage in any commerce for luxury goods. And to receive an education beyond the very basics, a *nuevomexicano* had to leave the province; in fact, Pino is believed to have "dictated" his work to someone else because he was insufficiently literate to compose it himself.[5]

Even though Pino pointed out the problems of his province, he explained that these could be worse by comparing them to those of central Mexico, which at the time was undergoing the upheaval of the Mexican independence movement: "The inhabitants of New Mexico are not reduced to such an unhappy state as are those [in the south]. . . ." Pino was amazed by the beggars and the bloodshed that he saw while making his trip to Veracruz. While New Mexico had its difficulties with Indians, it was at least being spared the civil disorder experienced in the south. New Mexico, Pino thought, avoided poverty and its accompanying problems because there was enough land and enough employment to support everyone. He felt so strongly about this that he advised the Spanish government: "The means of establishing permanent peace in New Spain lies in giving everyone an interest in the property of the territory, as is being done in my province." As a result of this policy, Pino claimed, New Mexican towns appeared neat; the people, clean, disciplined, and healthy; and everyone had shoes and clothes. With such advantages in comparison with the provinces to the south, New Mexico, Pino believed, could be and should be strengthened economically and militarily because it was vulnerable to attack from the United States.[6]

As early as 1812, nearly forty years before the North American conquest of the present Southwest, fear of Anglo-American aggression was a major concern in the region. Although some of the northern provinces had been established as buffers against French, Russian, and English incursions, by 1812 the United States had replaced France on New Spain's northeastern frontier. Pino specifically warned Ferdinand VII of the new danger from the north:

The purchase of Louisiana by the United States [in 1803] has opened the way for them to arm and incite the pagan Indians against us, and for them [the

Anglo-Americans] to invade the province; once lost the province will be impossible to recover; . . . there is still time for us to avoid this evil. . . .[7]

Pino also voiced the fear that if New Mexico were lost it would leave *"the other provinces to the same fate, one after another."*[8] The threat from the United States remained a major theme in Pino's work; he constantly referred to it whenever he needed a reason for the improvement of some phase of New Mexico life, from military preparedness to the education of professionals.

Of these needed improvements Pino saw an increase in the population and the expansion of trade, in addition to the granting of free land, as important ways of keeping the province under Spanish control. The opening of seaports in Sonora and Texas would permit the natural resources of the borderlands to be exported more easily, which would in turn lead to more imports. The increase in trade with the rest of the world would bring more merchants into the region; this increase in population would lead to the conquest and civilization of the nomadic Indians who would become "new consumers of merchandise, *new defenders of Spanish territory* against aggressions of the United States. . . ."[9]

Pino's concise economic scheme for furthering the progress of the region, while keeping it out of the hands of the United States, went unheeded until the independence of Mexico in 1821, and even then his plan was only partially implemented. As long as the central government continued to see New Mexico as a mere defensive outpost, there was little chance that Pino's "progressive" view of the province would affect policy. Mexico's independence led to a change in policy because the new nationalist spirit in Mexico City encouraged local initiative in the belief that this would strengthen the nation as a whole. This spirit and its effects appeared in a second work included in Escudero's *Noticias históricas;* this second work, entitled *Ojeada sobre Nuevo México,* was published in 1832. Its author, Antonio Barreiro, was sent to New Mexico by the central government to act as legal advisor to the territorial authorities. Later he was to be elected New Mexico's deputy to the congress in Mexico City.[10] From him, then, we get a picture of the province from both a local and national perspective. By 1832 some of the changes recommended by Pino had actually taken place in New Mexico, especially a tremendous increase in trade—though primarily with the United States.

One of the reasons Spain's American colonies rebelled was restrictive trade regulations. Spain's colonies could not trade directly with foreign countries because the mother country feared it would lose profits and taxes from such trade and perhaps even control of the colonies themselves. Despite attempts at reform in the late colonial period, Spain's monopoly on trade limited the growth of local economies, including those of the northern provinces.[11] When Mexico gained its independence, it opened its frontiers to foreign trade, and intensive commerce between the United States and the borderlands began, with California and New Mexico as the major northern participants. The immense distances that kept the frontier provinces isolated were overcome by steadily improving ships in the case of California and by wagon trains in the case of New Mexico. Access to New Mexico was easier by way of the plains from Missouri than by way of the mountains and deserts from Mexico City. Also, over forty years of independence from Britain had allowed the United States to develop its mercantile enterprises, while Mexico and the rest of Latin America had stagnated under rigorous economic controls. When the Spanish empire broke up, the United States was more than ready to supply the newly created markets in the former Spanish colonies.[12]

As expected by Mexican progressives, trade with foreigners strengthened the economy of northern Mexico, but as feared by the Spanish government, trade also increased the threat from the United States. By Barreiro's time fears of aggression were more immediate because many Anglo-American traders were now actually present within Mexico's far northern frontiers:

> Let us suppose for a moment that the United States brings her guns to bear upon us in the form of a military expedition of three or four thousand men. . . . add the large number of Anglo-Americans among us who are completely armed . . . [and] we can see . . . the seriousness of our unarmed condition.[13]

Even though increased trade had improved the economy of the borderlands, many of the old problems remained because the central government in Mexico City was not yet strong enough to deal with them. The removal of trade restrictions, though beneficial, had required little effort on Mexico's part, but positive action would be necessary if illiteracy, governmental disorder, and Indian warfare were to be eliminated and industry developed.

Barreiro was aware of his country's potential, and he vehemently encouraged economic progress: "What a wide field is open to industry in Mexico! What germs of prosperity are seen everywhere! Even those remote places occupied by wild Indians offer us rich products with which we are as yet unfamiliar." He raved about rivers full of beaver, virgin fields, a moderate climate permitting stock raising, and mountains—"bright blocks of marble [that] . . . seem to be outlining sketches of magnificent cities [which] are certainly powerful stimuli that should make us think seriously of developing the elements of true happiness which we have at hand!" Then, he condemned those who prevented Mexico from establishing a stable and progressive central government:

> Ambitious revolutionary men, infernal genii of discord, cast your eyes but once over your country, and, impelled by the force of furious remorse, you will run and bury yourselves forever in hell! You shall see that this soil, generously endowed by the loving hand of providence, is inviting Mexicans with its riches and variety of products which are not enjoyed nor even known because of your criminal and perverse designs![14]

From Barreiro's *Ojeada* we nevertheless gather that while New Mexico still suffered from isolation and neglect, Mexican rule had been an improvement over Spanish rule. In addition to increased trade, education had somewhat improved, and the population had risen. Though people in general were not rich, neither were they poverty-stricken: "Houses have apartments with warm, clean bedrooms where stoves are always kept burning and where one may spend the winter in comfort." In fact Barreiro's concern was for the future, rather than the present, of New Mexico. He feared that if Mexicans did not develop their own land, the Anglo-Americans would take it from them. While describing the promise of New Mexico's water power and admiring the way certain Anglo-Americans were taking advantage of it, Barreiro asked some prophetic questions:

> One Anglo-American company . . . has installed a privately owned plant for the distilling of whisky. Soon we shall learn in an experimental way how valuable and lucrative this establishment is going to be. How long shall we continue to be *foreigners on our own soil* [emphasis added]? When shall we see the true sources of wealth we have?[15]

Mexicans would never fully realize the extent of that wealth until it was no longer theirs, and until they were indeed foreigners on their own soil.

Ironically, owing in some ways to Mexico's ill-focused attempts to develop the borderlands, Mexicans in Texas as well as New Mexico were already becoming "native foreigners." In 1827 José María Sánchez, a draftsman, was appointed by the Mexican government to a commission that was to examine the eastern boundary between Mexico and the United States. In his capacity as boundary commissioner, he made a trip through Texas, leaving some astute observations. In Nacogdoches, the major town on the Mexican side of the boundary, he wrote of the Mexican population in a way that interestingly fits many of today's Mexican-Americans:

The Mexicans who live here . . . because of their education and environment . . . are ignorant not only of the customs of our great cities, but even of the occurrences of our Revolution. . . . Accustomed to the continued trade with the North Americans, they have adopted their customs and habits, and one may truly say that they are not Mexicans except by birth, for they even speak Spanish with marked incorrectness.[16]

Indeed by 1828, with Anglos having drifted into Texas even before Mexico gained independence, so many Anglo-Americans were in the province that Mexicans were already a minority. Realizing that preventing this illegal immigration was impossible, Mexico had decided to try to win over the Anglos by offering free land to those who would offer allegiance to the republic, respect its laws, and convert to Catholicism. In this way Mexico hoped to populate and develop Texas while keeping it loyal. This policy was in effect for a few years, but finally immigration from the United States was completely prohibited when Mexico realized that too many of the new settlers had no intention of accepting Mexican authority. Mexicans were too outnumbered to be taken seriously, especially in the area north and east of San Antonio.[17]

Using phrases ironically similar to those of modern complaints against "illegal" Mexican immigration, Sánchez commented on the influx of Anglo-Americans:

The Americans from the north have taken possession of practically all the eastern part of Texas, in most cases without permission of the authorities. They immigrate constantly, finding no one to prevent them. . . . Repeated and urgent appeals have been made to the Supreme Government of the Federation [of Mexico] regarding the imminent danger in which this interesting Department is of becoming the prize of the ambitious North Americans. . . .

Sánchez was even more vehement about the situation in Texas than Barreiro was about New Mexico because in Texas thousands of Anglo settlers, rather than small groups of traders, had moved into the province. Moreover, though Texas was a "most precious and interesting department," it was far less developed with regard to education, industry, and commerce than either New Mexico or California. Despite admonishing the central government to act, Sánchez was pessimistic that any action would be taken, and even predicted the Texas Revolution:

In my judgement, the spark that will start the conflagration that will deprive us of Texas, will start from this colony [Austin's]. All because the government does not take vigorous measures to prevent it. Perhaps it does not realize the value of what it is about to lose.[18]

The government, however, was not as oblivious to the value of the border-lands as Sánchez's statement might lead us to believe. Of course, only the future would reveal how truly rich such areas as California actually were, but that Mexico valued its northern provinces can be seen in its refusal to sell any of its territory to the United States, despite repeated offers, and in Mexico's active if ineffective moves to hold on to the far north, moves that finally included a major war with the United States. While New Mexico and California were considered more valuable territories than Texas, Mexico took more active steps to defend the latter simply because Texas was in the most imme-diate danger. California suffered from isolation, inefficient government, poor education, and most of the other difficulties that plagued New Mexico, but military threats were not as grave. The Indians in California were generally under control, and the few Anglo-American merchants in the territory were far from their homeland. Consequently, Mexico expended whatever energy it could on Texas, an area closer to the national capital and closer to the expand-ing North American frontier.[19]

In 1830 a special attempt was made to "Mexicanize" Texas, forbidding Anglos entry into the province and planning a string of forts with surround-ing settlements of Mexicans. These settlements bore Indian names, includ-ing Anáhuac, Lipantitlan, and even Tenoxtitlán, the former name of Mexico City. In using these names the central government was clearly promoting pride in the indigenous ethnic origins of the nation. By emphasizing the Indian background of the Mexican, the central government also hoped to strengthen its ties with the Indian tribes in Texas.[20] Independence from Spain had fos-tered pride in Mexico's native background, and the symbols of that back-ground were constantly used in attempts to unite the country and give the people a sense of nationality. Barreiro, for example, on viewing certain Pueblo ceremonies, wrote that

they recall generations that have disappeared, . . . days of calamity, oppression, and ignominy, in which a fierce nation [Spain] attempted to conquer the great Mexico, and with malicious tenacity, tried to exterminate its aboriginal races. Ancient Mexicans, now you belong to history alone, and your remains [the Pueb-los and other Indians] will shortly perish![21]

Although wrong in its prediction, Barreiro's comment revealed the pride in the native past that he felt and that he tried to impart to his readers. Nurturing such pride formed an important part of the plan to keep the borderlands Mexican, but this plan would fail, especially in Texas, because the central government would never find enough Mexicans able to settle in the area.

Because of Mexico's rigidly structured society, peculiar demographic development, and rugged geography, a mass movement north equal to the westward Anglo-American push was delayed until the twentieth century; prior to that time, Mexicans remained concentrated in the south. The steady immigration of uprooted individuals and families from Europe that characterized the United States did not occur in Mexico. In the United States every new wave of immigrants would tend to push the previous one westward. Having relatively weak ties within their new country, Anglo-Americans found it less difficult to move to new territory than did Mexicans. In the turbulent sixteenth century, during which a significant migration northward did occur, Mexico suffered a severe decline in population (largely due to disease) which made later migrations much smaller than they might have been. With a shortage of labor in the south, rich landowners did everything in their power to bind the poor to the land. As a result, various forms of servitude flourished, keeping the Mexican poor generally immobilized until the revolution of 1910 restructured Mexican society. Those people who migrated northward before 1848 frequently did so as part of official colonizing expeditions headed by rich entrepreneurs. Such enterprises, because so much of the north was too rugged to be easily crossed and too dry to be easily farmed, had limited success. People who migrated between 1848 and 1910 in general formed a steadily increasing stream that finally became a mass movement in the twentieth century.[22]

Given these factors, it is not surprising that the attempt to Mexicanize Texas failed. Texas under Mexican rule was confined to the green, wooded lowlands northeast of the Nueces River, an area more akin to Louisiana and states east than to the rest of the Mexican north. Though it was good farmland, Mexicans, who had become accustomed to aridity, found the area less amenable to their way of life than did Anglos, whose experience in a similar neighboring region made them feel quite at home.[23] The attempt to tie Texas closer to the rest of Mexico centered on the founding in 1830 of Tenoxtitlán, a settlement that was planned to be the future capital of the province. It was placed in the center of Texas, where it could command the major highway going south, and a garrison was placed there for the express purpose of preventing further infiltration of Anglo-Americans. Yet, strangely enough, some of the very first settlers turned out to be Anglos. Colonel Francisco Ruiz, commander of the fort and a native of Texas, allowed Anglos to settle because, as he put it, "I cannot help seeing the advantages which, to my way of thinking, would result if we admitted honest, hard-working people, regardless of what country they came from, . . . even hell itself."[24] Being a native, Colonel Ruiz was concerned with the improvement of the locale, his comments reflecting the position Mexico City took in the early 1820s when it first made land grants to Anglos. Ruiz probably realized that few Mexican colonists would be forthcoming since few Mexicans had ever settled north of San Antonio, except in the town of Nacogdoches. Indeed within two years the small Mexican population of Tenoxtitlán returned to San Antonio because not enough new settlers from the south appeared to make the central government's project worthwhile.

Despite its weak presence in Texas between 1821 and 1836, Mexico was intent on keeping the province within the nation. In 1834 Juan N. Almonte, a Mexican educated in the United States, was commissioned by the Mexican government to inspect Texas. In effect his job was to report on the strength of the Anglo-American colonists in case conflict should break out. By 1834 serious differences between Anglo-Americans and Mexicans had already arisen. In 1827 Mexican troops had suppressed an Anglo attempt to establish an independent republic in Nacogdoches. Certain Anglos, fearful that Mexico would not recognize their rights to lands they had occupied, had founded the short-lived Republic of Fredonia. It was after this episode that Mexico, naturally worried about the threat of insurrection, instructed Almonte "to paralyze the movements of the colonists, with the view of gaining time so that the supreme government, unburdened by the cares with which it today finds itself surrounded, may be able to dedicate all of its endeavors to the conservation of the integrity of the territory of the republic."[25] Almonte's report would be needed within two years.

Both Anglos and Mexicans had serious complaints about each other, grievances that finally led to the Texas Revolution of 1836. Anglo-Texans were dissatisfied with their representation in the government; they felt the tax system was unfair, the government inefficient, and immigration, land, and antislavery laws too restrictive. Mexicans felt that Anglos had violated Mexican hospitality. Even though the legitimate colonists had been orderly enough (some had helped suppress the Fredonian revolt), the more numerous recent arrivals had entered illegally, squatting on others' lands, bringing in more slaves, failing to accept Catholicism, and, most seriously, refusing to submit to the authority of local Mexican officials. Conflict finally broke out when the Anglo-Americans received news that the dictator, Antonio López de Santa Anna, was forming a new, highly centralized government. Since Anglos had been lobbying for separate statehood for Texas (within Mexico), they were outraged by Mexico's impending abandonment of federalism, seeing no hope thus for achieving a measure of self-government peacefully. Of course, many Anglos saw this as exactly the excuse they needed to separate from Mexico. Many Mexicans both inside and outside Texas sympathized with the Anglos because the new dictatorship was unpopular among liberals, who supported the federalist constitution that Santa Anna was discarding.[26] After a few months of warfare, however, the Anglos declared Texas independent and consequently lost most, though not all, of their Mexican supporters.

A large Mexican army, commanded by Santa Anna himself, had entered Texas in early 1836 in a campaign to enforce the authority of the central government. One of Santa Anna's officers, José Enrique de la Peña, later narrated a surprisingly objective account of the campaign. Though de la Peña opposed the independence of Texas, he praised the courage of the Anglo colonists and condemned the political and military policies of Santa Anna, one of the most infamous dictators in Mexican history. Though in sympathy with the liberal cause, de la Peña marched with the army because he thought the colonists had gone beyond partisan politics and, indeed, were attempting to dismember the nation itself. He believed the Anglo-Texans' declaration of independence had revealed their true intentions and had clarified the issue for everyone concerned:

> This declaration was also useful to the Mexicans, for, once they saw these incidents [Anglo dealings with U.S. land speculators] in proper perspective, they knew exactly where they stood. The cry of independence darkened the magic of liberty that had misled some of the less careful thinkers, and the few who had cast their lot with the colonists, believing them to be acting in good faith, disassociated themselves immediately, there remaining with the colonists only Don Lorenzo de Zavala and the Béjar [San Antonio] natives, Don Antonio Navarro and Don Juan N. Seguín, the only intelligent men who incurred the name of traitor, a label both ugly and deserved. At least they are the only ones that we know about.[27]

Four days after Texas declared its independence, Santa Anna's army defeated the Texans at the Alamo. Among the defenders of the Alamo were a number of *tejanos* (Texas Mexicans) who died supporting the liberal cause, but who did not favor separation from Mexico. On the other hand, there were *tejanos* and other Mexicans at the Alamo and elsewhere who did want independence. Dr. Lorenzo de Zavala, whom de la Peña considered a traitor, was one of the most prominent of the Mexican separatists. In addition to being highly educated, Zavala had been governor of a state, minister to France, and a member of the president's cabinet; however, he was an exile in Texas because he had criticized Santa Anna. He subsequently became interim vice-president of the Texas Republic.[28]

Don Antonio Navarro, another signer of the Texas declaration of independence, had served in the state legislature of Coahuila y Texas, of which Texas was a part, and he had been chosen to serve in the Mexican congress. Don Juan N. Seguín, who commanded a *tejano* cavalry unit in the army of Texas, came from a wealthy *tejano* family, as did Navarro. These men, admiring the liberal institutions of the Anglos and especially the stability of the United States, felt that Texas would never develop economically under unstable Mexican rule, and since they had important business interests in the province, they desired the prosperity that Anglo rule seemed to promise. They seemed unaware of or unconcerned with the racial and cultural impact that Anglo dominance would eventually have on their people and on themselves.[29]

In the attitudes of these men, and other leaders like them in New Mexico and California, we find the beginnings of what we might call the Mexican-American image of the Southwest. The loss of the cultural and racial traits that marked them as indigenous to the region seemed a small price to pay for the prosperity that Anglo rule promised. Mexicans would succeed in the region if they adopted the practical values of the Anglo and left the old ways behind. From the beginning these views conflicted with those of Mexican nationalists, a conflict that would continue throughout Chicano history: "Because of his [Navarro's] friendship with Stephen F. Austin and the Anglo colonists, those Mexicans who could not be reconciled to the presence of Anglo-born citizens in Texas commenced to refer to Navarro as an 'Anglocized-Mexican.' "[30]

Significantly, Santa Anna's victories in Texas took place at San Antonio and Goliad in the southwestern part of the province, a part where Mexicans formed a majority of the population. In this area the Mexican army was still on familiar terrain amidst a populace that was generally loyal to Mexico, even though divided with regard to Santa Anna and his government. However, when Santa Anna's forces pushed northeastward, they entered essentially alien and hostile territory.[31] After their initial defeats, the Texans retreated farther and farther into their own terrain, in the process gaining the support of many formerly indifferent Anglos who now felt their homes were in danger. At least one historian, Eugene C. Barker, has commented that until the threat of military action by the central government became real, "Most of the [Anglo] rank and file, perhaps, were merely indifferent to the alleged abuses of Santa Anna."[32] Santa Anna himself helped incite Anglo public opinion when he ordered all prisoners captured at San Antonio and Goliad executed. De la Peña and other officers were outraged by Santa Anna's brutality, warning that it would only stiffen resistance, but the dictator refused to listen. Santa

Anna's words and actions, according to de la Peña, were unnecessarily harsh: "The language that General Santa Anna employed . . . displayed the most unfortunate ideas regarding Texas, expressing in the strongest way his opinion that it should be razed to the ground, so that this immense desert, he said, might serve as a wall between Mexico and the United States."[33]

Santa Anna's opinion reflected the old Spanish view of the borderlands as a defensive frontier of little intrinsic value. De la Peña, on the other hand, exhibiting the new Mexican nationalism, was

> astonished and saddened to think that such a man was at the head of a great people. When he spoke thus, he was completely ignoring the importance of the country, its prodigious fertility, its geographic situation, and its channels of communication to the sea. When Texas is populated and governed by good laws, it will be one of the most enviable places in the world. . . .[34]

Unfortunately for Mexico, Santa Anna disagreed, and his harsh attitude together with his cruelty only succeeded in inspiring Anglo hatred.

Roused by this hatred and positioned near their homes, the Anglos surprised Santa Anna's fatigued army and defeated it in the Battle of San Jacinto. Captured by the Texans, the dictator recognized their independence, and so ended the last opportunity for a Mexican Texas. This first loss of territory to Anglo-Americans deprived Mexico of a rich land that her people would later need when her population exploded. Thus, the independence of Texas in 1836 meant the loss of a potential rather than an actual homeland—with the important exception of the San Antonio area. Although there were Mexicans throughout Texas, including a sizable community in Nacogdoches, only in San Antonio were they a substantial majority. Also, San Antonio, unlike Nacogdoches, would always remain a Chicano city, a conquered bit of settled Mexico continuously inhabited by the Spanish-speaking.

Even though Santa Anna recognized Texas independence, the Mexican congress repudiated the treaty he had made under duress. The congress not only refused to acknowledge Texas independence, it emphatically rejected the boundaries claimed by the new republic. This boundary issue would finally lead to war between Mexico and the United States, and is especially important to Chicanos because Texas, in its claim, strove to acquire *settled* Mexican lands, besides the San Antonio area. Throughout the periods of Spanish and Mexican rule, Texas had never extended beyond the Nueces River in the south nor beyond San Saba Mission in the west, yet in the treaty that Santa Anna signed the southern and western boundary of Texas was established at the Rio Grande. This meant that the border was pushed over a hundred miles

south of the Nueces along the Gulf of Mexico and over four hundred miles
west of San Saba. The Texas Republic, therefore, claimed not only the area of
the present state but over half of the present state of New Mexico and parts of
Colorado, Wyoming, Kansas, and Oklahoma as well. Although vast sections
of this territory were unsettled, the extra land Texas claimed included three
important areas of Mexican settlement that would eventually become centers
of Chicano population. These were the South Texas area around Laredo, the
West Texas area including present-day El Paso, and upper New Mexico around
Santa Fe.[35]

Mexicans saw the separation of Texas as a deliberate attempt on the part of
the United States to expand at their expense. The constant agitation to have
Texas annexed to the United States naturally aroused strong feelings against
the latter in Mexico. Even though the Battle of San Jacinto had effectively
established Texas independence, a state of war continued to exist, and conflict along the "border" was incessant. At the center of this conflict were the
Mexican settlements claimed by Texas. Although Nacogdoches was deep in
Anglo Texas, according to historian Joseph Milton Nance, in the late 1830s,
"the Mexican military commanders sought to stir up the discontented Mexicans around Nacogdoches, as well as . . . Indians to war on the Texans. . . ."[36]
This plan met with some success, especially when the Indians saw Anglos
encroaching on their lands. In 1842 the Mexican army recaptured San Antonio and held it briefly; this was the most successful Mexican operation in
Texas after San Jacinto, and it is no surprise that it occurred in the heavily
Mexican south. The people of this area were, with some cause, suspected of
disloyalty from the beginning by the Anglo independence movement. In 1836
the *Telegraph and Texas Register* called for "the Mexican citizens there to manifest their intentions with respect to the war."[37] That these people supported
Mexico seems probable given a statement made in 1837 by a Texan who had
just returned from a raid near Mexican-occupied Laredo: "'No shout of exulta-
tion welcomed our return to Béxar [San Antonio],' reported Smith, 'the
inhabitants plainly evidencing that their sympathies were with the enemy.' "[38]
While fear of Anglo-American expansion raged throughout Mexico, in the
borderlands Mexicans were beginning to feel the reality of conquest; in Texas
they were now a suspect minority ruled by an alien power in their own land.

Even though Texans claimed territory beyond San Saba and the Nueces,
their attempts to enforce the republic's authority there were no more successful than Mexico's attempts to retake Texas. Laredo, the major town between
the Nueces and the Rio Grande, remained under Mexican control until war
broke out between the United States and Mexico in 1846. Although Texan
forays south of the Nueces were common enough, only one real attempt was

made to assert Texas rule in the west before 1846. In 1841 an expedition, ostensibly for trade, was sent to Santa Fe by the Texas government. Fortunately for Mexico, the Texans experienced such hardships on their long march that they were easily overcome by Mexican forces near Santa Fe. This episode, more than any other, convinced Mexicans that Anglos were a threat to all of Mexico's territory. Not only had they separated Texas from the nation, in crossing the Nueces they had invaded the state of Tamaulipas, and now they had actually crossed hundreds of miles to attack the territory of New Mexico. Even though these actions had been taken by the Texas Republic, Mexicans felt that that republic was merely a front for the expansionist United States. This belief was furthered by events at the other end of the borderlands, in the valuable and vulnerable territory of California.[39]

Like Texas, California was an underpopulated province in the Mexican north, yet large numbers of Anglos had never settled there. Mexico, however, began to fear for California when the United States made repeated offers to purchase it. Mexico's fears would prove reasonable, for while the dispute over territory around Texas would lead to war with the United States, the grand prize of that war would be California. Although there were fewer than a thousand Anglo residents in California by the time it was occupied by the United States, Anglo-Americans had visited the province as early as 1796 when a U.S. vessel had anchored near Monterey.[40] After that, ships from New England regularly stopped in California on their way to China. Later, trappers arrived overland, and some farmers, diverted from the Oregon Trail, found themselves in California's valleys. The Mexican government never encouraged Anglo immigration in this province as it did in Texas. Though some Anglos did receive land grants, no large colonies of settlers were established; California's distance from the U.S. frontier was one reason why few Anglos arrived early. Because of this distance Mexico felt little need to populate the province with loyal Anglo settlers, since the territory was in no immediate danger of invasion by squatters. But by the late 1830s and early 1840s Mexico began to feel that distance was no safeguard. Although Anglos were few in California, many were entrepreneurs who had gained influence on account of their wealth. Because of the Texas Revolution, the presence of these men in California seemed more dangerous. Furthermore, several incidents occurred that further threatened Mexico.[41]

In 1840 Isaac Graham, an Anglo-American trapper, was suspected of plotting to overthrow the government of California. He and forty-five of his associates were arrested and shipped to central Mexico for trial. Although Graham was found innocent of the charge, the affair did little to improve Mexico's opinion of North Americans. In 1842, a far more ominous episode occurred.

Because of tensions over Texas, relations between Mexico and the United States had deteriorated to the point where rumors of war were constantly repeated. On hearing one such rumor, Commodore Thomas Ap Catesby Jones, in command of the U.S. Pacific squadron, landed at Monterey and raised the Stars and Stripes, declaring the province U.S. territory. To his embarrassment and that of the United States, he found that war had not been declared. Although he sailed away soon after, Jones's action betrayed his country's wishes concerning the borderlands, and in Mexican eyes, this action was especially ominous because it had been taken directly by the U.S. Navy, rather than by an army of the Texas Republic.[42]

In 1843 another violation of Mexican territory took place when John C. Frémont, an officer in the U.S. Army, illegally entered and mapped sections of California and other parts of the borderlands. The alarm these actions caused in Mexico was well founded. In 1845, several months before the outbreak of the U.S.-Mexican War, Frémont was back in California; in March 1846 he built a fortification twenty-five miles from Monterey and raised the flag of the United States, which naturally angered the authorities. Before he could provoke an incident that might lead to war, he was advised by the North American consul to leave for Oregon. On his way north, however, he received instructions from Washington that caused him to turn south again. Shortly after, in June 1846, by rather suspicious coincidence, a small group of Anglo-Americans in Sonoma declared their independence and established what they called the "California Republic." Their excuse was that the government was planning to expel all foreigners (which was not true). After several skirmishes between Anglos and Mexicans, the "Bear Flag Republic" came to an end when the U.S. Navy, now officially notified that war had been declared, occupied Monterey on July 7, 1846.[43]

Although the annexation of Texas to the United States, which was made official on December 29, 1845, led to war, four months passed before hostilities began. Interestingly, General Zachary Taylor's army had entered Texas in the summer of 1845, yet had never been attacked by Mexico despite its claims to the province. Indeed Mexico realized by then that Texas would never be recovered; in fact in the spring of 1845, Mexico had offered to recognize Texas independence if it would not join the United States—this had been one last attempt to make Texas a buffer against the northern aggression that Spain and Mexico had feared for centuries. What finally started the war was Taylor's crossing of the Nueces and his advance to the Rio Grande. Since Mexico, and Spain before her, had always regarded this area as part of Tamaulipas (called Nuevo Santander under the Spanish), Taylor's advance was an invasion of territory that had never been Texan, and whose small population was overwhelmingly Mexican (and remains predominantly Chicano to this day). Even though the Mexican government again delayed before taking action, it finally decided that further territorial losses would be unavoidable unless the United States realized that Mexico would actually fight. In late April 1846, a detachment of Mexican troops crossed the Rio Grande and attacked a part of Taylor's army—whereupon President James K. Polk claimed that "American blood" had been shed on "American soil."[44]

Why would Mexico, which had been unable to subdue Texas, go to war with the far more powerful United States? Some historians have argued that Mexico could have avoided a futile war if she had simply sold her northern provinces, territory which she scarcely controlled anyway. While this may be true, these historians fail to realize the importance that Mexicans attached to the national domain. In a country badly divided in many ways, according to historian Gene M. Brack, upon one issue "there was general accord: maintaining territorial integrity."[45] While Mexicans were very regional-minded in practice, an attitude that later hampered the war effort, the idea of any part of the national domain being detached, especially by a foreign power, threatened the very ideal of a Mexican nation.

This frame of mind was evident in California where in 1836 the natives rebelled and won autonomy within the Mexican Republic. Despite this semi-independent status, in late 1845 Governor Pío Pico warned *californios* that a united effort would be necessary in case of foreign invasion; he warned that this would not be another of California and Mexico's frequent internal conflicts: "Fellow citizens, united we can save our country . . . but if by misfortune we are divided, we will be victims. . . . Let us then unite and assure the integrity of the national territory. . . ."[46] Though Mexicans distrusted the central government, they sensed that the loss of territory, especially to the United States, meant more than the loss of land. They sensed that their way of life was in danger. Brack has argued that Mexicans discerned

a direct relationship between American expansion and ethnocentric, even crassly racist, elements within the United States. Over the years Mexicans had become increasingly aware that many Americans, especially those who most vociferously advocated Southwestern expansion, looked upon Mexicans as inferior beings. This had frightening implications, for Americans had respect for neither the rights nor the culture of those whom they considered inferior. They had been merciless in their treatment of the Indian and had reduced blacks to a brutal form of servitude. Mexicans were perceptive enough to recognize that a similar fate threatened them should they fall under American domination.[47]

Although peonage and ill-treatment of the Indian were common in Mexico, Mexicans who recognized the Indian background of their nation were aware that Anglos respected this heritage even less than Mexico's Spanish Catholic heritage. They were afraid that wherever Anglos gained control a caste system, with Mexicans, Indians, and Blacks in inferior positions, would be established. They even feared cultural extinction; according to Brack, in 1836:

> A pamphlet urging war with the United States declared that Mexico must triumph, for she had no other choice. The day that the United States acquired dominion in Mexico would be the day "when the Catholic religion would disappear from Mexican soil," and her fate would be similar to that of the "natives of that country," who had been "stripped of the last traces of their civilization."[48]

Because Mexicans imagined themselves being pushed off their land and culturally extinguished,[49] in 1846 they chose against heavy odds to go to war to defend the largely empty borderlands. By 1846 Mexicans, unlike the Spaniards who surrendered Florida and Louisiana before them, no longer saw the borderlands as a mere buffer; the region was part of the national territory where Mexican culture must flourish. Unfortunately for Mexico, domestic turmoil prevented the national government from obtaining the men, money, and resources necessary to wage even a defensive war effectively.

Although the decisive operations of the war were conducted in what is today Mexican territory—at such places as Tampico, Monterrey, Veracruz, Mexico City—conflict occurred in the far north as well. The arrival of North American forces in both California and New Mexico at first resulted in little violence, but this situation changed as the Anglo-Americans attempted to consolidate their rule. As in Texas, a number of Mexicans collaborated with the Anglos, a fact which has led to the myth that U.S. forces were greeted as liberators from Mexican tyranny. In New Mexico, Governor Manuel Armijo was divided between his political obligations and his economic interests. Armijo and other *nuevomexicanos* had made their fortunes in the lucrative commerce that developed with Missouri after Mexico permitted trade with the United States. He realized that hostilities would be bad for business, especially since some of his wagons were moving slightly ahead of Colonel Stephen W. Kearny's advancing army. While Armijo and others, engaged in the trade with Missouri, were reluctant to fight, an army of four thousand was gathered in Santa Fe under the command of Diego Archuleta and supported by other Mexicans, including the sons of Pedro Bautista Pino. Armijo, however, still first in command, refused to engage the enemy despite the fact that his army outnumbered the North Americans and held a strong defensive position. Instead, he disbanded his troops, and allowed New Mexico to be occupied by the United States. Abandoned by their governor, many *nuevomexicanos,* nevertheless, soon plotted resistance against the occupying force. An attempted revolt in Santa Fe in December of 1846 failed to come about when the U.S. governor, Charles Bent, was informed of it. However, thinking he had suppressed all resistance, Governor Bent made a trip to Taos on business; there on January 19, 1847, he was assassinated by *nuevomexicanos,* including Pueblo Indians. U.S. troops were sent from Santa Fe to suppress the rebellion, which had spread through much of northern New Mexico, but were successful only after several skirmishes with the rebels.[50]

In California North American forces occupied the major ports with little trouble, but when they began to move farther inland, *californios* feared they would confiscate property. Guerrilla warfare soon broke out in areas that had formally surrendered. In Los Angeles a full-scale revolt occurred when the North American commander imposed a curfew, closed stores, banned most social gatherings, and in general intimidated citizens. José María Flores, a former Mexican officer, led a group of rebels against the occupying troops and forced the commander to sign surrender terms. Flores then defeated groups of Yankees in Chino and Santa Barbara, virtually liberating southern California from foreign troops. Soon after, Stephen W. Kearny arrived in California from New Mexico, and at the Battle of San Pascual, which took place between Los Angeles and San Diego, he was defeated and wounded by a Mexican force under Andrés Pico. Despite these victories, the Mexicans were forced to surrender when Frémont arrived from northern California with reinforcements. By the spring of 1847, the United States had secured its conquest of the Mexican far north, and only awaited events in central Mexico to make the acquisition official.[51]

On Feburary 2, 1848, with Mexico City occupied by the United States, the Treaty of Guadalupe Hidalgo was signed. With the exception of a strip of territory in what is now southern Arizona and New Mexico, the present Southwest was ceded to the United States. Fortunately for Mexico and for the United States as well, the cries of those who wished to annex all of the southern republic remained wisely unheeded. In exchange for the land, the United States paid $15 million, assumed claims of its citizens against Mexico, promised to restrain Indian raids from the Southwest into Mexico, honored Mexican land grants, and offered U.S. citizenship to Mexicans remaining in the ceded territories.[52]

Because this treaty officially separated the first Chicanos from their mother country, it permanently changed their image of the homeland, which had now become the Southwest. No longer was the region a threatened defensive outpost of Mexican civilization or a potentially fertile part of the Mexican nation. Mexicans in the Southwest were now a conquered people in a conquered land.

# 3

## The Lost Land

We can date to 1848 the modern Chicano image of the Southwest as a lost land. The conquest of the present Southwest severed the region from the control of Mexico City and the local Mexican elites. In some places the Anglo-Americans seized complete political power almost immediately after the military conquest, but in other areas, notably New Mexico, the native leadership managed to maintain some influence after the occupation. Command of military power, of course, determined that Anglos would hold the major positions everywhere in the Southwest, but the factor that decisively undermined Mexican political strength was the enormous growth of the Anglo population. We have already seen that the increase of that population in eastern Texas destroyed local Mexican dominance even before the revolution of 1836. *Nuevo-mexicanos* were more fortunate because they remained a majority in New Mexico well into the twentieth century. In northern California, on the other hand, where the Gold Rush of 1849 resulted in a huge influx of Anglos, *californios* were left powerless almost immediately. Once having lost control of the government, Mexicans soon found themselves losing their economic base to the newcomers. Owing to the quagmire of litigation created by the requirement that Spanish and Mexican land grants be verified, Mexican elites in many parts of the Southwest lost their lands and with them they lost the social position that helped sustain the prestige of Mexican culture in the region.[1] Finding their culture steadily declining with the increasing influence of Anglo society, Mexicans began to see themselves as *"foreigners in their own land,"*[2] a self-image that appeared repeatedly in their writings and that affected their relations with the dominant group for much of the nineteenth century. One result of that alienation was the appearance, in both legend and reality, of the often well-born native hero who, victimized by Anglo society, rebelled against it.[3] Yet, though Mexicans felt themselves increasingly alienated from the Southwest, they continued to see it as their homeland. The fact that Mexico had once embraced the region was still too recent for Southwest Mexicans to have forgotten; not yet separated from their history in the borderlands, they still recalled their dispossession.

A week before the signing of the Treaty of Guadalupe Hidalgo, gold was discovered in northern California, a discovery that was to cause unprecedented immigration to the area. Although a Mexican ranchman had found gold in southern California in 1842, his find had been too small to attract people from far outside the locality. The discovery of 1848, however, increased the overall population of California from under 10,000 before the North American occupation to over 90,000 by 1850. The U.S. Census of 1850, which excluded Indians, listed 91,635 people in the state, of which approximately 7,500 were native, "white" Spanish-speaking Californians. In addition to these *californios* there were about 6,500 other Mexicans who had recently arrived in the gold fields from areas south of the new international boundary.[4] Furthermore, in the first year of the Gold Rush 5,000 South Americans came to California, bringing the total Spanish-speaking population up to roughly 20,000.[5] Despite this increase and the arrival of many foreigners who spoke neither Spanish nor English, by 1850 Anglo-Americans outnumbered the Spanish-speaking three to one. In two years the Latin Americans went from a large majority to a minority.

The *californios* were, needless to say, amazed at the numbers of new arrivals and felt threatened. Mariano Vallejo, a *californio* who had long supported annexation to the United States, left a largely unfavorable description of the newcomers, a description which incidentally revealed his own ethnocentric and even racist sentiments:

> Australia sent us a swarm of bandits. . . . The Mormons, lascivious but very industrious people, sent the ship *Brooklyn*. . . . Mexico inundated us with a wave of gamblers. . . . Italy sent us musicians. . . . [who] lost no time in fraternizing with the keepers of gambling houses. . . .

Although Vallejo emphasized the negative, he did praise those he considered good workers, such as the Mormons and Italian gardeners who became small farmers. He had nothing but praise for the Germans, and he held the Chileans in high regard: "Chile sent us many laborers who were very useful and contributed not a little to the development of the resources of the country." On the other hand, reflecting the extreme prejudice against Asians in nineteenth-century California, Vallejo wrote, "I believe that the great Chinese immigration which invaded California in '50, '51, and '52 was very harmful to the moral and material development of the country, . . . the Chinese women, . . . it seems had made it a duty to keep the hospitals always filled with syphilitics." Though this racial slur was vicious, Vallejo saved his most bitter remarks for the non-Mormon, Anglo majority from the rest of the United States:

But all these evils became negligible in comparison with the swollen torrent of shysters who came from Missouri and other states of the Union. No sooner had they arrived than they assumed the title of attorney and began to seek means of depriving the Californians of their farms and other properties.[6]

At first the population increase was confined to the mining region in the interior of northern California, which permitted *californios* to retain some political control along the coast, especially south of Monterey. Because of this political strength, eight Mexicans participated in the constitutional convention that in 1849 formed the first state government of California; their experience at the convention reflected their people's position in relation to the Anglo-American majority. Since the proceedings were conducted in English, the *californio* delegates, finding it necessary to use interpreters in their native country, felt like foreigners; at one point one of the Mexicans became angry when he sensed that an Anglo representative had called him a foreigner. Even though they declined to vote as a block on all matters, in general the *californio* delegates did promote the interests of their people. Realizing that Mexicans were now a minority, the Spanish-speaking representatives engaged in many maneuvers to make the Mexican position under the new regime more secure, but their success was limited.[7]

Since *californios* continued to own most of the land in the proposed state, they feared that the highest taxes would be placed on them. Their representatives gained a concession on this matter when it was decided that assessors would be elected locally, thus permitting Mexicans, in counties where they were numerous, some control over their own taxation. The *californio* delegates also succeeded in having the new constitution require that all laws be translated into Spanish. With regard to the franchise, they confronted the serious threat of racial discrimination when the question of Indian voting rights arose; since some of the Mexican delegates were mestizos, and one was an Indian, they strongly opposed the effort to deny Indians the vote. Despite this resistance, the convention decided that only certain Indians would be allowed to vote and only by direct action of the legislature. Given the large white majority at the convention, this has to be regarded as a small victory for the *californios*.[8]

Though the Mexican delegation managed these few successes, the five southern California members failed to achieve perhaps their most important objective, that of separating their area from the north. By creating a territory in the south where they were the majority (and would be until the 1870s),[9] the *californios* of that area hoped to escape domination by the Anglo majority that had settled in the north. To achieve this the *californio* delegates from the south engaged in several complex maneuvers. One was to push for territorial status rather than statehood for all of California, thus keeping the boundaries less rigid and permitting future division. Another was to include within the state, if such it was to be, as much as possible of the land considered at one time or another part of California by Mexico, in other words all of present California and Nevada, and fractions of other present states. By creating such a large state, Mexicans from the southern counties hoped it would eventually become unwieldy and subsequently be divided, possibly leaving the Spanish-speaking in control of southern California. Though these mechinations met with no success and were carried out by the Mexican delegation from the south, they revealed the desire all *californios* had for a land where they might retain a measure of independence. This desire did not disappear with the Constitutional Convention of 1849; movements for the division of the state continued for years.[10]

One of the most articulate agitators for such a division, and for other actions beneficial for California's Mexicans, was Francisco Ramírez, editor of *El clamor público,* the Spanish-language newspaper of Los Angeles during the 1850s. Ramírez was a progressive who hoped for full participation of his people in the brilliant future he predicted for California. Despite the unrest caused by the Gold Rush and the threat that the mines might be exhausted, in June of 1855 Ramírez optimistically wrote:

> As great as California's mineral resources are, its livestock and the invaluable products of its agriculture are no less notable. . . . Adding to these great elements of prosperity, a clear and glossy sky and a healthy climate, it can be said that California is the paradise of America. In regard to natural beauty, the sublime picturesque scenes of lovely Italy and Switzerland do not equal it.

With an increase in the number of respectable citizens, the improvement of highways, and the building of railroads, Ramírez saw California becoming the center for commerce with the Orient, trade which would result in the riches necessary to raise great cities. In this picture we find elements of earlier images of the Southwest: the natural paradise of the Aztecs, the early Spanish land of gold, and the Mexican land of promise. Interestingly, we also find an Anglo vision of prosperous cities built by commerce, especially commerce by rail.[11]

Ramírez drew this optimistic sketch of California in an early issue of his newspaper (published from 1855 through 1859). Though he never doubted the state would reach greatness, he always suspected Mexicans would have little share in the prosperity. By August 1856 he bitterly commented that "the faith that [*californios*] had in the new government that had just established itself on the shores of the Pacific has vanished forever." And he added, "All are convinced that *California is lost to all Spanish-Americans. . . .*" The more he dealt editorially with issues directly affecting his people, the more publicly pessimistic he became. His early public optimism may be attributed to the knowledge that many of his first subscribers were Anglos, whom he was hesitant to offend; certainly he was privately aware of the abuses Mexicans and other Latin Americans had suffered in California since 1848. In fact Ramírez complained in August 1856, "Despotism, [and] crime have existed here since the day of the discovery of gold. . . . Brute force is the only law that is observed." Unfortunately for Latin Americans much of that brutality and despotism was directed at them. [12]

Because of their proximity to the mines, *californios* were some of the first to reach the gold fields. They were followed by other Mexicans, collectively called Sonorans, who trekked from northern Mexico, across the southern California deserts to the coast, then north to the mines. Chileans and Peruvians found it relatively easy to reach the state by ship directly up the Pacific coast. Because these people arrived early and possessed the rich mining tradition of Spanish America, they were more successful in the gold fields than were the Anglos who were forced to learn from them. As a result, animosity between Anglos and these "foreigners" developed to such a point that the legislature passed the Foreign Miners' Tax Law of 1850, a law whose "avowed purpose," as Josiah Royce sarcastically remarked, "was as far as possible to exclude foreigners from these mines, the God-given property of the American people." When officials attempted to collect the exorbitant tax in Mexican mining settlements, they encountered resistance. Before long, rioting between Anglo and Latin American miners broke out; eventually the Latin Americans were expelled, with many of the Mexicans fleeing to southern California. The violence of the gold fields, which often amounted to race war, soon spread throughout California; and some Mexicans, chased from their claims, became bandits as a way of getting revenge. Before long almost any crime was blamed on Mexicans, and the lynching of Mexicans became common through much of the third quarter of the nineteenth century. [13]

Interestingly, much of the so-called banditry took on the character of a guerrilla resistance movement. Among the bandits and those who gave them aid were Latin Americans of all types, peons and aristocrats, native *californios* and newcomers. Of the native poor, historian James Miller Guinn commented:

a strange metamorphosis took place in the character of the lower classes of the native Californians. . . . Before the conquest by the Americans. . . . There were no organized bands of outlaws among them. . . . The Americans not only took possession of their country and its government, but in many cases despoiled them of their ancestral acres and their personal property. Injustice rankles, and they were often treated by the rougher American elements as aliens and intruders, who had no right in the land of their birth.[14]

Of the disinherited native elite, Josiah Royce wrote, "those numerous degraded Spanish or half-breed outlaws, the creatures of our injustice, the sons some-times . . . of the great landowners whom we had robbed, if one remembers how they infested country roads . . ., one sees at length in full how our injus-tice avenged itself upon us. . . ."[15] While many of the California bandits were simply criminals who preyed on all ethnic groups, at least two gained reputations as resistance fighters; these two were the legendary Joaquín Mur-rieta and Tiburcio Vásquez.

The facts of Joaquín Murrieta's life are obscure; he so successfully concealed his identity from the authorities that they were never quite sure who he was even after they claimed to have killed him in 1853. According to one version of his life, he was a Mexican miner whose claim was jumped by a group of Anglos who had already killed his brother; they knocked him unconscious, raped his wife, then murdered her. Murrieta became an outlaw, swearing to avenge himself on all Anglos.[16] He became a legend during his own life: soon crimes all over California were attributed to his efforts, and other ban-dits were mistaken for him. Though Anglos regarded him as a curse, Mexi-cans and other Latin Americans saw him as a hero; long after his exploits, corridos, popular ballads, were sung in praise of him. In one of these, sung in the first person, we find a clear statement of the Mexican's view of himself in relation to the conquered Southwest of the 1850s:

> I came from Hermosillo [Sonora]
> In search of gold and riches;
> With fierceness I defended
> The noble and simple Indian.
>
> . . . . . . . . . . . . . . .
>
> Now I go out on the roads
> Americans to kill,
> You [who] were the cause
> Of the death of my brother.
>
> . . . . . . . . . . . . . . .
>
> I am neither gringo nor stranger
> In this land where I walk;
> California is Mexico's

Because God wished it so;
And in my serape . . . I carry
My certificate of baptism. [17]

Clearly the anonymous balladeer, and many of those who repeated the song, refused to acknowledge the presence of the new boundary. This ballad suggests that Mexicans, even those born south of the new border, continued, in opposition to the Anglo conquerers, to identify with the land of the Southwest, and to some extent with the native Indians.

Though Murrieta was a half-mythic character, the motives that supposedly drove him to crime are similar to those of the very real Tiburcio Vásquez, captured in 1876. While Murrieta seems to have been a Sonoran miner, Vásquez belonged to a relatively well-off *californio* family. He became an outlaw because of the repeated insults he and other *californios* suffered when courting their own women in competition with Anglo men; as he put it, "A spirit of hatred and revenge took possession of me. I had numerous fights in defense of what I believed to be my rights and those of my countrymen." Apparently he felt this spirit was widespread because he once claimed he could revolutionize southern California if he had $60,000 to buy arms and recruit men. Indeed the condition of the Spanish-speaking in California was such that many prominent *californio* families were represented among the bandit rebels who roamed the highways in the third quarter of the nineteenth century. [18]

One reason for the rebellion of some of the younger members of the elite was the Land Law of 1851. Although, as *El clamor público* noted, "The first occupants of this soil were of Spanish descent [sic]" [19] and were entitled to their property by the Treaty of Guadalupe Hidalgo, the Land Law of 1851 required them to prove ownership of their estates. Anglo squatters, believing in a "right of conquest," had challenged the validity of Spanish and Mexican land grants. Since the boundaries of the original grants were often loosely drawn, the *californios* were soon caught in what seemed endless difficulties: an unfamiliar judicial system conducted in English, unscrupulous lawyers who demanded exorbitant fees often payable only in land, squatters who refused to pay rent until grants were validated, raising money through profitable sales or low-interest loans while claims were being processed, and making land productive without sufficient cash. The Land Law of 1851 together with the *californios'* unfamiliarity with the competitive Anglo economic system eventually led to the loss of their property. (Because the population there was smaller, the process was slower in southern than northern California.) [20]

In the articles of *El clamor público* protesting the land losses and other injustices inflicted on Latin Americans, Francisco Ramírez proposed a variety of possible solutions to these problems. Besides advocating division of the state, which would free southern California from a legislature heavily influenced by squatters, *El clamor público* suggested even more extreme measures. At one point Ramírez helped promote an unsuccessful plan to settle *californios* and other Mexicans in Sonora where they might escape Anglo domination. (He himself left Los Angeles and lived in Sonora between 1860 and 1862.) In one issue an article was published arguing that California be made a protectorate of the European and Latin American nations whose citizens had settled in the state. This was argued on the grounds that California had been "grabbed from Mexico," "that the Hispanic-American and European population, spread throughout the territory, . . . [had] established unchangeable customs," and finally that the United States threatened to "infest" the Pacific region of the world that was the heritage of Latin Americans "emanating originally from the Inca." In a tone of surrender, *El clamor público* once also commented:

> We are now under the American flag, be it through our own choice or by force, and it is probable that we will remain thus always. We should then accept the events and vicissitudes of our age and familiarize ourselves with the new language, habits, and customs; thus we will not be dominated but equal in everything. This is best for us and our posterity.

Surely, however, Ramírez never truly agreed with this statement since his more extreme ideas were published after he had written it.[21]

In order to participate fully, especially economically, in California's brilliant future, Ramírez feared Mexicans would have to assimilate, cutting completely their ties with Mexico, the nation which "to insure its independence, and [to insure] that its name did not disappear forever . . . was forced to part with a great portion of its territory," and was forced to leave its northern citizens "strangers in our own country."[22] Though Ramírez and other *californio* progressives fervently believed in economic development, they did not wish to renounce Mexican culture, a renunciation that U.S. society demanded before it would allow them to feel at home in their native country. Even Mariano Vallejo, who had desired annexation to the United States, feeling it would bring prosperity to California, did not give up all ties to Mexico. In 1877 when he went to Mexico City to lobby for a railroad between that capital and his state, he commented,

> I am an American because the treaty of Guadalupe placed me on the other side of the line dividing the two nations, but I was born a Mexican, my ancestors were Mexicans. . . . I have both Mexican and American children and I desire

for my native land all the prosperity and progress enjoyed by the country of some of my children and mine by adoption. The day that Mexico has a railroad which devouring distance unites it with California, commerce and industry will progress.[23]

Even as Vallejo sought closer ties with Mexico, however, a railroad was being planned from the East to southern California, a railroad that would destroy Mexican dominance in its last major bastion in the state. The boom of the 1880s would bring thousands of Easterners to Los Angeles.

Though they often admired the political ideals and the material advances of the United States, Mexicans throughout the Southwest were at the very least uncomfortable with Anglo civilization because, like Ramírez and Vallejo of California, they saw the damage this civilization was inflicting on their people and their culture. Even those like Vallejo who favored North American rule felt that their property, their way of life, and even their lives were too often threatened. Despite these threats, most Mexicans tried to make the best of their difficult situation. Even in Texas, where relations between Anglos and Mexicans had been hostile since before the Texas Revolution, a San Antonio newspaper, *El bejareño,* found positive things to say about *tejano* life in 1855:

> As a consequence of one of those changes that are daily observed in the destiny of nations, Texas was violently separated from the Mexican nation. . . . Did this change result in good or evil for the country? The liberty that we enjoy, the wealth and general prosperity, the moderation and fairness of our laws on one side, on the other, the military despotism, the poverty, the edicts, the political convulsions that prevail in Mexico . . . peremptorily answer the question for any intelligent and rational man.[24]

Yet we do find that at least one thing disturbed *El bejareño:* "The majority [of *tejanos*], we must confess, lacks education, and they frequently pay for this deficiency, finding themselves strangers in the land of their birth. . . ." The newspaper clearly saw education, especially education that would teach the ways of the Anglo, as a means toward greater acceptance and participation in the society that had taken possession of Texas. From this we may infer that *El bejareño* saw the retention of Mexican culture as an impediment to success in the new society, as excess clothing merely serving to alienate *tejanos* from the United States. But such was not the case. The newspaper wanted *tejanos* to be able to function comfortably in the new society, but not to abandon the "old ways." We find this attitude clearly evident in a brief description of the schools *El bejareño* desired: "We will always persist in promoting the foundation and stimulation of the *Public Schools* in which, without losing the language of Cervantes, Mexican-Texan children will acquire the national language. . . ."[25] Thus, as early as 1855, Southwest Mexicans were calling for an educational system that would teach them English, and by extension other Anglo ways, without depriving them of their own language and culture.

Even though *El bejareño* claimed that life was much better in Texas than in Mexico, many *tejanos* disagreed. Juan Nepomuceno Seguín, one of the *tejanos* whom José Enrique de la Peña had labeled traitors for their support of the Texas Republic, later found life in Texas so difficult that he left and lived in Mexico for several years. Although he had been a cavalry officer during the Texas Revolution and had served as mayor of San Antonio under the Texas Republic, he was accused by certain envious Anglos of disloyalty. A general in the Mexican Army, in a deliberate attempt to discredit him, had announced that Seguín was actually a loyal citizen of Mexico; using this statement against him, Seguín's Anglo rivals succeeded in destroying him politically. Fearing for his life, Seguín left Texas in 1842 and did not return until 1848, by which time he was no longer a serious threat to his rivals, who by then controlled San Antonio. In his memoirs in 1858, Seguín described his decision to flee Texas: "A victim to the wickedness of a few men, whose imposture was favored by their origin, and recent domination over the country; a foreigner in my native land. . . . Crushed by sorrow . . ., I sought for a shelter amongst those against whom I had fought. . . ." Though Seguín clearly felt no loyalty to Mexico, he found that being a "Mexican" in Texas was far from comfortable; so true was this that even in 1858 he was writing his memoirs to counter the attacks that were still leveled against him.[26]

Many *tejanos* went to Mexico after the Anglo occupation because, for decades after San Jacinto and Guadalupe Hidalgo, it was simply unsafe in Texas. Bandits from both the United States and Mexico roamed South Texas, making harmonious ethnic relations difficult. Several times, "wars" between Anglos and *tejanos* broke out across the state. Between San Antonio and the Gulf, commercial rivalry between teamsters of the two groups became open conflict in 1857. In 1877 months of interracial violence over rights to salt beds near El Paso ended with the flight of many *tejano* families into Mexico. The Civil War, which found *tejanos* generally opposed to the slave-holding Confederacy, also led to much racial warfare. But the most important episode was the revolt of the Texas equivalent to California's Murrieta and Vásquez— Juan N. Cortina. Cortina was born in the lower Rio Grande Valley into a wealthy Mexican family. In 1859, when a marshal arrested and mistreated a former employee of the family, Cortina shot the officer, declaring war against those Anglos who were persecuting *tejanos*.[27] Cortina sought redress for the ills inflicted on his people and called for armed rebellion against the oppressors: "Mexicans! My part is taken; the voice of revelation whispers to me that to me is entrusted the work of breaking the chains of your slavery. . . ."[28]

Indeed Cortina had done his part; for before making this statement he had occupied Brownsville and punished a certain group of Anglos he considered especially cruel. In late 1859 his forces gained much support in the area between Rio Grande City and Brownsville, a distance of a hundred miles. Though he carried the Mexican flag, Cortina attempted neither to regain South Texas for Mexico nor to establish an independent state, but to improve the conditions of his people by threatening Anglos with violence if they failed to respect Mexican rights. During this Texas rebellion from September to December of 1859, Cortina failed to liberate *tejanos,* but he did win several victories over forces sent against him by the governments of both Mexico and Texas. However, he was defeated by U.S. troops at Rio Grande City in December 1859 and fled to Mexico. In 1861 he made one more raid into Texas to avenge several Mexicans who had been killed by Confederates, but was again forced across the border.[29]

After his intrepid but unsuccessful Texas revolt, Cortina spent the rest of his life involved in the maelstrom of Mexico's politics, where he acted as daringly as he had in Texas.[30] Significantly, Cortina had carried on his anti-Anglo activities in the old, Mexican-settled sections of Texas, sections that remained extensions of Mexico. Since these areas contained Mexican majorities, Anglo dominance seemed especially unjust; consequently resistance was stronger and more successful. Like Seguín, Cortina was forced into Mexico after experiencing the problems of being a "Mexican" in Texas, but unlike Seguín, he resisted before he left and briefly continued his fight from Mexico paying little attention to a boundary that to him, as to most Mexicans, was unjust and artificial.

By the 1880s, because of better enforcement on the part of U.S. and Mexican authorities, open conflict along the border had temporarily lessened, yet the life of *tejanos* continued to be difficult. Since they had long been outnumbered, their political power in the state was minimal; even in their enclaves in South and West Texas, the constant pattern of violence and intimidation that had driven many to Mexico prevented those who remained from being sufficiently assertive. Land grant difficulties of the sort experienced in California had occurred in Texas after the revolution, and later *tejanos* lost other property when they were unable to compete effectively in the aggressive Anglo economy. With their political and economic base undermined, *tejanos* made little progress even in such areas as education.[31]

In 1879 we find *El horizonte,* a Corpus Christi newspaper, still asking for
the public schools that *El bejareño* had requested in 1855:

> Mexican children in Corpus Christi are not even foreigners. . . . [and yet] innu-
> merable are the Mexican heads of family with their children who have been
> turned away from the door of the school covered with shame, turned away from
> where they were going to demand the completion of the faultless obligation
> [*sic*] to which thay have a right as citizens.

This lack of education made *tejanos* a "disinherited-class" subject to harassment by Anglos merely because "the former [the Mexican] is the son of
Guatimoc [*sic,* last emperor of the Aztecs] and the latter are sons of Washington." To remedy this situation *El horizonte,* going beyond the earlier position
of *El bejareño,* argued not only that public education be extended to Mexicans but that it be bilingual. Otherwise it would be completely ineffective:
"It would be convenient to appoint a professor who speaks English and is
Mexican, because otherwise, that is to say, to appoint a teacher who does not
know Spanish perfectly, we believe no result would be obtained at all, and
the children would do nothing more than waste precious time." *El horizonte*
realized that if *tejanos* were ever to live comfortably in Texas, they had to
learn the language and ways of the dominant group, but the newspaper did
not believe this could be done by ignoring Mexican culture.[32]

While Mexicans in Texas and California by 1850 found themselves and
their civilization inundated by Anglo immigrants, the situation in New
Mexico, which then included most of Arizona and part of Colorado, was at
first different. New Mexico attracted few Anglo immigrants soon after 1848
because it had little gold, less arable land than neighboring areas, problems
with the Apaches, and a native Mexican population about ten times that of
either Texas or California. In fact, because U.S. troops provided a market for
local goods, the initial North American occupation of New Mexico brought a
measure of prosperity to the province. This prosperity and the promise of
improved defense for the territory even permitted *nuevomexicanos* to expand
their areas of settlement so that in the early 1850s the Spanish-speaking were
able to found their first permanent towns in present-day southeastern Colorado,
an area formerly belonging to but never really occupied by Spain and Mexico.
Present-day Arizona north of the Gila, also left unsettled by Spain or Mexico,
was made part of the U.S. territory of New Mexico after Guadalupe Hidalgo.
With the Gadsden Purchase of 1854, a sliver of land, including Tucson and
the Mesilla Valley, was added to the territory. The United States thus incorporated another though smaller group of Mexicans within its boundaries; these

new residents, especially those in the Tucson area, also benefited initially from the Anglo-American occupation.[33]

The relationship that Anglos and Mexicans saw between themselves and the geographical space they occupied strongly affected events in the territory of New Mexico from 1848 until statehood was achieved by Arizona and New Mexico in 1912. The division of the huge territory of 1854 into the present-day states, the location of the various state capitals, the promotion of public schools, the building of railroads, as well as the writing of constitutions, the adjudication of land claims, and the perpetration of interracial violence were all heavily influenced by the Anglo desire to minimize Mexican control of the area. As Anglos moved into the territory, the problems that were experienced in California and Texas eventually occurred in New Mexico also, becoming severe in the 1880s. By this time, with the Apaches subjected by the military, *nuevomexicanos* had pushed out of their Rio Grande enclaves east into the Texas Panhandle, and also southeast and southwest within present-day New Mexico. However, this expansion ceased when confronted by the movement of Anglo Texans in roughly the opposite directions. The traditional animosity between Texans and Mexicans together with the competition for space led to widespread violence. In the Panhandle a Mexican folk hero of French-Mexican descent, Sostenes l'Archevêque, avenged the murder of his father by killing more than twenty Anglos. Unfortunately, these killings resulted in wholesale retaliations against Mexicans who were forced to retreat into New Mexico, but this retreat did them little good since throughout the territory Mexican sheepherders and Anglo cattlemen constantly fought each other. For example, in southern New Mexico the entrance of Texans caused violent competition for pasture land. As a result, many Mexican families, fleeing Texan terrorism, abandoned their homes and ranches in the Socorro and Doña Ana areas and went to Mexico.[34]

The movement of Anglo cattlemen into New Mexico was followed by a wave of farmers in the mid-1880s, increasing the struggle for land, the best acres of which were usually the legal property of *nuevomexicanos,* the first settlers. As in California, Mexicans gradually lost their property through unfamiliarity with the new legal and economic systems so that by the turn of the century four-fifths of the early Spanish and Mexican grants were in Anglo hands. Outraged by their deteriorating situation, *nuevomexicanos* in the 1880s organized several groups of nightriders who vandalized the property of those they held responsible for native losses. In New Mexico an additional factor depriving Mexicans of land rights was a congressional act of 1891 setting aside large tracts as national forests, tracts that had formerly been considered land held in common by ranchers and villagers for grazing purposes. As a result of this act, *nuevomexicanos* were forced to reduce their flocks of sheep, thus cutting the production of wool and causing a depression in the industry. (To this day grazing rights in the national forests are an important issue to Chicanos in New Mexico.) Yet in spite of the loss of land and the dwindling of their economic base, *nuevomexicanos* were able to maintain and have continued to maintain some political power in New Mexico because they have always formed a large percentage of the population. Also, the delay in the arrival of significant numbers of Anglos permitted *nuevomexicanos* to gain some political and economic expertise before the major conflict of the 1880s. Finally, a small number of the elite, who were able to hold on to their economic position, kept a measure of political power and prevented their people from losing all social prestige.[35]

New Mexico then is the one place where Southwest Mexicans succeeded in keeping a modicum of permanent control over their homeland. In fact, partly because Mexicans seemed to have too much power in the northern Rio Grande Valley, Anglos in other parts of the territory constantly tried to escape the rule of Santa Fe by proposing divisions of the huge territory of 1854. (As we have seen, Mexicans had unsuccessfully tried a similar scheme in California, but in that case to escape Anglo dominance.) From as early as 1854, attempts were made to create a territory of Arizona with a boundary running east-west from Texas to California, thus including present southern New Mexico and excluding present northern Arizona. In 1861–62 an invading Southern army actually established such a territory under the Confederacy. Many Mexicans actively opposed the short-lived new government because it derived from Texas, legalized slavery, and specified that English would be the language of the legislature, thus severely limiting Mexican participation.[36]

In 1863, after the Confederate withdrawal, the federal government organized the Arizona territory that would eventually become the state. This new territory was formed and controlled by Anglo businessmen who hoped to build railroads and develop the mineral resources of the area without interference from Santa Fe. Although Mexicans were more numerous than Anglos, and Indians heavily outnumbered all the settlers, Anglos were able to take immediate control because of their connections with big business in the East. The small Mexican elite, nominal owners of much land that was often in Indian hands, had some influence but not nearly as much as their counterparts in New Mexico.[37] The separation of the Mexicans in Arizona from their compatriots in New Mexico deprived the former of the protection of Santa Fe; yet since they were still a majority of the settlers in the new territory, they could at least hope to wield more power in the future. This was not true of the many Mexicans who were separated from Santa Fe when they were included within the boundaries of Colorado Territory in 1861.

Unlike the isolated group in and near Tucson, Mexicans in southeastern Colorado lived close to Santa Fe; their separation from that capital by an unnatural boundary weakened them by making them a minority in Colorado rather than part of the majority in New Mexico. The division of the Mexican population in this way permitted Anglos to gain more leverage in Santa Fe by increasing their own percentage of the voters in New Mexico. Though the usual reasons given by Anglos for the new boundary involved slavery and land speculation,[38] this division of the Spanish-speaking at the very least revealed a disregard for, if not a deliberate denial of, the Mexicans' desire to govern themselves in the areas where they lived. Indeed fear of undue Mexican political strength in the Southwest also influenced the placing of capitals in Anglo towns rather than Mexican settlements. Tucson was passed over in favor of Phoenix, and an attempt was made to replace Santa Fe with Albuquerque, where Anglos had settled in large numbers. This followed the pattern set in Texas and California, where Austin had replaced San Antonio, and Sacramento had replaced Monterey and Los Angeles.

In spite of such geopolitical maneuvers and the support of the military, Anglo-Americans in New Mexico Territory could not completely exclude *nuevomexicanos* from government, simply because the latter made up a vast majority, especially in the first years after the conquest. Consequently, from the beginning the U.S. officials appointed Mexicans, even those who had not cooperated in the conquest, to important positions in the government. Interestingly, one of the results of this policy was to further the cleavage between those *nuevomexicanos* who favored Anglo-American rule and those who opposed it.[39] As time passed, this cleavage developed into one between those who favored "Americanization" and those who wished to retain Mexican culture—a cleavage that persists.

Two of the more noteworthy supporters of Americanization were Miguel Antonio Otero I, New Mexico's delegate to Congress from 1855 to 1861, and his son, Miguel A. Otero II, who served as territorial governor from 1897 to 1906. Though born in New Mexico, the senior Otero attended college in Missouri and New York, entering the legal profession in 1852. His family's business ties with merchants in Missouri oriented him toward acceptance of the customs and political rule of the United States. He married a woman from a prominent Southern family and was a successful businessman, becoming vice president of the Atchison, Topeka & Santa Fe Railroad. According to his son, politically Otero "represented the progressive American element in the Territory. The Otero, Chaves and Armijo families were all for the American Party as against the Mexican Party. . . . a powerful anti-American priest-ridden party." The Oteros sided wholeheartedly with the forces of economic development and thus supported the coming of the railroad, which they must have realized would undermine Mexican culture.[40]

In 1882, at the opening of the Montezuma Hotel in Las Vegas, New Mexico, the senior Otero praised the railroad as a civilizer. His rhetoric curiously mingled symbols from the Indian, Mexican, and Anglo traditions of the territory:

> The Pecos Indians. . . . implicitly believed that their mighty but ill-fated emperor, the glorious Montezuma, disappeared from view amid the clouds of their native mountains, that he promised to return . . . that he would come in glory from the east. . . . The last remnant of the faithful old tribe has disappeared . . ., but we who fill their places, have lived to see the return of the mighty chieftain [the train from Chicago later named the *Chief* and the *Super Chief*]. With power and majesty he comes, with the ancient sun-god from the east, and tonight we hail his coming in the new and splendid halls of the Montezuma![41]

In this speech Otero alluded to a southwestern Indian legend, incorporated from the Spaniards and Mexicans who thought the Aztecs had originated in New Mexico, a legend that paralleled the Aztec myth of the beneficent god, Quetzalcóatl, who was to return gloriously from exile in the east to rule Mexico City. In 1519 the Aztec emperor Moctezuma (confused with Quetzalcóatl in the Southwest) mistook Cortés for the returning god and allowed the Spaniards to seize his palace unopposed. Ironically, Otero was similarly welcoming a conquering god from the east, the beneficent railroad that would help New Mexico.

That other *nuevomexicanos* disagreed is evident from a statement made in 1872 by Francisco Perea, who once ran for office on a platform opposing the building of railroads. "We don't want you damned Yankees in the country," he said, realizing that the trains would bring immigrants from the East; "We can't compete with you, you will drive us all out, and we shall have no home left us." In 1880 at Cow Creek Hill, railroad construction workers and local Mexicans actually fought a pitched battle because the natives feared the trains would bring an invasion of their lands.[42]

During his terms in Congress, Miguel A. Otero I tried to have New Mexico admitted as a state but failed. From the time of the conquest until 1872, both traditional and progressive Mexicans hoped for statehood, the former because it would bring them home rule, the latter because it would mean full acceptance in the Union. Early movements were frustrated not only by the national struggle between the free and slave states but also by the eastern view of New Mexico as a foreign land. The Civil War ended the slavery issue, but the prejudice against "foreign" New Mexico persisted. In 1872 traditional *nuevomexicanos* made a final effort to gain home rule through statehood; they were opposed, according to historian Howard Roberts Lamar, by Anglos in the southern counties who thought New Mexico should wait "until enough Americans were there to balance the Spanish influence effectively."[43] Later, because the Anglo population greatly increased in the late 1870s and the 1880s, *nuevomexicanos* lost interest in statehood. Territorial status then had the advantage of preventing the growing local Anglo population from gaining more political power. In 1889, in an important referendum in which education was a major issue, *nuevomexicanos* as a whole voted against statehood because it seemed untimely to progressives and a definite threat to traditionalists. Progressives, including the younger Otero, thought, because few nonsectarian public schools teaching English and modern democratic (Anglo) ideals existed, that *nuevomexicanos* were unprepared for statehood. Traditionalists, knowing that such schools would be promoted under a new government, voted against statehood because they wanted, at best, schools supported but not administered by the state.[44]

Although the Catholic Church vehemently opposed secular public school education, the issue, as far as Mexicans were concerned, was not simply religious. In 1889 the Archbishop of Santa Fe proposed a system of state-supported church schools like that of Quebec, a system that permitted French Canadians to preserve their language and customs as well as religion.[45] In 1884 Archbishop Jean Baptiste Lamy had condemned those Catholics who refused to send their children to Catholic schools (which composed the majority of schools in the territory) because English was not used to the exclusion of Spanish. He had argued that though English was the language of commerce, "we cannot but recommend that they [the schools] neglect not to perfect the children in the knowledge and use of their beautiful native castilian [*sic*] language, of which they should always show themselves proud. . . ." Since the language and customs of *nuevomexicanos* reflected and reinforced their Catholicism, the church sought to preserve much of their culture. To most Mexicans, religion, language, and ethnic identity were inseparable. In 1873 *El clarín mejicano,* a Santa Fe newspaper, had argued that it was practically the sacred duty of Mexicans to subscribe to the paper because it was in Spanish: "Little can be said in favor of the Spanish people of this country . . . who do not wish to support a newspaper written in the language of their parents who

gave them birth and taught them the Holy Faith, which . . . is so . . .
respected by *nuevomexicanos.*" Mexicans saw secular public schools as a threat
not only to their religion but to their culture.[46]

By the turn of the century *nuevomexicano* opposition to statehood lessened
primarily because the number of Anglos increased to the point where they
could draft a constitution and have the territory admitted with a minimum
of Mexican help. If *nuevomexicanos* hoped to have any influence on the educational and other policies of the new state, they would have to participate in
the statehood movement. The administration of the younger Miguel A. Otero
as governor from 1897 to 1906 was instrumental in winning *nuevomexicano*
support for statehood. Otero was born in St. Louis of a Mexican father and an
Anglo mother, educated in the East, and raised in close contact with Anglo
businessmen and politicians. It is not surprising that on his appointment one
Chicago newspaper praised Otero as "thoroughly American in every way."[47]

Although he spoke Spanish, Otero considered his Mexican culture of minor
importance. From his lengthy memoirs, we can infer that he saw assimilation
of Mexicans into the larger society as an inevitable consequence of progress.
To him, the decline of Mexican culture was unimportant as long as *nuevomexicanos* advanced economically and politically with the rest of society. In
fact, in his memoirs he regarded antagonism between Anglo and Mexican
interests as a thing of the past. He claimed that with increased (Anglo)
immigration, new railroads, new industries, and Americanized cities, New
Mexico in 1881 "became one of the great territories of the Union" and that
"even such old prejudices as the racial discrimination between Americans and
Mexicans were gradually wearing off. . . ."[48] Nevertheless, being the first
*nuevomexicano* appointed governor, Otero was very popular among Mexicans,
and having become an advocate of statehood, he soon had their support for
that cause as well as his administration. Governor Otero rewarded them for
their support by paying special attention to local disputes and by pardoning
criminals liberally, two policies that were especially appreciated because they
made the Governor appear accessible to the "little man" in the way governors
had been during Spanish and Mexican rule. Otero also gained Mexican support by keeping the capital at Santa Fe and by opposing the admission of
New Mexico and Arizona as a single state.[49]

Much of the opposition in Congress, and in the East, to New Mexico statehood resulted from the belief that the Spanish-speaking were too powerful in
the territory. Consequently, in 1906 an attempt was made to join predominantly Anglo Arizona to New Mexico, thus making Anglos the majority in
the new state. This plan, Lamar has commented, appealed to Anglos in New
Mexico and progressive *nuevomexicanos,* but most

Spanish-Americans in New Mexico did not care to become a minority in a giant state when they could be a majority in a smaller one. Using the same reasoning, the Anglo-American citizens of Arizona were opposed to an increase in the proportion of their own Spanish-American minority.[50]

Although Anglos and progressive Mexicans had enough votes to pass "jointure" in New Mexico, Anglo-Arizonans overwhelmingly rejected the idea in the referendum held in their territory. Even though Otero had opposed jointure, fearing his political machine would lose control in a larger state, his position also served the interests of traditional *nuevomexicanos*. Because jointure was defeated, in 1912 New Mexico was admitted separately to the Union with a constitution heavily influenced by the Spanish-speaking. Since Mexicans still made up much of the population within the boundaries of the new state, they were able to safeguard their culture, at least in writing, in a number of ways. Among the numerous guarantees were the recognition of Spanish as an official language and the promise of bilingual education.[51]

Although Otero had indirectly helped preserve Mexican culture in the Southwest, the real credit belonged to those who intentionally sought that end. Casimiro Barela, leader of the Spanish-speaking in Colorado for decades, definitely earned such credit. Like his counterparts in New Mexico's legislature and constitutional convention, Barela consciously advanced the interests of his group; he once stated: "When it comes to my people, especially if it concerns discrimination, I abandon my political ideas and dedicate myself to their defense at any time or place." In 1847 Barela was born into a wealthy New Mexico family; in 1867 he migrated to southern Colorado at the head of a Spanish-speaking colony. Although this area had never been permanently settled by Spain or Mexico, Barela still regarded it as his native land, constantly reminding Anglos: "Mexicans were the legitimate owners of this country which came to them through their inheritance from their ancestors." In defending the rights of his people, he repeatedly based his arguments on the Treaty of Guadalupe Hidalgo, a treaty in which he believed Mexico had desperately sought to protect "her own children, who in their own land, in their own country were to be left like strangers. . . ."[52]

Barela served continuously in Colorado's territorial and state legislatures for over forty years after his first election in 1871, and was also a delegate to the Constitutional Convention in 1875–76. At that convention the major social cleavage was between the Protestant, English-speaking, northern counties and the Catholic, Spanish-speaking, southern counties. An attempt by Mexicans to have the state support Catholic and other private schools failed miserably; however, Barela succeeded in having laws published in Spanish for at least twenty-five years, and also prevented a knowledge of English from being required of all voters. Barela spent his long career facing the problems that confronted Mexicans throughout the Southwest: land grant disputes, prejudiced courts, gerrymandering, discriminatory election laws, and interracial violence. His success and that of others like him was limited, but because of them Mexican culture in the Southwest lived to be rejuvenated in the twentieth century.[53]

Next to the heavy invasion of Anglo settlers, the most serious attack on Mexican culture in the Southwest during the nineteenth century was the assault on native landowners, an attack that almost uprooted Mexicans from the region. Though the loss of an exploitive elite's huge estates may seem deserved, the loss was also experienced by the common man because the native upper class was replaced by an even more oppressive foreign elite, more oppressive because it had little respect for the culture of the ordinary Mexican who would continue to do much of the heavy labor throughout the Southwest. Outside of New Mexico and Colorado, the loss of land destroyed the native leadership, leaving the average Mexican without representatives in the prestigious positions of society. Without such representation he gradually became alienated from the Southwest and increasingly looked south of the border for cultural reinforcement. Constant and easy communication across the artificial border made thoroughly "Mexican" Mexico seem more of a homeland even to the native whose family had been in the Southwest for generations. The common Mexican began to forget his history, to forget that he was indigenous to the Southwest as well as Mexico. For a time during the twentieth century, this loss of historical memory would obscure the Chicano's image of the Southwest as lost, and of himself as dispossessed.

# 4

## Occupied Latin America

Even though Mexico lost the present Southwest in 1848, in some ways the region became more closely bound to the motherland as the nineteenth century progressed. As a result, the image of the Southwest as lost and of Mexicans as dispossessed developed another dimension; although the region had been occupied by the United States, it was still perceived as an extension of Mexico and Latin America, while its indigenous Spanish-speaking people were still seen as Mexican, despite the U.S. citizenship of many.

As the political, social, and economic strength of the indigenous local elites declined, Mexicans, U.S. citizens or not, looked south for cultural reinforcement, and with improved communications Mexico City was increasingly able to provide that reinforcement both directly and indirectly. Better roads and railroads within the Southwest, together with the construction of railroads between Mexico City and the U.S. border in the 1880s, allowed a degree of cultural contact that had not been possible previously. The political stability prevalent in Mexico during the dictatorship of Porfirio Díaz from 1876 to 1911 tied such formerly isolated northern states as Sonora and Chihuahua more securely to the national capital. As a consequence, the Southwest was also to some degree drawn back into the political orbit of Mexico City. The influence of Mexican politics on the Southwest had always been present, but it reached a high point immediately preceding and during the Mexican Revolution of 1910–20. Furthermore, Mexicans in the Southwest became so involved in the revolutionary events of the motherland that Mexico itself was strongly affected by political activities in its lost provinces.[1]

This constant and increasing contact with Mexico permitted Southwest Mexicans to maintain their culture, despite the Anglo invasion from the East, until the masses of refugees from the tumult of the revolution resecured the place of Mexican culture in the Southwest. Because of their location, Southwest Mexicans in the late nineteenth century saw their land as an outpost of Mexico and Spanish America, an outpost that had been overrun militarily but that remained strategically important for the defense of Latin American culture. Politically and economically the Southwest was a lost land, and the cultural battle was nearly decided when the heavy migration began to arrive from Mexico in 1911. Though the refugees strengthened Mexican culture in the Southwest,[2] ironically they also had the effect of further alienating that culture from its northern homeland. Because so many exiles fled to the region, they soon far outnumbered the earlier settlers in Texas, Arizona, and California. As a result of the preponderance of newcomers, both newcomers and older residents began to forget their local history as a native people of Mexican origin, to think their Mexican culture alien to the Southwest and thus to believe Mexicans were truly foreigners in their own land.

Although the migration of Mexicans into the Southwest reached a high point with the coming of the revolution, the movement after 1910 was only part of the constant flow of people from central Mexico, a flow that had begun centuries earlier and had continued after 1848 despite the new international boundary. We have already seen that the Gold Rush of 1849 brought thousands of Mexicans to California, many of whom stayed. Throughout the rest of the nineteenth century the need in the United States for cheap labor constantly drew Mexicans across the border. In Texas the cattle industry needed vaqueros (cowboys); in southern New Mexico and Arizona, skilled miners were in demand, and the railroads throughout the Southwest called for a steady supply of workers. How many Mexicans migrated to the region between 1848 and 1911 is not clearly known because few official counts were kept for the entire period, and since the boundary was crossed with few or no legalities until the 1920s, the remaining records appear even less accurate than similar counts are today.[3] The general public has recognized the importance of workers from Mexico for the development of the Southwest in agriculture and related industries during the twentieth century, but the nineteenth-century contributions of this labor have frequently been forgotten. For example, the importance of "imported" workers for the development of mining in Arizona is not generally known, and yet such labor was critical for the territory. The dependence of Arizona on Mexican workers developed largely as a result of the territory's continuing geographical ties to Mexico, ties that became more important after the North American occupation than ever before.[4]

Modern Arizona grew out of that area south of the Gila that was purchased from Mexico in 1854, rather than the larger northern portion of the state that was acquired as a result of the conquest of 1846–48. Despite this, Chicanos today regard southern Arizona as conquered territory because Mexico was intimidated into selling it by threats of larger "involuntary" annexations to the United States. Anglo-American designs on Mexican territory did not cease with the Treaty of Guadalupe Hidalgo, and at least until the 1920s Mexicans on both sides of the border continued to fear further losses to the expansionist United States. This fear was especially acute before the Civil War, when various groups of armed Anglo adventurers, imbued with the doctrine of manifest destiny, made numerous attempts to set up republics within Mexico and other Latin American countries, with the hope of eventually seeing these republics annexed to the United States.[5]

Because of the region's geographical connections with the Southwest, during the 1850s northern Mexico, especially the state of Sonora, was a target of the filibusters (as the Anglo adventurers were called). Sonora, including southern Arizona before 1854, was geographically important to the Southwest because it had possibilities as a southern route for a railroad between the East and California and because its ports on the Gulf of California could serve the interior area between the Rio Grande Valley and the Colorado River. Of course, Sonora's mineral wealth, together with the state's supply of skilled miners, provided a purely economic inducement to foreign interests as well.[6] Though their methods were somewhat different, both filibusters and the U.S. government wanted more Mexican territory, and Mexico was fortunate in 1854 to lose only that area known in the United States as the Gadsden Purchase.

In the early 1850s border difficulties arising from implementation of the Treaty of Guadalupe Hidalgo led the U.S. government to realize that the international boundary of 1848 unnaturally divided the Southwest from Mexico, especially from the northern parts of that country. Consequently, the United States sent James Gadsden to negotiate a settlement with Mexico, a settlement that would supposedly solve the problems of uncontrollable filibusters, of Indian raids into Mexico, and of a disputed boundary line by establishing a more natural frontier between the two countries. This more natural border, if the wishes of the United States were met, would be drawn farther south, leaving Baja California, northern Sonora including ports on the Gulf, and vast sections of other northern Mexican provinces in North American hands. Despite its defeat in the recent war, Mexico was unwilling to discuss any sale of territory except that immediately adjacent to the boundary as set in 1848, yet Mexico realized that it had to sell something or risk another losing war with the United States.[7] According to Santa Anna, once again the Mexican president, Gadsden threatened that if Mexico did not sell enough land for at least a railroad route, the United States would "take it."[8]

This possibility was made especially vivid to Mexico when in the midst of negotiations William Walker, a filibuster who would in 1856 seize control of Nicaragua, established himself in Baja California and declared that territory and Sonora an independent republic. The United States denounced

Walker's expedition because it placed Santa Anna in a position where he could not sell Lower California without appearing to have surrendered it to armed force. On the other hand, the expedition reminded Mexico that it could barely defend its northern frontier and that it had to make the best possible deal with the United States. As a result, Mexico sold present-day southern Arizona and a corner of present New Mexico in return for a sorely needed $10 million,[9] which Santa Anna squandered in attempts to prop up his faltering regime.

Thus in 1854 Tucson, an outpost founded in 1776 to defend the silver of Sonora,[10] became an outpost of Latin American civilization under Anglo political control. Though few Anglos moved to southern Arizona until the late nineteenth century, by 1877 Mexicans realized that they were in a cultural combat zone. In that year *Las dos repúblicas,* a Tucson newspaper, described the situation vividly:

> We are here, then, the advance guard of Latin civilization in America, and our duty is to maintain our post against the attack of the hordes from the north. . . .
>
> It would be nice if this were not so, but the fact is that the United States has already taken a great part of Mexico; because of this should we abandon the land and retreat step by step until they cast us into the sea, as they did with the aborigines? No, Sir. We must learn from the Southerners, who accepted the judgment of arms and surrendered but only to change their tactics from the field of battle to that of politics and the halls of Congress. Thus should we also act; if we are defeated by force, we should take refuge at those points where we are strong, and take possession of their own [the Anglos'] arms to ultimately conquer the conquerer. Our customs, our faith, our language, activity, industry, education, taking part in politics, influencing the legislature, and naming the governors: these are the arms with which Latin civilization must conquer the Saxon.

If these arms were not taken up, the newspaper warned, "they will hurl us from the native land," and "our race and language will disappear.[11]

Even though more Mexicans than Anglos lived in Arizona during the nineteenth century, Mexicans feared for their way of life because the Anglo minority had political control. Also, because Arizona was of special importance to mining and railroad interests and to the suppliers of the military, this minority had powerful contacts in Washington and the rest of the East. Moreover, the Mexican majority could not even control the voting booth because, for one thing, few Mexicans were citizens. Most Mexicans migrated to Arizona after 1854 in successive waves to work in the mines and were thus technically aliens. Since the larger Arizona towns were so close to the border, Mexicans would cross over from Sonora or Chihuahua, scarcely aware that they had entered the United States, and would rarely bother to change citizenship. Their contributions to mining in Arizona were critical; for instance, in the early 1870s their labor and technical skills resulted in the first copper smelting operation in the territory, a major breakthrough in a copper-rich area.[12] Yet, despite their numbers and contributions to the economy, their lack of political power resulted in their being denied basic rights and services. In 1889, for example, a law was passed denying "aliens," who were overwhelmingly Mexican, admission to hospitals in the territory.[13] It is little surprise that *Las dos repúblicas* saw the Mexican situation in Arizona as a matter of life or death.

Throughout the Southwest, Mexicans saw this struggle for racial and cultural survival within the United States as part of the larger conflict between the Latin and Anglo-Saxon civilizations, a conflict that dated at least as far back as the defeat of the Spanish Armada in 1588. Mexican elites in the United States were aware of events throughout Latin America and of North American involvement in those events. Since they perceived their own situation under Anglo dominance as oppressive, they warned other Latin Americans about U.S. aggression and constantly opposed North American intervention south of the border, especially in Mexico. That Latin Americans as far away as Chile and as early as 1855 paid attention to the plight of their cousins is evident from the following lines, reprinted in *La crónica* of San Francisco, from a Valparaíso newspaper:

> No one doubts . . . the hostile and ambitious spirit manifested by that nation [the United States] toward the republics of the south, that all are more or less threatened by . . . annexation that is the article of faith which it seems the Anglo-Saxons of North America have adopted with respect to any state inhabited by the Spanish or their descendants. . . . it should not be surprising that the cabinet in Washington is presently striving to advance that which a few years back . . . its predecessors left planned in the annexation of Texas and California, acquisitions which if they have not been able to justify on the basis of any . . . human law, it has not mattered, since the territory of the Union has been made larger.
>
> But have they not every excuse . . . if they come to make us moral with their virtues, making us also participants in the well-being which . . . the Spanish-American communities that today are under their magnanimous and philanthropic government enjoy?

> But . . . we ask these justifiers of rapine if the troubles, systematic robberies
> and barbarous cruelty carried out by them in the midst of these communities is
> not living proof of the unhappiness that causes the subject Spanish population
> to groan. . . .[14]

Chileans realized that the spirit of manifest destiny had not died with the
Treaty of Guadalupe Hidalgo. Even as that treaty was before the Mexican
congress in 1848, some officials in Washington were pushing for the annexation of Yucatán; in 1850–51 several filibustering expeditions were launched
against Cuba from U.S. territory; and the Walker expedition was neither the
first nor the last to attack Sonora from the United States.[15]

Latin Americans, both in the Southwest and elsewhere, were especially concerned with threats against Sonora because despite the Mesilla (or Gadsden)
Treaty, it seemed the United States would still seize the province. The acquisition of Tucson had only made Guaymas and other ports seem more desirable,
the fastest commercial routes to the East and San Francisco being by sea until
the arrival of the railroad in the late 1870s.[16] For this reason and because the
military was dependent on supplies arriving through Mexican territory, the
United States periodically renewed efforts to buy or otherwise induce Mexico
to part with Sonora. *El clamor público* of Los Angeles was adamant in its opposition to further seizures of Mexican land, and in 1858, shortly after the
failure of another filibustering expedition into Sonora, Francisco Ramírez
published a series of articles arguing against any Anglo-American attempts
to acquire the state. One of these articles, reprinted from a Sonoran newspaper,
revealed that Sonorans feared annexation to the United States because of what
they had seen happen to Mexicans in the occupied lands to the north:

> Let us now suppose that the United States were to acquire Sonora . . . what
> would be our fate? We have only to look toward Alta California to know the
> future. . . . The rapacity of the new settlers of that privileged country has left
> the former possessors in the most miserable condition imaginable. . . .

Despite their internal problems, the article continued, Mexicans were independent and could solve their own difficulties, and unless and until Sonora
were finally given by providence to the United States, the article stressed,
"WE DO NOT WANT TO BE AMERICANS."[17]

As in the Southwest before the U.S. conquest, however, this sentiment
was not unanimous. *El eco del Pacífico* of San Francisco commented on a letter
by a Sonoran student at Fordham in New York who favored the annexation of
his home state. The student argued that the problems of the area were so

severe that the president of Mexico had no "recourse *but the sale of Sonora.*" The student further remarked that as for himself the sale would be of little significance since he was prepared for the inevitable. *El eco,* beside itself with anger, asked the student, "and you, what will become of you, you big imbecile?—a wandering Jew without a country in this vast world." The newspaper concluded by scolding the parents of Spanish descent who sent their children to learn such ideas in North American schools.[18]

The most serious threats of annexation, at least of Mexican territory, came to an end with the beginning of the Civil War in 1861. The United States became too preoccupied with its own affairs to involve itself in Latin America. Mexico, however, received no reprieve from intervention; in 1862 it was invaded by French troops establishing a monarchy and placing the Hapsburg, Maximilian, on the "imperial throne." Since the United States opposed this violation of the Monroe Doctrine, relations with the republican government of Benito Juárez, which had fled Mexico City, were friendly. The cordial relations between the two governments during this period were reflected in the sympathies of the Mexican population of the Southwest. Because the Confederacy sought the aid of France, Mexicans considered the South to be in league with the French in Mexico, as was indicated by this statement from a Brownsville newspaper: "From the beginning of the war [the Civil War], the Confederates have regarded France as their ally, Mexico their last refuge, and the [French] Imperial army as in reserve in case of a forced emigration."[19]

Consequently, many Mexicans perceived the Lincoln and Juárez governments as united in a common effort against European and Southern, particularly Texan, imperialism. Most threats against Mexico's territorial integrity had come from the South, and Mexicans feared further aggression from that quarter, whether by a conquering or retreating Confederate army, especially since such an army could aid and be aided by the French. Mexicans also feared Texan incursions into those areas of the Southwest where Mexicans had managed to retain some control. As a result, the Confederate invasions of 1861 and 1862 into New Mexico were defeated by Union armies with large contingents of Spanish-speaking troops. Several battalions of "native," Spanish-speaking cavalrymen (of whom a half or more had migrated to the Southwest from Mexico and South America) from as far off as California were deployed at the Rio Grande in southern New Mexico. That troops arrived from California should be little surprise since pro-Union, pro-Juárez sentiment was strong in that state, especially in San Francisco.[20]

As might be expected, not all Mexicans in the Southwest agreed with the supporters of Juárez and the Union. In New Mexico a faction, including such wealthy landowners as the Armijo and Otero families,[21] sympathized with

Confederate attempts to occupy the territory. This faction feared that the progress of New Mexico would be retarded if it remained tied to the Union. Since peonage, a form of servitude, remained an important economic institution in the territory, some landowners feared a Union victory would lead to the loss of their cheap labor supply, with a consequent decline in the economy. In California, even in pro-Union, pro-Juárez San Francisco, a Mexican minority believed the French intervention would bring stability to Mexico. *El eco del Pacífico,* a San Francisco newspaper with strong ties to the city's French community, served as the organ of Mexican conservatives, a role not very consistent with *El eco*'s earlier opposition to North American intervention in Sonora.[22] *La voz de México,* on the other hand, was the outspoken organ of republicans, and, when a representative of Juárez sought money, arms, and men in San Francisco, the newspaper was instrumental in obtaining that assistance.[23] The significance of Maximilian's final defeat was underscored by another pro-Juárez newspaper: "On North American soil a descendant of the House of Hapsburg has been judged, condemned, and executed by the descendants of the Aztecs."[24] San Francisco's liberal activists were proud of their part in the victory of Juárez, an Indian, over a monarch whose family had once ruled the Spanish Empire. Such political activism, especially in support of liberal causes, was to be common throughout the Southwest well into the twentieth century and would be of special importance during the Mexican Revolution.

After the 1860s the friendly relations that had existed between the United States and Mexico during the civil wars in both countries began to deteriorate because of lawlessness along the Texas frontier. Neither country seemed able to control the raids of bandits back and forth across the Rio Grande. Though some annexationist sentiment rose again in the United States, the Grant administration was too involved with the difficulties of Reconstruction to risk another war seriously. In 1876 Porfirio Díaz, who had planned his takeover in Texas, gained control of the Mexican government and gradually stopped Mexican raids across the northern border. The stability imposed on Mexico by the Díaz dictatorship ended threats of further annexation of Mexican territory; ironically, however, this stability left the country completely open to North American economic exploitation.[25]

Almost immediately after his rise to power, Díaz entered into agreements with North American capitalists that gradually allowed them to control Mexico's railroads, mines, and much of its land. Though this policy led to unprecedented development of the Mexican economy, only the upper class and U.S. industrialists benefited. After it became apparent that Díaz's policies were leading to the economic colonization of Mexico by the United States, opposition to Díaz arose, especially in the southwestern Spanish-language press, which was beyond the control of the dictatorship. The Díaz men, wrote *La república* of San Francisco as early as 1882, "in their blind desire to acquire, in their devouring thirst for riches, sell everything, sacrifice everything, . . . handing over the shackled nation to the yankee speculators. . . . Those who make up the dominant circle will be left immensely rich: the people as a whole will be disinherited." And again Mexicans saw the situation as a struggle for cultural and racial survival: "Just as a small lake disappears when crossed by the current of a rich river so shall the Latin race that peoples Mexico be engulfed by the impetuous torrent that is unleashed from the north. . . ." Unless Díaz became more careful, economic penetration by the United States could eventually lead to political annexation and finally to the disappearance of Mexicans as a people. Opposition to Díaz and United States capitalists was especially strong in California, where many prominent Mexican exiles had come to live, but it was also common throughout the Southwest, growing stronger as time passed. In 1889 El Paso's *El valle del Bravo* attacked those in the United States who were trying to create a North American empire. In 1891 Albuquerque's *El defensor del pueblo* actually recommended the assassination of Díaz.[26]

However, some Spanish-language newspapers did support Díaz. In San Francisco, where opposition to the dictator was strong, *La voz del Nuevo Mundo* in 1882 defended him against the attacks of the city's anti-Díaz newspapers. That such criticism, wrote *La voz*, should appear "in organs that are published in a country where there is so little sympathy for anyone, especially Mexicans, and anything connected with the Spanish race . . . is undignified and indecorous. . . . that men who were born under the sky of Mexico, here on foreign soil, and obeying sentiments of personal vengeance, would denigrate the men who are at the head of the [Mexican] government, provokes our indignation." Strangely, the editors of *La voz* seemed more concerned with what North Americans thought of Mexicans than with the actual condition of Mexico's people. The newspaper was satisfied that the Díaz government was "progressive," stable, and dignified.[27] (Interestingly, while other Mexicans were still referring to the Southwest as their native land, *La voz* wrote of California as "here on foreign soil." This suggests that at least some Southwest Mexicans were beginning to see themselves as North Americans saw them—as aliens on "American" land.)

With the sweeping concessions granted to U.S. capitalists by Díaz in the 1880s, the threat of direct United States aggression against Mexico lessened, but as the effects of the Civil War wore away, the United States once more became interested in other parts of Latin America. The Caribbean and the

possibility of a canal across Central America attracted North American attention. As in the 1850s, the Spanish-language press in the Southwest became
wary of North American intentions; however, since the threat was more distant both in time and place, the attitude of this press was somewhat less
hostile than it had been earlier. For example, *La gaceta* of Santa Barbara,
California, while opposing Anglo diehards who still wished to invade Mexico
in 1879, advocated North American control over the canal that Ferdinand de
Lesseps had just begun in Panama. But this is not surprising given Mexico's
then recent experience with French imperialism; if the canal had to be built
by foreigners, *La gaceta* preferred the United States to less predictable European powers. By 1892, with the United States about to embark on a new era
of conquest, North American influence in Panama was more threatening.
Consequently, the *Revista hispano-americana* of Los Angeles reprinted an article from an eastern paper warning Colombia that it could lose Panama to the
United States, which is more or less what happened in 1903.[28] Except during the Spanish-American War, from the 1890s until the advent of Franklin
Roosevelt's Good Neighbor Policy in the 1930s, the Southwest Mexican press
would constantly criticize the frequent U.S. interventions in Latin America.

Before the United States embarked on the "dollar diplomacy" that characterized its relations with its southern neighbors in the early twentieth century,
it established its hegemony over the Caribbean by defeating Spain, its major
rival in the region, and gaining control of the last Spanish colonies in America.
As soon as the possibility of war with Spain arose, Mexicans in the Southwest,
especially in New Mexico, became suspect "aliens."[29] Since New Mexico was
the one area in the Southwest where the Spanish-speaking remained a significant percentage of the population *and* still maintained some political power,
there was some doubt about their loyalty, and they themselves became concerned with what the rest of the nation thought of them. As a result, Spanish-
language commentary on events leading to the war with Spain had a tendency
to be moderate, especially as actual conflict drew closer. *La voz del pueblo* of
East Las Vegas, New Mexico, reflected the cautious attitude of *nuevomexicanos*
in its editorials and even in its news articles. Rather than offering its own
opinions, this newspaper would often reprint articles and editorials from other
papers around the country; nevertheless, the selection suggested the editors'
opposition to North American intervention in Cuba.

Cuba, which had failed to gain its independence in the early nineteenth
century when most of Spanish America did so, had rebelled periodically, but
always unsuccessfully. A revolt that started in 1895 was especially bloody,
and severe measures were taken by Spain in suppressing it. The public in the
United States, roused by the Anglo-American press, sympathized with the

rebels and called for intervention. *La voz del pueblo,* however, suspicious of U.S. intentions, reprinted an antiinterventionist article from a San Francisco newspaper. Just a week before the declaration of war on April 11, 1898, this article warned Cubans that if they accepted North American aid, they would only be replacing one ruling power with another more vigorous one—a prediction not far from the truth. Significantly, this article was reprinted weeks after the *Maine* had been blown up while visiting Havana harbor. The destruction of this U.S. vessel, which was blamed on Spain (though Cuban rebels were most likely responsible), finally started the war that the general public desired. The administration of William McKinley, aware that North Americans had important economic interests in Cuba, refused to accept significant concessions offered by Spain and declared war.[30]

Nevertheless, until the day of the declaration, *La voz del pueblo* refused to side openly with any of the disputing parties. Needless to say, once the war had started, the newspaper supported the United States, but only under the slogan of "our country right or wrong." Up to that time, the newspaper hid its true sentiments behind a pacifist position:

The inhabitants of New Mexico are not in favor of war against Spain or any other nation [but]. . . . If, by misfortune, a war truly comes to pass between Spain and the United States, on the part of Hispanic-Americans we can say sincerely, *without inquiring into or fixing the blame, concerning who or what is the cause of the war between the two nations* [emphasis added]. . . . we will demonstrate one more time that that element which has prospered least, that those children who have gone unknown and belittled—*we are Americans in reality* because this soil is ours by origin: *we are Americans because we love the sacred bird of liberty.* . . .

Despite its remark about the culpability of the parties involved, only a week earlier, *La voz del pueblo* had reprinted an article boldly stating:

There is not, nor has there ever been, on the part of slandered Spain, the least threat against the United States. The provocations have come from the other side: in the federal congress, in the vociferous press, in the outgoing expeditions of men, arms, and powerful explosives destined to destroy the wealth of Cuba. . . .[31]

The insecurity that Mexicans felt about their status as "Americans" kept the editors of *La voz del pueblo* from airing their opinions freely, thus impelling them to reveal such opinions only through articles borrowed from other sources. This early pose of impartiality allowed them to move safely to the Anglo-American position, once war seemed inevitable: "We have no reason to be ashamed of our origins and antecedents, on account of the Spanish blood that runs through our veins;" and despite earlier pro-Spanish articles on Cuba: "The Cubans also have Spanish blood, and today they fight with unprecedented heroism to obtain their liberty from this very Spain." Once war began, the newspaper completely dropped pro-Spanish material and became unabashedly patriotic, openly exhorting its readers to forget the past conflicts with Anglos and to unite against the common foe: "The true greatness of man does not consist of desiring . . . to avenge infamous acts of ungrateful persons such as those which New Mexico has suffered on various occasions; but it does consist . . . of downplaying such acts [in time of war]. . . ." Finally, *La voz del pueblo* appealed to the *nuevomexicanos'* bicultural republican traditions in the war against the Spanish crown:

> Do not forget that the strong and glorious blow of independence against the despotism of Spain was delivered heroically by your predecessors. The beneficent light of liberty illuminated the mind and touched the heart of Hidalgo as well as Washington.

Such appeals, when repeated by influential Spanish-speaking leaders, won over the Mexican population to the war effort.[32]

Both legislator Casimiro Barela of Colorado and Governor Miguel A. Otero of New Mexico, despite the differences between them with regard to acculturation, urged their people to show their loyalty in the war against Spain. Governor Otero, who was a friend of President McKinley, enthusiastically offered the territory's men and services for the war effort. In response to an early inquiry from eastern journalists concerning New Mexico's potential contribution in case of hostilities, Otero stated, "New Mexico will furnish, as she did during the war of the rebellion, more men in proportion to her population, than any [other] state or territory in the Union; a large majority of her soldiers are Spanish-speaking and are as loyal to this country as any New England troops; they will rally round the stars and stripes. . . ." In fact, because *nuevomexicanos* spoke the language of the enemy, Otero telegraphed the Secretary of War offering "a full regiment of cavalry, 95 percent Spanish-speaking. . . . Can send more regiments if desired. It occurs to me that our volunteers would be very desirable in a Spanish-speaking country [Cuba]."[33]

New Mexico fulfilled the Governor's promise, as both Mexicans and Anglos volunteered in large numbers. Otero's Spanish-speaking troops formed a numerous and important part of Teddy Roosevelt's Rough Riders, a circumstance that made all Southwest Mexicans feel they were verifying their citizenship. In the county of Las Animas, Colorado, on July 4, 1898, Casimiro Barela spoke proudly of these troops, "Today, you will find in the battlefields two companies of Hispanic-Americans from the territory of New Mexico," and added with regret, "The Hispanic-Americans of Colorado have offered . . . Governor Adams the services of a company, but . . . the Governor declined to accept." These volunteers, Barela concluded, demonstrated that "we Hispanic-Americans feel proud to live under the American flag, [and] are ready to die in defense of our nation's honor. . . ."[34]

Ironically, the conclusion of the Spanish-American War caused an unexpected problem for the Spanish-speaking in New Mexico, and to some extent in Arizona. Since these two territories had not yet achieved statehood, serious questions arose as to their status in relation to the already admitted states and especially in relation to the possessions newly acquired from Spain. Cuba, Puerto Rico, the Philippines, and Guam were colonies inhabited by "civilized," "foreign" peoples who could never be incorporated into the United States, or so argued Theodore Roosevelt and the other proponents of the "new" imperial approach to recently acquired areas. Either these new possessions should be kept indefinitely as strategic and economic colonies of the United States, or they should be prepared for independence rather than statehood. Unfortunately for New Mexico and Arizona, since the new possessions had been acquired from Spain, the United States began to see its southwestern Spanish-speaking territories as colonies also.[35]

Both the new possessions and the two territories came to be regarded as backward lands, retarded by their long association with Catholic, monarchical, unprogressive Spain. Because Roosevelt's territorial appointees were imperialist-minded as was the chairman of the Senate's powerful Committee on Territories, Albert J. Beveridge, statehood for the two "Spanish" territories was postponed for over a decade. In 1902 Senator Beveridge made a brief tour of Arizona and New Mexico, and on noting the extensive use of Spanish in the region concluded that the territories, particularly the latter, were insufficiently "American" for statehood. "Thus," as historian Robert W. Larson has said, "an unfortunate but instinctive distrust of New Mexico's essentially foreign [sic] culture was the last and most durable brick added to the strong wall of opposition that prevented the territory from joining the Union until 1912." Despite their overwhelming enlistment in the armed forces during the Spanish-American War, nuevomexicanos had not won the trust of their fellow citizens.[36]

Mistrust of Mexicans during the Spanish-American War was focused on New Mexico because that territory still contained the core of Southwest Mexican population and culture at the end of the nineteenth century. But this situation was soon to change; Texas by 1900 was already receiving a large

number of arrivals from Mexico, and California would soon become the desti-
nation for thousands of refugees once the Mexican Revolution broke out.[37]
Many of the newcomers, even before the beginning of the revolution, did not
come to seek their fortunes in the United States, but to escape the oppression
of the Díaz regime. Among these exiles were some of the men who would be
most influential in the flow of events and ideas that finally brought about the
revolution.

One of these men, Ricardo Flores Magón, left Mexico in 1904 after openly
criticizing the Díaz government. In the United States and Canada he moved
from one city to another trying to avoid the harassment of the dictator's agents
who tried to prevent him from publishing material against Díaz and from
organizing any resistance. Despite their efforts, Flores Magón managed to
publish his opposition newspaper, *Regeneración,* in several cities including San
Antonio and Los Angeles.[38] His newspaper commented on the condition of
Mexicans both in Mexico and the Southwest, and as time passed it became
increasingly radical. Referring to exiles from Mexico, implicitly including
himself, Flores Magón in 1905 lamented "the serious problem of the depopula-
tion of Mexico, of that alarming emigration that seeks refuge in the United
States fleeing . . . despotism. . . ." Not only were the oppressive tactics of
the dictatorship causing the flight of peons and intellectuals, they were
responsible for bloody Yaqui Indian uprisings in Sonora. Because these uprisings had resulted in the loss of Anglo-American lives, *Regeneración* feared that
United States troops would intervene on behalf of Anglo interests in Sonora.[39]

In time Flores Magón gained a following among Mexicans in the Southwest and a true resistance movement against Díaz developed there. (Eventually
it became anarco-communist in ideology and had an important impact on
labor and the Mexican Constitution of 1917.)[40] In 1906 this movement indirectly influenced the Cananea, Sonora, strike against U.S. mining interests,
a strike that revealed once and for all that Díaz was a virtual pawn of North
American capitalists. Díaz's troops together with Arizona state police aided
Anglo owners in crushing a Mexican strike for pay comparable to that of Anglo
workers at a mine located in *Mexico itself.* This event, however, led to further
harassment of the *magonistas,* which weakened them to the point where they
were unable to bring about the revolution that would finally explode a few
years later. That honor would belong to Francisco I. Madero, a former student at the University of California, born and raised in Coahuila.[41]

It is not surprising that Madero and most of the other major Mexican
revolutionary leaders—Francisco Villa, Venustiano Carranza, Alvaro Obre-
gón—came from the far northern states of Mexico. The north was the region
traditionally least under central control and also closest to the arms, money,

volunteers, sympathizers, and safety of the U.S. Southwest. After campaigning on a moderate reform platform and being defeated by Díaz in a rigged election (in late 1910), Madero exiled himself to San Antonio, Texas, where he called for the overthrow of the dictator. Madero's proclamation was initially sufficiently vague in ideology to attract a variety of dissidents, including the *magonistas*. Because of this vagueness, Mexicans on neither side of the border were sure what the revolutionaries stood for, except the ouster of Díaz.[42] At first *La voz del pueblo* of New Mexico actually thought Madero was a tool of North American capitalists; according to the newspaper, these capitalists hoped to gain control of Mexico by supplying filibustering expeditions initially to aid the revolution, but finally to betray it. Since Madero was a rich landowner and had unsuccessfully sought financial aid from businessmen in the eastern United States, this view was not as outrageous as it may seem. Moreover, in California non-Mexican volunteers who had joined a *magonista* armed force preparing to attack Baja California made this legitimate revolutionary group seem like an old-fashioned filibustering expedition.[43]

Even after the revolution was four months old, *La voz del pueblo* remained confused about the issues involved and concerned itself mainly with warnings of possible North American intervention:

This newspaper does not especially sympathize either with the rebels or the supporters of the government. Neither do we believe that certain American newspapers of this country sympathize with the rebels and their cause as much as they pretend: what they would like is for the rebellion to continue for an indefinite time until this country, with the purpose of protecting American interests in Mexico, sees itself obligated to intervene and use the occasion of intervention as a pretext for taking all or a part of Mexico.[44]

Later *La voz del pueblo* gave lukewarm support to the revolution, but even such support would never be easy for Mexicans anywhere because the revolution was so beset by factionalism. Even before Madero had occupied the national capital, the *magonistas,* who had captured parts of Baja California, found him too conservative on social and economic issues. Shortly after Díaz's capitulation on May 21, 1911, Emiliano Zapata's guerrillas in southern Mexico broke with Madero because land reform was not immediately forthcoming. By early 1913 a counter-revolution, assisted by the North American ambassador, toppled Madero, and chaos overwhelmed Mexico.[45] As different groups fought for control, Southwest Mexican opinion on the revolution again became confused.

The impact of fighting in Mexico was immediately felt in the Southwest.

In Arizona, for example, where revolutionary activities had been going on since before the Cananea strike of 1906, different groups of exiles moved into the state during the first years of the revolution. At first small parties of belligerents crossed the border to organize resistance. Among these men was Madero's provisional governor of Sonora, who held meetings with supporters in Tucson and Nogales. From there his men dispersed to various other points in Arizona and California to muster further aid. Once the fighting intensified, Mexicans from every class sought escape from the violence, the financial insecurity, the unemployment, and the threat of conscription brought by the upheaval. At times retreating troops from both sides would cross over to Arizona where their wounded could be cared for. With Madero's triumph in May of 1911, hundreds of Díaz's supporters then found it expedient to move north. Ironically, as these various groups moved back and forth across the boundary they revealed the cultural unity existing along the border even as they transferred the deep divisions of Mexican society to the Southwest.[46]

Despite these divisions, one thing all Mexicans, even those who had once supported Díaz, agreed on was that foreign, particularly North American, intervention would not be tolerated. This resolve was soon tested. For several years the United States Navy had patrolled the eastern coast of Mexico to protect North American and European oil installations in Tampico. In the early spring of 1914, while the revolutionists under Venustiano Carranza fought the counter-revolutionary government of Victoriano Huerta for control of the port, several North American sailors were mistakenly arrested by Huerta's men. Despite their quick release, the United States demanded a formal apology and a twenty-one-gun salute to the Stars and Stripes. Since such an act would have meant political ruin for Huerta given the intense antiforeign sentiment in Mexico, the salute was never given. President Woodrow Wilson then ordered U.S. forces to occupy Veracruz. Though Huerta's troops offered little resistance, the civilian population, released prisoners, and young cadets battled the invaders with some success for two days. Both Huerta and Carranza protested the intervention, reflecting the anger most Mexicans felt at this new violation of their territory.[47]

It is more than coincidence that after this event deep in Mexico, conflict along the United States border, which had been relatively quiet during the Díaz era, broke out once more, culminating in a raid by Pancho Villa on Columbus, New Mexico, on March 9, 1916. Though that raid received the most publicity, it was only one of many raids on U.S. territory conducted by politically diverse groups of Mexicans from both sides of the border who had one thing in common—anti-Americanism. As in the past, the violence was focused in Texas south of the Nueces in the lower Rio Grande Valley. This valley, as geographer D. W. Meinig has so aptly said,

> remained an area almost entirely Hispano-American, isolated and alien, annexed entirely through extrinsic interests, sheltering refugees . . ., and responsive in some degree to recurrent secessionist schemes in northeastern Mexico. It was a severed half of old Nuevo Santander [Tamaulipas], a vivid exhibit of the truth of Texas as an empire: a people and a country conquered and ruled but restive and unassimilated.[48]

In 1915 a secessionist and irredentist proposal known as the Plan of San Diego gained the support of a surprising number of Mexicans from both the United States and Mexico. That their extraordinary plan led to as much action as it did was due to Mexico's instability and to the politics of World War I.

In early January of 1915, a few months after President Wilson had effectively deposed Huerta by cutting off money and supplies at Veracruz, a small group of *huertistas* imprisoned at Monterrey signed the "Plan of San Diego," which had supposedly been smuggled to them from San Diego, Texas, "by a friend."[49] This ambitious plan, doubtless motivated in part by a desire to avenge Wilson's intervention at Veracruz, called for "the independence and segregation of the States bordering upon the Mexican Nation, which are: TEXAS, NEW MEXICO, ARIZONA, COLORADO, AND UPPER CALIFORNIA, OF WHICH States the Republic of MEXICO was robbed in a most perfidious manner by North American imperialism." Though the first known signers of the plan were *huertistas,* the proclamation made an appeal for a base of support far greater than that partisan group, and to a degree succeeded. It not only made an appeal to Southwest Mexicans, who indeed may have been its source, but also to blacks, American Indians, and Japanese. A "LIBERATING ARMY FOR RACES AND PEOPLES" was to be formed against "Yankee tyranny." A stranger could be recruited into this army only if he belonged "to the Latin, the negro or the Japanese race." For their participation in the movement, Indians were to receive the "lands which have been taken from them," and blacks were to be aided "in obtaining six States [outside the Southwest] of the American Union" from which they could form their own independent republic. The appeal made to the Japanese was an attempt to solicit aid from Japan, which was periodically at odds with the United States, especially over the mistreatment of Japanese in California. Though the plan was thus conceived in terms of what would today be called a Third World mentality, few non-Latins participated, realizing that their own goals would be secondary to those of Mexicans.[50]

However, among Mexicans from both sides of the border and of various political beliefs, the Plan of San Diego gained significant support because, besides its separatist goals, it was vague with regard to political, social, and economic ideals. For example, the plan stated that after gaining independence, the new southwestern republic would request, "(if it be thought expedient) annexation to MEXICO, without concerning ourselves at that time about the form of Government which may control the destinies of the common mother country."[51] The expressed motive behind the plan was the desire for revenge for territorial losses and other indignities suffered at the hands of the Anglos. As one signer put it, "If it [the plan] were not the grandest idea in America, it was at least a challenge unto death of *decapitated* Latin America [emphasis added] to the whitefaced hogs of Pennsylvania."[52] A handbill used to recruit men for the cause reminded them of the decades of oppression *tejanos* had suffered and called for them to rebel: "Enough of tolerance, enough of insults and deprecations, we are men . . . who know how to think just as well as 'the gringos;' who can be free and will be. . . ." This handbill was endorsed by Aniceto Pizaña, a *tejano* and former *magonista,* who gave the movement the rudiments of anarchist ideology and led many raids in Texas.[53]

Though the Plan of San Diego was first signed on January 6, 1915, actual raids in its name were not carried out until July 4, a month after Aniceto Pizaña and Luis de la Rosa, a resident of Laredo, organized paramilitary companies for that purpose. Until the last of about twenty-seven raids was conducted on June 16, 1916, the *sediciosos,* as the raiders came to be known, disrupted the economy of four counties, destroyed thousands of dollars worth of property, and killed or wounded about sixty Anglos, while suffering about the same number of casualties themselves. The main attack pattern was to destroy railroad bridges and track and to rob and kill Anglos. These attacks were aided by the fact that the Texas Rangers and the U.S. Army found it difficult to patrol so long a border. Although the plan was first taken lightly by U.S. authorities, as the violence increased they became more alarmed, especially when an investigation suggested that Germany was providing the *sediciosos* with funds and propaganda and the Carranza government in Mexico City was giving tacit support. Germany, it seems, hoped to keep the United States out of Europe by keeping the Southwest in turmoil, while Carranza refused to control his northern border unless the United States recognized his government.[54]

Unfortunately for Southwest Mexicans, the inability of the regular authorities to control the situation led to vigilante activities on the part of Anglos against innocent *tejanos*. Though *tejanos* sympathized with the raiders, they realized that they themselves would face the reprisals of the Anglo community. "Los sediciosos," a corrido sung by the common people of South Texas, revealed this clearly:

> In that well-known place called Norias,
>   it really got hot for them [the Rangers];
> a great many bullets rained down on
>   those cursed *rinches* [Rangers].
>
> Now the fuse is lit by the true-born
>   Mexicans,
> and it will be the Texas-Mexicans who
>   will have to pay the price.[55]

Between July and October of 1916, some sixty local Mexicans were killed on the mere suspicion of being raiders. Such retaliations caused many *tejanos* to move to Mexico where some naturally joined the *sediciosos*. Ultimately, the basic motive of the uprising was not to regain territory previously lost (though that was symbolic of Mexican grievances), but, as Flores Magón stated, to defend "the oppressed against the oppressor." Unfortunately, even though the movement may have given Southwest Mexicans some vengeance for Anglo racism and exploitation, it increased their oppression in the end.[56]

After the United States recognized Carranza, the raids of the *sediciosos* gradually ceased as the Mexican president withdrew his support and pressured the raiders to desist. However, occasional raids occurred until the U.S. Army was allowed to pursue the guerrillas into Mexico under the same agreement that allowed General John J. Pershing to chase Pancho Villa after Villa's raid on New Mexico. That raid, unconnected with those of the *sediciosos*, outraged the North American public because it was comparatively large and was carried out by an important Mexican leader. On March 10, 1916 in the early morning, about four hundred *villistas* crossed the border and attacked the town of Columbus, where they set fire to buildings, shot innocent civilians, and skirmished with a cavalry patrol.[57]

Villa hoped to show that the United States had made a mistake in recognizing his rival, Carranza, by demonstrating, for one thing, that the latter had little control over the northern frontier. He hoped that such a demonstration would not only lower Carranza's prestige but rally the intensely antiforeign Mexican public behind Villa himself. Indeed Villa's raid was seen by Mexicans as a long-overdue retaliation for the North American occupation of

Veracruz—even though the raid led to further intervention by the United States. Under an old agreement that allowed U.S. forces to pursue Indians into Mexico, Carranza, under some protest, initially permitted General Pershing to move against Villa. However, since the Mexican populace considered Pershing's expedition an invasion, within a month Carranza ordered his own troops to resist. This led to a skirmish in Carrizal, Chihuahua, where a detachment of U.S. troops was defeated. Had it not been for the threat of war with Germany, this incident would probably have brought a declaration of war from the United States. Instead President Wilson decided to defuse the situation by gradually withdrawing U.S. troops since they had not succeeded in even dispersing Villa's forces. This withdrawal of Pershing without the capture of Villa led Mexicans to consider the episode a victory for Mexico.[58]

As can be imagined, these events left Southwest Mexicans in a precarious position. The treatment they had received in South Texas as a result of the *sedicioso* raids left Mexicans throughout the region apprehensive about their fate in case of war with Mexico. *La voz del pueblo* of New Mexico, which had consistently opposed intervention for years, meekly acceded to Pershing's invasion: "This will not be considered in any way as armed intervention; it is but an isolated case to punish Villa, which the government of Carranza is powerless to do." The newspaper claimed that though it refused to support any one Mexican faction, when it came "to the assassin and bandit Villa, the day he ceases to exist, one of the most horrendous creatures of evil will disappear from this world. . . ." Since Villa had just raided New Mexico, *La voz del pueblo* could hardly take any other stand, nor, for that matter, could Southwest Mexicans in general. The following report from *La voz* gives some indication of the tension caused by the raid:

> In all the border towns where the Mexican element is numerous, extraordinary precautionary measures have been taken [by whom and against whom is not made clear]. A large number of the Hispanic-American citizens of El Paso . . . have offered their services for whatever is necessary.[59]

Southwest Mexicans felt impelled to prove their loyalty; and indeed they were loyal, yet the subsequent popularity in New Mexico itself of a corrido called "Pancho Villa" revealed a latent pride in the "bandit's" handling of Pershing:

> When the "gringos" arrived
> To pin him to the door
> Villa, not even a matador,
> Turned them away.[60]

The entry of the United States into World War I on April 6, 1917, allowed relations with Mexico to relax somewhat, even though German activities in Mexico had been a major reason for the U.S. declaration of war. In February, Germany, in the notorious Zimmermann Note, had offered Carranza the return of lost Mexican territory in the United States if Mexico would ally itself with Germany. When it learned of this note, the Wilson administration was naturally outraged, but since Carranza (knowing Germany was too distant to be much of an ally) refused the offer, relations between the United States and Mexico improved.[61] Later there were rumors of Mexico siding with the United States in the World War, but the history of North American conquest and intervention in their country made that possibility repugnant to Mexicans—as one balladeer of the time reminded:

> In 1847
> Date of dark memory,
> They took all,
> All of Alta California
> Leaving sad recollections
> In the books of history.[62]

While these memories may have prevented Mexico from allying itself with the United States, they did not prevent U.S. citizens of Mexican descent from joining the United States Army and Navy. During World War I volunteers from this minority proportionally exceeded the number of any other ethnic group.[63]

Because Southwest Mexicans lived in an outpost of Latin America, they were naturally defensive about U.S. involvement south of the border, yet by 1917 Mexicans had lived within the United States long enough for many of them to have become "Americanized" to the point where they felt little attachment to Mexico. However, the revolution caused a large increase in the number of Mexicans living in the Southwest, an increase that paradoxically renewed the entire Spanish-speaking population's ties to Mexico, even as it partially alienated that population from the Southwest. The revolution had the effect of strengthening the nationalism of Mexican citizens. The Constitution of 1917, which was the culmination of the revolution, incorporated the anti-foreignism of the period: Mexico was to be for Mexicans. And more than ever the Indian was to epitomize the Mexican while the Spanish, the French, and the North Americans were scorned as intruders. Mexicans who went to the Southwest carried the new nationalism with them and to some extent renewed the ethnic pride of the older residents there. Yet the most recent arrivals, imbued with a new love for the motherland, found it more difficult than did earlier settlers to identify with the Southwest, a land now indelibly marked by Anglo culture. On reaching a border now more real than ever before, the migrant protagonist of one corrido lamented:

> Goodbye! beloved country,
> . . . . . . . . . . . .
> And so I take my leave
> of my country, Mexico.
> I have reached Ciudad Juárez.
> Oh, Virgin of Guadalupe![64]

To these newcomers, the Southwest, with its barrios and pueblos, was familiar, but it was not the motherland.

Some of the older residents accepted the newcomers warmly just as they had accepted the people of the previous smaller migrations; however, the most recent migrants were so numerous that they threatened the socioeconomic position the earlier settlers had made for themselves vis-à-vis the Anglos. As a result, many older residents refused to admit they had anything in common with these "Mexicans," a name which ironically became a dirty word among earlier Mexican residents of the Southwest. This break between the old and new groups did severe damage to the region's Spanish-speaking people as a whole, and would affect the future regional image of Chicanos. The image of the Southwest as lost and of the Spanish-speaking as dispossessed was modified by the older residents to deny, for one thing, that the newcomers had any native claim to the region. As a result, while the newcomers were coming to feel like foreigners, a people without a history in their northern homeland, the older residents were to an extent cut off from the vibrant, incoming currents that could rejuvenate their culture. Consequently, the earlier settlers became a curious anachronism studied by Anglo anthropologists, especially in New Mexico, while the recent arrivals were treated like aliens in California and Texas.[65]

# 5

# The Spanish Southwest

About 1920 the break that developed between the earlier settlers, who began to call themselves Spanish-Americans or Hispanos, and the new arrivals, who were now especially proud of being Mexicans, led to a division in the image of the Southwest perceived by the Spanish-speaking as a whole. While the image since 1848 had included the features of conquest and dispossession, Hispanos, in their desire to accommodate Anglos, deemphasized those aspects; instead they focused on the less controversial, late colonial image of the region as simply a homeland, and of themselves as native descendants of Spanish settlers. On this traditional background, however, they superimposed the new idea that because of their land's early isolation from central Mexico, they had remained pure Spanish in ancestry. Confronted with this exclusive "Spanish" perspective, Mexican newcomers after 1900, though as a group still vaguely aware of the conquest and dispossession, frequently accepted the Anglo image of themselves as aliens in a new land.

Mexicans who came to the Southwest between 1848 and 1900 generally came in numbers small enough to be absorbed by the population that had settled there before the North American occupation. These earlier groups, especially in California, New Mexico, and Colorado, had accommodated themselves to the Anglo immigrants by borrowing from their culture, even learning their language. In other words, by "Americanizing" to some extent, they found a place, albeit an uncomfortable one, within the new political and social order. Of course, the elites were able to do this much more easily than the poor, to the point where in some areas, as in California, many members of the upper class intermarried with the Anglos and were completely assimilated. In general the settlers arriving before 1900 accommodated themselves just enough to minimize discrimination and other disadvantages resulting from their background, without sacrificing their culture. By becoming sufficiently Americanized and by emphasizing those things about their people that Anglos found commendable, these earlier settlers were able to maintain some status within the new society. Those features considered commendable were associ-

ated with Spain: the Mexicans' European ancestry, their history as conquistadores, their old aristocratic rural society, and their former wealth. Conversely,
those features considered objectionable by Anglos were deemphasized: the
Mexicans' Indian and mestizo heritage, their history as a conquered people,
and their current socioeconomic inequality. The Mexicans who arrived in the
Southwest after 1900, and especially after 1910, threatened the accommodation the earlier settlers had made because they were numerous and mostly
poor, were not at all Americanized, and had a renewed pride in their Indian
background. [1]

Because the newcomers exemplified the poor Indian peon and outnumbered
the earlier settlers, Hispanos feared with justification that Anglos would perceive all Mexicans in the Southwest unfavorably, with a consequent increase
in discrimination. As a result, Hispanos as a group tried to disassociate themselves from the newcomers, an attitude that made the new arrivals feel alien
in the Southwest despite the familiar geography and Mexican culture of the
region. Intercourse between the two groups never slacked, but with the older
residents claiming that they were Spanish, the newcomers were denied any
connection with the previous history of Mexicans in the region. This division
among Mexicans unfortunately lessened their ability to resist the attacks of
the dominant culture. Though the Hispano elites could have provided leadership for and gained support from the newcomers, no such union occurred. In
California much of the upper class assimilated with the Anglos, leaving the
poor to merge with the overwhelming migration of newcomers in a leaderless
working class. [2]

As a result, the exploitation of Mexican labor in the 1920s and particularly
the 1930s increased and forced the Mexican community to develop new
leadership. This was necessary even in Texas and Arizona, where contact with
Mexico was closest, because although the old elites in those states never fully
developed a Spanish-American mentality, they left the United States when
their economic fortunes declined. In Colorado and New Mexico the division
between Hispanos and newcomers generally followed geographical lines. The
newcomers took up residence in Denver and southern New Mexico, leaving
upper New Mexico and southern Colorado to the still numerous older residents. This limited the political effectiveness of both groups and isolated
Hispanos of all classes in these states from Mexicans in the rest of the Southwest, where the new arrivals eventually predominated. Because Hispanos saw
themselves as "Spanish" and "American," they came to see the international
border between the United States and Mexico as a more genuine cultural and
ethnic boundary than it actually was, a perception that had unfortunate
economic, political, and social consequences for all Mexicans. [3]

The Spanish-American image of the Southwest was, curiously enough, largely a creation of the Anglo rather than the Mexican imagination. In California an Anglo literary movement romanticizing the state's early past became popular in the 1880s. Significantly, this movement, despite having its roots in pre-1848 Anglo travel narratives, gained impetus just as *californios* were losing their last strongholds to Anglos in southern California. Before then, except in a few works such as those of Bret Harte, Mexicans in Anglo-American literature were most often treated in a thoroughly negative way, as a racially inferior, ignorant, half-savage people blocking the advance of the U.S. frontier in the same way as the Indians. In southern Arizona and South Texas, where Mexico and its population remained a constant threat to Anglo influence well into the twentieth century, the earlier picture of Mexicans as half-barbaric continued with little modification. But in California, where the Mexicans' percentage of the total population and their overall influence had declined steeply by the 1880s, it was much easier for Anglos to feel sympathy for the passing of an "older, simpler way of life." As Anglo settlement of California increased, the earlier Anglo conception of the state changed; by the 1880s California was no longer the wilderness frontier of the Gold Rush, but a booming agricultural wonderland. This new conception colored the Anglo view of California's past. Anglos began to think of the state before 1848 not as a wild country peopled by Indians and half-savage Mexicans, but as a bountiful land occupied by pastoral peoples living in a "half-civilized Spanish" society.[4]

This new image of California served the Anglo psychology by "explaining" the prior settlement of Mexicans in California, indirectly justifying the Anglo conquest, and in general alleviating guilt feelings. With regard to Mexicans themselves, the new image was merely a change in emphasis rather than substance. While Mexicans were still seen as racially inferior, ignorant, and half-savage, the positive side of these qualities was stressed because of the guilt Anglos now felt over the destruction of the old society. Indolence, one of the main "biological traits" of the Mexican, and ignorance were now seen as contributing factors to the "blissful" state of affairs existing in early California. The Mexicans' half-savage nature, attributed to their Indian background, was now seen as modified by their Spanish blood. The Spanish side of their mixed nature provided a civilizing influence that permitted the development of a certain refinement in early California society, which nevertheless remained unspoiled by "advanced" civilization.[5]

This image of the Mexican, which was just a minor revision of the earlier view, fit into the new picture of the California landscape. Since by the 1880s the Anglo had found California's land and weather extremely amenable to agriculture, he began to think that the place had never truly been a wilderness and that the early Mexican must have had an easy time settling the land. Hubert Howe Bancroft, the renowned historian of the West, furthered this myth in his *California Pastoral* published in 1888:

> This California country, about as well as any could, suited the Mexican settler, with his inherent indolence, relieved only by slow spasmodic energy. With the richest of soil around him, which to the scratching of the wooden plough would yield sixty and a hundred to one, he disdained tillage. . . . More suited to the chivalric instincts of the Mexican, coming to him honestly in his Spanish blood, was general domination over animals, with lordly command of . . . vast herds and flocks.

In this pastoral landscape the Mexican had an easy life: "Roaming his native hills, breathing the pure air of the Pacific, the horse his companion, the lasso his weapon, he carries about him and into all life's commonplaces the chivalrous bearing of the cavaliers of old Spain."[6]

Though Bancroft was aware of the *californio*'s mixed ancestry, he emphasized the group's Spanish heritage and believed that, strengthened by the healthy environment, this heritage made the *californio,* at least in physical appearance, "vastly superior to the people of the other Mexican states."[7] Despite this, the *californio*'s inherent indolence prevented him from taking full advantage of California, prevented him from making it, that is, a modern progressive land. This could only be accomplished by the biologically superior, energetic Anglo, and even though Bancroft lamented the decline of the *californio* and castigated the Anglo for his part in that decline, he considered the *californio*'s fall an inevitable consequence of man's evolution. Ultimately, Bancroft therefore exonerated the Anglo for the conquest since the United States was fulfilling human destiny by taking the Southwest.

Although Bancroft did much to spread the myth of pastoral Spanish California, he was neither the first nor the most influential of the "romanticizers." The first to make significant use of the myth was Helen Hunt Jackson, who wrote the extremely popular novel *Ramona,* published in 1884. Although Jackson's main purpose was to condemn the injustices committed by Anglos against the Indians, she also protested the injustices suffered by Mexicans.[8] In the latter case, however, she was somewhat less sympathetic because she believed the arrogance, indolence, and inflexibility of Mexicans were as much to blame for their decline as the Anglo invasion. Although Jackson always referred to her Spanish-speaking characters as "Mexicans," she emphasized that these people were aristocrats of pure Spanish descent.

In describing the life of Señora Moreno, owner of the huge hacienda that serves as the setting of *Ramona,* Jackson made the lady's Spanish origin apparent: "Her life, the mere surface of it, if it had been written, would have made a romance . . . : sixty years of *the best of old Spain* [emphasis added] and the wildest of New Spain. . . ." Jackson's description of the hacienda also emphasized the romantic Spanish aspects of California's early rural society: "The Señora Moreno's house was one of the best specimens to be found in California of the representative house of the half barbaric, half elegant, wholly generous and free-handed life led there by Mexican men and women of degree in the early part of this century, under the rule of the Spanish and Mexican viceroys, when the laws of the Indies were still the law of the land, and *its old name, 'New Spain,' was an ever-present link and stimulus to the warmest memories and deepest patriotism of its people* [emphasis added]."[9]

Because it was fairly well-written and had a moving plot, *Ramona* sold very well and was soon followed by many similar romances which so emphasized things Spanish that the term "Mexican" was scarcely even used. Critic Raymund Paredes has commented that to Gertrude Atherton, one of the most successful of the novelists to write on Spanish California,

> The term "Castilian" was crucial . . ., because she emphasized the racial distinctiveness of the Californios more than other novelists. She ignored the *mestizo* altogether, concentrating her attention on the "high bred Castilians". . . .

Bret Harte, who had dealt with Spanish California topics as early as the 1860s, continued to write about the subject until his death at the turn of the century. He too stressed the pure blood of his aristocratic *californio* characters.[10] In "The Devotion of Enríquez," a short story about a rich *californio* who courts the prim niece of a New England minister, the main character is described as "a scion of one of the oldest Castilian families," and even the landscape is treated as though it were actually a part of Spain: "The Plaza de Toros was reached through the decayed and tile-strewn outskirts of an old Spanish village."[11] Significantly, Harte used "Mexican" only when referring to servants and other members of the lower class.

It is interesting that the myth of Spanish California received its first boost in the 1880s from Jackson and Bancroft, two people who knew some of the surviving members of the old elite. Though Jackson's contact with the elite was cursory, Bancroft and his staff systematically collected documents about and from the elite and even interviewed many of the old leaders concerning life before 1848. Despite his thorough research, Bancroft seemingly ignored his sources when it came time to describe the character of early California life. The accounts of early California given by older members of the upper class, such as Pío Pico and Angustias de la Guerra Ord (collected in the 1870s), were generally straightforward, unromantic narrations of the past.[12] In romanticizing that past, Bancroft, therefore, abandoned the spirit of his historical sources and substituted the tone of a genre of fiction that was gaining in popularity while he was writing his works. Even though his sources at times revealed a nostalgic quality, the romantic tone of his *California Pastoral* went far beyond any nostalgia felt by the early *californios*.

Not only was the myth of Spanish California strong enough to influence Bancroft, it was eventually strong enough to color the memories of Mexicans themselves. *Californios* in the 1880s were flattered by the attention and even "respect" their culture was getting after so many years of Anglo hostility and indifference. The myth also gained popularity among *californios* because it appealed to their nostalgia, their caste consciousness, and their provincial pride. The new interest in old California led to a movement among Anglos to preserve the missions and other early historical sites, a movement that gratified Mexicans who had feared that all signs of their past would disappear forever. The new emphasis on things Spanish, and especially on the notion that *californios* were predominantly if not purely Spanish, appealed to *californios* because in their society as in other Latin American societies, pure Spanish blood was a mark of gentility.[13]

Even though early documents clearly reveal that California's original settlers were not even predominantly Spanish,[14] the belief that those settlers were European increased among *californios* as time passed, since both their own and Anglo culture saw such ancestry as desirable. The notion that the first settlers were more or less pure Spanish was accompanied by another fiction. Because California was so distant from the large concentrations of Indian population in Mexico, it was believed that the descendants of the early settlers had been largely spared the evils of miscegenation, even though a few generations had been born and had lived in close contact with the California Indians. Closely allied to this belief was the idea that California's healthy environment had combined with the *californios'* purity of stock to make them physically superior to Mexicans farther south. *Californios,* needless to say, were also flattered by the idea, especially since regionalism had been strong in California before 1848 (a period, as we have seen, in Mexico's history marred by the struggle between those who wanted a strong central government and those who preferred more local control). As a result, *californios* began to deemphasize and even deny their ties with Mexico and with those Mexicans who were more recent arrivals.[15]

As early as 1890, at least one Mexican had adopted the myth of Spanish

California. In that year Guadalupe Vallejo, nephew of Mariano Vallejo, published a description of early California in English in the *Century*, a New York magazine devoted to the preservation of the genteel tradition in the United States. In that article Vallejo used the word "Spanish" almost to the complete exclusion of "Mexican." Up to this time Mexicans in the Southwest had used the words "Spanish," "Spanish-American," and "Mexican" (or their Spanish-language equivalents) more or less interchangeably: "Spanish" when referring to themselves as a linguistic group, "Spanish-American" when linking themselves to the other Spanish-speaking peoples of the Western Hemisphere, and "Mexican" most other times. (In individual states, especially California, the respective self-designations were also common: *californio, nuevomexicano,* and *tejano.*) This gradually changed as the Spanish California myth spread, until "Spanish" (or Hispano) became the preferred designation (now referring to race rather than language), "Spanish-American" came to mean a U.S. citizen of "pure" Hispanic descent, and "Mexican" applied only to recent arrivals from south of the border.[16]

Vallejo confined his use of "Mexican" strictly to the lower class and to articles and customs that came from Mexico. Otherwise his article was a litany of hispanizations: "Spanish ranches," "Spanish ancestors," "Spanish life," ". . . people," ". . . families," ". . . households," and of course "Spanish ladies" and gentlemen. Vallejo also picked up the other fallacies of the early California romanticizers; for instance, he commented, "No one need suppose that the Spanish pioneers of California suffered many hardships or privations, although it was a new country." Thus by virtually denying the frontier ruggedness of his own ancestors, Vallejo ingratiated himself with his Anglo readers, who were imbued with the idea that such ruggedness was unique to the Anglo-American character. This concession was part of the overall attempt by Southwest Mexicans to accommodate themselves to the dominant culture, to find a place in U.S. society despite their distinct background. Vallejo reflected this sentiment clearly in the following words: "No class of American citizens is more loyal than the Spanish Californians, but we shall always be especially proud of the traditions . . . of the long pastoral age before 1840." However, that pride did not extend to "an old Mexican flag [on the property of the Vallejo family] which was used as an awning."[17]

Though Guadalupe Vallejo claimed to have gleaned his description from the memories of elderly *californios,* he admitted his familiarity with the many travel books written about California, books that in the 1880s were promoting the Spanish California myth. After the 1880s this myth became increasingly popular, reaching a high point between 1900 and 1910, and continuing to the present day. Most significant for Mexicans in the United States, however, was the myth's eventual adaptation and application to the rest of the Southwest, particularly to New Mexico and Colorado. One of the first to romanticize New Mexico was Charles F. Lummis. In his travel book, *The Land of Poco Tiempo* (1893), he described the territory as a "New Spain" where "sheep . . . doze . . . on the mesas." "'Picturesque,'" he continued, "is a tame word for it. It is a picture, a romance, a dream, all in one." Though he regarded Mexicans in the territory as "inbred and isolation-shrunken descendants of the Castilian world-finders," Lummis glorified the Spanish conquistadores and in other ways opened the way for the thorough romantic hispanization of the people, culture, and history of New Mexico and Colorado.[18]

Twenty years after *The Land of Poco Tiempo,* New Mexico had become every bit as Spanish as romantic California. By 1914 an Anglo columnist in *Harper's Weekly* wrote, "These Spanish people of New Mexico . . ., are not of the mixed breed one finds south of the Rio Grande, or even Arizona. . . . Indeed it is probable that there is no purer Spanish stock in Old Spain itself. . . ."[19] In 1916 the author of a travel book entitled *Our Hispanic Southwest* remarked,

> I must confess . . . that the new [restored in 1909] colonnade of the Palace of the Governors [Santa Fe's centuries-old former center of government] is, to my mind, a fatal mistake. Why this so-called Mexican Pueblo style grafted upon the front of a venerable Hispanic building? Why should the palace of the Spanish governors adopt the architecture of the Indian when it was built as castle and fortress to protect the settlers from these very Indians?[20]

This writer clearly failed to understand the mestizo nature of the *nuevomexicano,* a mestizo nature that had left its indelible mark on the architecture, the land, the history, and the people of New Mexico.

Despite this mark, the myth of Spanish New Mexico had so permeated the state that in 1914 the author of the *Harper's Weekly* article was able to say, "the Spanish people of New Mexico. . . . will not allow any one to call them Mexicans. They are New Mexicans, if you please. Better still, they are Spanish-Americans. . . ."[21] The desire to be accepted as "Americans," which reached a high point with New Mexico's admission to statehood in 1912, and the fear of further social ostracism represented by the influx of Mexican exiles from the revolution merged in the second decade of the twentieth century with the attraction to the myth of the Spanish Southwest. This apposition of feelings inculcated the earlier Mexican residents of the state with a Spanish-American mentality that would divide them, together with the early Spanish-speaking Coloradans, from other Mexicans until the 1960s.

This division became quite serious at times. In 1967 Enrique Hank López, a Chicano lawyer, described his early life as a new arrival in Denver around 1920. As a child, López came to the United States with his parents; his father, who had served under Pancho Villa, was forced to leave Mexico when the fortunes of the *villistas* declined. On the family's arrival in El Paso, López's parents realized that with so many exiles in that city there would be little work. As a result, they moved to Denver:

> There we moved into a ghetto of Spanish-speaking residents who chose to call themselves Spanish-Americans and resented the sudden migration of their brethren from Mexico, whom they sneeringly called *surumatos* (slang for "southerners" [*sic*]). These so-called Spanish-Americans claimed direct descent from the original conquistadores of Spain. They also insisted that they had *never* been Mexicans, since their region of New Spain (later annexed to the United States) was never a part of Mexico [*sic*]. But what they claimed most vociferously—and erroneously— was an absence of Indian ancestry. It made no difference that any objective observer could see by merely looking at them the results of considerable fraternization between the conquering Spaniards and the Comanche and Navaho women who crossed their paths. Still, these *manitos* [for *hermanitos*, little brothers], as they were snidely labeled by the *surumatos*, stubbornly refused to be identified with Mexico, and would actually fight anyone who called them Mexican. So intense was this intergroup rivalry that the bitterest "race riots" I have ever witnessed—and engaged in—were between the look-alike, talk-alike *surumatos* and *manitos* who lived near Denver's Curtis Park. In retrospect the harsh conflicts between us were all the more silly and self-defeating when one recalls that we were all lumped together as "spiks" and "greasers" by the Anglo-Saxon community.[22]

López and his fellows were especially sensitive to the claims of the Hispanos because they were extremely proud of the roles they or their parents had played in the Mexican Revolution. Consequently, for them any Mexican who denied his heritage was committing an act tantamount to sacrilege.

Hispanos, on the other hand, trying desperately to keep their precarious position in society, resented any insinuation that they were related to the incoming Mexicans. The upper class in New Mexico, as in California and Latin America as a whole, was most conscious of its "Spanish" ancestry. The more the elite's estates and power diminished, the more it sought to maintain the trappings of an aristocracy. The well-known New Mexico writer Oliver La Farge, who had married into the upper-class Baca family, described an incident in his wife's early life that revealed the emphasis Hispanos had come to place on the "differences" between themselves and "Mexicans." While showing a rather unwelcome visitor around her financially troubled family's estate,

Consuelo (La Farge's future wife) became upset over her charge's insulting questions and insinuations:

> Unfortunately, Miss Tisdale had betrayed the fact that she thought the natives of Rociada [the local village] were Mexicans, which suggested that she might think the same thing even of the Bacas. Consuelo treated her with a smooth, dire politeness that is profoundly Spanish, the meaning of which was quite lost on the recipient.

Miss Tisdale continued her questions, and despite the irritation Consuelo felt, she answered as patiently as possible,

> No, there were no Indians at Rociada; the people were all *Spanish-Americans* except [for one Anglo]. . . . There was a *Mexican* who had settled just outside the village some years ago, but he had wound up in the penitentiary.[23]

As this incident implies, few of the newly arrived Mexicans settled in the rural areas of northern New Mexico and southern Colorado, and even fewer intermingled with the elites anywhere in the Southwest. However, in urban areas such as Denver and Albuquerque and everywhere else in the Southwest, middle– and lower–class Hispanos came into direct contact with the new-comers who arrived during the revolution of 1910–20 and the following dec-ade of instability in Mexico. In fact during the 1920s migration from Mexico reached a high and did not slow until the crash of 1929.[24] This was such an interesting phenomenon that in 1926 the U.S. Social Research Council com-missioned Dr. Manuel Gamio, a Mexican anthropologist, to study the new arrivals firsthand. He interviewed these people along with some of the earlier residents, and many of the resulting autobiographical documents were col-lected in his volume called *The Mexican Immigrant: His Life Story* (1931).[25]

Luis Albornoz, one of those interviewed by Gamio, was born in New Mex-ico of *nuevomexicano* parents. About 1914 he moved to Los Angeles and mar-ried a woman from Mexico "of a markedly Indian type" who as "obstinately pro-Mexican." Significantly, according to Gamio:

> Sr. Albornoz says that he would never have married an American [Anglo] because his blood is Mexican and he doesn't care about the geographical-political division. He looks at the two countries with love, and he condemns the treason of Santa Ana [*sic*] and his followers who dismembered Mexico. He says that he who sells is to be criticized more than he who buys, and that he admires the United States

for having made of the part which they acquired a productive land with magnificent living conditions [apparently Albornoz was unaware of or chose to ignore the force exercised by the United States in its acquisition of the present Southwest].

Albornoz was not as hostile toward the newly arrived Mexicans as were other Hispanos, probably because he himself was a newcomer in Los Angeles and had become isolated from other *nuevomexicanos*. In fact, as his marriage indicates, he felt more at home among these "foreigners" than he did among his fellow citizens of Anglo descent. Indeed, he had joined several Mexican cooperative societies; also he often went to Mexican patriotic festivals and even kept "a picture of Hidalgo as a decoration with a little Mexican flag." Nevertheless,

> Sr. Albornoz feels proud of being American and deplores the fact that the Mexicans who come to the United States are uncultured immigrants, so that they are despised; this makes him feel ashamed of being of Mexican descent. . . . [then, correcting himself, Albornoz] says that in reality his grandparents were Spanish so that when he is asked what he is, he says he is "Spanish-American."[26]

Working class Hispanos outside rural New Mexico and Colorado may have felt ambivalent toward the refugees from Mexico; however, they had little choice but to adapt to the ways of the more numerous newcomers. In Arizona and Texas working class Hispanos adapted quite easily since they had always had close contacts with Mexicans in the towns across the border. Elena Cortés de Luna, another of Gamio's informants, was not at all disturbed by the migration from Mexico because she had never adopted many Anglo-American customs:

> I am seventy-one years old [about 1927]. My great-grandparents, my grandparents and my parents were all from Arizona. We don't know when our family came, nor if we have Spanish, Mexican or Indian blood in our veins. . . . I didn't learn any English . . . on the other hand I do know how to read and write Spanish well.

Despite or rather because of her deep roots in Arizona, Doña Elena never lost contact with Mexico: "My husband was from the district of Altar, Sonora, . . . [though] he has been almost brought up here." She herself had spent several months in the Sonoran capital of Hermosillo, and her son had been "well fixed" in Mexico for a time. Though her children had learned to speak

English, they still spoke Spanish and loved Mexican food. As a result, even though Doña Elena was not sure whether there was much difference between peoples on either side of the border, she did "feel more akin to the Mexicans [rather than the Anglos] for they are my people since I have Mexican blood in my veins. . . ." Interestingly, she made no open distinction between "Hispanos" and "Mexicans."[27]

By the 1920s and especially the 1930s, the myth of the Spanish Southwest had become so pervasive that often educators, scholars, and scholarly publications uncritically accepted the myth as fact. Among Anglo scholars, Herbert E. Bolton, the leading historian of the early Southwest, succumbed to the myth in 1921 in his landmark *The Spanish Borderlands*. Though otherwise a solid scholar, at times Bolton slipped into the romantic tone then common to his subject; he wrote for instance that: "The life of the Californians presented phases not always seen in Spanish colonies. The beauties and graces of the Spanish character flowered there. . . ." His influence was widespread, and of his protégés, at least one reiterated the myth. In a work entitled *Spanish Arcadia* (1929), Nellie Van de Grift Sánchez, who had married one of the early California residents, described the social life of the province as "the glamour of the day that is gone, when the Spanish *caballero* jingled his spurs along the *Camino Real*."[28]

Among the tiny group of Mexican intellectuals in the United States, the myth of the Spanish Southwest predictably gained a following among Hispano writers, but was usually ignored by the expatriates from Mexico. In 1935 the *Historical Society of Southern California Quarterly* published an article titled "Old San Juan: Last Stronghold of Spanish California," written by Alfonso Yorba, a descendant of the old elite. Yorba's theme was that San Juan Capistrano, where a number of Hispano families still resided, was all of California's "Spanish" heritage that still survived:

> The last of the old Spanish pueblo towns sleeps on into 1935 almost untouched by the modern world. A long row of old adobe houses lines the main street—U.S. Highway 101—and in all corners of the little town one finds the crumbling adobes of yesterday.

From Yorba's account one could infer that once this last stronghold crumbled away, "Spanish" culture in California would be a thing of the past. Sadly, Yorba and other Hispanos resigned themselves to the demise of their culture and comforted themselves by recalling the glories of their history. They could not accept the idea that the waves of Mexicans who arrived between 1900 and 1930 were no less "Spanish" than earlier migrations from Mexico and that these waves would rejuvenate "Spanish" culture in the Southwest. This attitude was especially unfortunate in California, where Hispanos were numerically in no position to carry on "their" culture by themselves.[29]

In New Mexico, however, Hispanos were numerous enough to save their traditions on their own, and they used the myth of Spanish New Mexico as a resource in the fight to preserve their identity. Adelina Otero Warren, a county superintendent of schools and member of the old Otero family, used the myth for just that purpose. In 1931 an article she wrote romanticized New Mexico and implied that bicultural education would help the state keep its romantic quality. As superintendent, Otero Warren often visited small village schools in the mountains of northern New Mexico. While at one of these schools, she once wondered "how to encourage them to preserve the arts, the customs, and the traditions of *this New Spain* [emphasis added] in an effort to save its charm, which is its very life."[30]

She complained that state laws prohibited uncertified personnel from teaching the traditions which certified teachers did not know; that students could not get credit for subjects which did not conform to those taught in schools in the rest of the United States; and that "teachers are instructed to keep the children from conversing in it [Spanish] on the playground [or in the classroom], thereby conforming to the national system of education" (despite the bilingual education provisions of the state constitution of 1912). Thus, even though Otero Warren called her people Spanish-Americans, she was fighting the same cultural battle Mexicans have fought in the Southwest from 1848 to the present: "Is it not a question of our gradual merging, of our assimilation, into this great nation, but at the same time of conserving our distinctive contribution through the preservation of the customs, traditions, the arts and crafts of the Spanish Southwest?"[31]

In 1936 Otero Warren wrote *Old Spain in Our Southwest,* a book including songs, stories, and other traditions of New Mexico. In portions of that work the myth of Spanish New Mexico is so strong that New Mexico appeared not only more Spanish than Mexico but more Spanish than Spain itself:

Like Castile, northern New Mexico is a high mountain country, 7,000 feet above sea level. This New World has a grandeur that everyone, native or stranger, recognizes, and the descendants of the *Conquistadores* still feel that it is an "echo of Spain across the seas." In the 16th and 17th centuries, Spain called in outside artists, and the resulting fusion made the folk art of Spain less crude. In New

Spain [read New Mexico], however, the folk art which the people loved as part
of their inheritance remained unchanged.[32]

According to the myth, after its founding in the late sixteenth and early seventeenth centuries, New Mexico was so isolated that it preserved the purity
of Old Spain, even as the mother country itself changed. Though totally unre-
alistic and harmful in many respects, the myth of Spanish New Mexico had
its positive side. It permitted Mexicans in the state to feel some pride in their
culture even if they rejected that culture's indigenous aspects, and it prevented Hispanos from becoming completely Americanized. Even though the
myth caused hostility for the Anglo to be displaced and aimed at the newcomer from Mexico, it also permitted Hispano intellectuals to take positive
steps towards preserving the Mexican subculture of their "gentle, industrious,
and intelligent people, brown-eyed and *suntanned* [emphasis added]."[33]

     One of the areas of *nuevomexicano* culture (including that of Colorado) most
closely studied by Hispano and other Mexican scholars was folklore. Aurelio
M. Espinosa, born in southern Colorado in 1880, was one of the first in the
field. Dr. Espinosa taught Spanish at a number of universities including the
University of New Mexico, the University of Chicago, and Stanford, and
besides his research in folklore, his publications included Spanish grammars
and studies in linguistics. In virtually all this work, he perpetuated the myth
of Spanish New Mexico. For example, in a beginning Spanish reader which
he called *España en Nuevo Méjico* (1937), Espinosa wrote:

> Spanish New Mexico has remained to this day like a lone sentinel of Spanish
> civilization in the northernmost frontier of the old Spanish Empire in Amer-
> ica. . . . everywhere within its confines we find living evidences of the blood,
> the language, the religion, the laws, and the traditions of Spain.

Furthermore, he added, "New Mexico is still an integral part of Spain." As
for New Mexico's Indians, "they have not given the state its true and permanent character. They have intermingled [read intermarried] very little with
the Hispanic element. . . ."[34]

     Espinosa relied heavily on linguistics and folklore to prove his assertion
that New Mexico was pure Spanish. Because of the state's former relative
isolation, New Mexican Spanish had retained some seventeenth-century words
that had died out elsewhere, a phenomenon that Espinosa believed gave New
Mexico a special tie to old Spain.[35] Furthermore, New Mexico's folklore
seemed to be traceable directly back to that nation. As early as 1910 Espinosa

claimed: "the character of all my New Mexican folklore material; . . . is Spanish in every sense. . . . The Indian and English elements have no importance whatever. . . ."[36] Although he claimed that New Mexico was no different from most of Spanish America in that respect, he did think that the state differed from Mexico and Central America, which were more influenced by the Indian.[37]

One of Espinosa's major reasons for collecting *nuevomexicano* folklore was his fear that "Spanish" culture would disappear from New Mexico. At one point in *España en Nuevo Méjico* he asked rhetorically: "Will the Spanish tradition in New Mexico remain forever vigorous? It is not easy to answer this question. It depends a great deal on the problem of language." Even though Spanish, which Espinosa thought could be a cultural bond stronger than race or religion, was at a disadvantage in the face of the economic power of English, he believed New Mexico would continue to be bilingual. His reasons for believing this, however, were rather romantic; Spanish would survive because it was "the language of the descendants of conquerers and colonizers of noble Spanish blood, men and women conscious of their glorious past and of the spiritual force of their people." Hispano culture as a whole would survive because *nuevomexicanos* "are Spain in New Mexico. They have the power, the privilege and the duty to conserve, fortify and perpetuate all the beauty, . . . of the great and glorious Spain of bygone centuries."[38]

Another Mexican who studied *nuevomexicano* folklore extensively in the 1930s was Arthur L. Campa. Although Dr. Campa followed Espinosa in the field, the fact that Campa was born in Sonora (1905) made his interpretations different from Espinosa's. Campa arrived in the Southwest with the influx of refugees from Mexico when he was about ten. He was fortunate enough to get an excellent education and went on to teach at Columbia, the University of New Mexico, and the University of Denver. In his folklore studies Campa argued that while the influence of Spain was important, that influence had been filtered through Mexico. To ignore the latter country was not only an injustice but also an affront to good scholarship. In an article written in 1933 Campa stated this pointedly: "Many folklorists, in an effort to prove their preconceived idea that everything in New Mexico is pure Spanish, have gone astray in their conclusions because of the lack of sufficient evidence." As examples, Campa listed several words that Espinosa had taken from folksongs and classified wrongly, several words that Espinosa, despite his background in linguistics, could not or would not recognize as being of indigenous Mexican origin. Furthermore, in another article (1934) Campa challenged Espinosa's belief that New Mexican folklore was more Spanish than that of Mexico: "In matters of origin hardly any distinction can be made between Mexico and

New Mexico. Culturally, these two regions are seldom separated by the Rio Grande. . . ."[39]

Later, in an introduction to a collection of New Mexican folk poetry (1946), Campa discussed the myth of Spanish New Mexico at some length. With regard to race, he pointed out that Hispanos were not at all pure Spanish since from earliest times entire Indian villages had been absorbed by the settlers; and Indian prisoners of war, especially women and children, had often been enslaved and subsequently made integral parts of the Hispanic population. With respect to geography, Campa admitted that the relative isolation of northern New Mexico and southern Colorado had allowed the area to originate certain customs and to preserve others that had died out elsewhere; nevertheless,

> The real cultural differences between the region north of the Rio Grande and that below are those which the New Mexican has acquired by close contact with American life. In a sense, it is his dehispanization, his falling away from Spanish, that stamps him as a different individual. The Mexican is different in that he preserves his Spanish language, literature, and menu [sic] The New Mexican is educated in English and naturally acquires traits and habits that are American.[40]

Finally, concerning nomenclature, Campa commented after going through the various terms applied to the Spanish-speaking: "The whole thing is characterized by anomalies which attempt to justify prejudices and defense mechanisms." And he concluded:

> It is not a matter of what people are called by others, nor what they would like to be called, but what they call themselves when speaking in an unbuttoned frankness. They are all Americans; they know it, yet they never speak in Spanish of themselves as *nosotros los americanos* any more than they say *nostros los españoles*. . . . They conceive of their own kin in realistic terms such as *nosotros, nuestra gente, la raza,* and *nosotros los mexicanos*. By *mexicanos* they do not mean Mexicans; neither can it be translated as such. . . . [By *mexicanos,* they mean] the culture that still nurtures them when out of school. Mexican art, dress, music, and food are still the rule among these *mexicanos* north of the river. *Mexicano de México,* is the phrase that distinguishes the Mexican national. By inference it admits of a *mexicano* on either side of the river.[41]

In spite of the pervasiveness of the myth of the Spanish Southwest, not all Hispano writing promoted it. In 1928 Francisca López de Belderrain, the great-granddaughter of a man who had once managed San Gabriel Mission, wrote a matter-of-fact account of early Los Angeles, an account that completely ignored the Spanish California myth. Though Doña Francisca made a subtle distinction between Californians and Mexicans, it seemed more a distinction between natives and newcomers than between pure-blooded Spaniards and half-breeds. In 1940 Dr. George I. Sánchez wrote *Forgotten People,* the first important sociological study of *nuevomexicanos.* In this work Sánchez referred to his fellow *nuevomexicanos* as "New Mexicans" and admitted that "The Pueblo, the Navajo, the Mexican Indian tinged . . . life with indigenous colors, adding their quota to the blood and to the culture of the colonists." Although he accepted the belief that *nuevomexicanos* before 1848 felt little attachment to Mexico and welcomed the North American conquest, he criticized the U.S. government for ignoring the past and contemporary needs of these loyal citizens. Of even more significance is that Sánchez also criticized the public preoccupation with the romantic history of *nuevomexicanos* at the same time that their current culture and needs were ignored.[42]

Among Mexican intellectuals in the United States, those least likely to promote the myth of the Spanish Southwest were the recent arrivals, though few of these directly challenged the myth as did Campa. Among those intellectuals born in Mexico but educated in the United States were the historian Carlos E. Castañeda and the playwright Josephina Niggli. Both were born just south of Texas and had strong family ties in that state; they were, therefore, beyond the region most affected by the myth. This location combined with their arrival in the United States about the time of the Mexican Revolution to make their works more favorable toward Mexico. Even though Dr. Castañeda specialized in the early history of Texas and translated many Spanish documents from the colonial period, one of his most enduring works was *The Mexican Side of the Texas Revolution* (1928), a translation of Mexican documents that helped give a more well-balanced picture of a conflict that meant so much to Mexicans in the Southwest. Josephina Niggli, writing in a genre requiring less objectivity than Castañeda's field, proudly depicted the history and life of Mexico. Two of her plays published in 1938 were titled *Soldadera* and *Azteca,* both written in English. The first dealt with the heroic women who accompanied and often fought in the armies during the revolution. The second play was a tragedy set in pre-Hispanic Mexico and revealed Niggli's interest in the Mexican nationalistic art movement resulting from the revolution, a movement that put heavy emphasis on that country's Indian heritage.[43]

While such writers, relative newcomers to the Southwest, and their Hispano counterparts emphasized different aspects of their history, there was little open hostility between the two groups. At times, in fact, the new arrivals, though they saw no real difference between themselves and the Hispanos, paid tribute to the latter's accomplishments in settling the region. In 1926, for instance, *La opinión,* a Los Angeles newspaper, expressed the hope in one of its early issues that its articles would "succeed in awakening the Mexican blood that runs through the veins of the Astudillos, the Guerras, the Alvarados, the Vallejos, the Picos, and the other descendants of our 'pioneers' to the promise of the new daily's Mexicanism. . . . And that the editor and his newspaper will become a bond of unity among the Mexicans of the north so that these will each day increase in their love for the motherland."[44]

That Hispanos and more recent arrivals could cooperate under the right circumstances was demonstrated in 1918 when a native of southern Chihuahua, Octaviano Larrazolo, was elected governor of New Mexico. Larrazolo settled permanently in New Mexico in 1895, shortly before the increasingly heavy migration of Mexicans to the Southwest began in 1900, but he ran for governor at a time when animosity toward the newcomers was high. Strangely enough Larrazolo won the election by appealing to the ethnic pride of *nuevomexicanos,* and by emphasizing the similarities between himself and them. Larrazolo was born in 1859, came to the Southwest as a child in 1870, and received most of his education in the United States. Before settling permanently in New Mexico, he lived in Tucson and El Paso, where he participated in local elections. As a result, by 1895 he was sufficiently Americanized to be accepted by *nuevomexicanos* and was also aware of the difficulties Mexicans were having throughout the Southwest. In New Mexico he moved up the political ladder in the Democratic party, to which he had always belonged, but in 1911 he joined the Republicans because he believed certain elements in the Democratic party were denying the Spanish-speaking "an equal measure of the rights and privileges in a land that is the common heritage of us and our children." Larrazolo had been especially angered because the "native citizens" had been severely underrepresented in the Democratic delegation to the state constitutional convention. Since the constitution involved the future of the "sacred heritage in the land hallowed by the blood of . . . [the *nuevomexicano}* forefathers who fought to protect it," to deny representation to *nuevomexicanos* was to threaten their survival as a people.[45]

After the convention and his shift to the Republicans, Larrazolo took up the "race issue," as his enemies called it, and fought for the betterment of his people. Among the heavily Hispano Republicans, Larrazolo's appeals for the rights of the natives eventually brought him to the leadership of the party despite the circumstances of his birth. When he ran for governor in 1918, he was accused of being a foreigner meddling in New Mexico politics and trying to "Mexicanize" the state. Fearing his ethnic appeals to *nuevomexicanos,* the predominantly Anglo Democratic party nominated a Hispano, Félix García, to run against him. During the campaign, the Democrats suggested that despite Larrazolo's "nativist" rhetoric, he could make no claim to the heritage of the conquistadores since he was Mexican-born. Nevertheless Larrazolo won the closely fought election. (He was, however, unseated in his bid for a second term.) During his administration he bettered the position of his people by supporting bilingual education and by paying special attention to the problems of small farmers and farm workers. He was, on the other hand, not as sensitive to the problems of industrial labor because he feared radical unions were organizing miners and other industrial workers.[46]

Larrazolo sympathized with New Mexican agricultural labor because around 1920 such labor still followed the patterns of traditional Mexican society. But labor of all types was changing in New Mexico and throughout the Southwest: the dependency between peon and *patrón* was fast becoming a conflict between worker and boss. Ironically, the influx of workers freed from peonage by the Mexican Revolution created a large pool of mobile unskilled labor in the Southwest, labor that could be exploited by employers who lacked even the condescending paternalism *hacendados* had shown for their peons. From 1900 to 1930 Mexican labor was the fuel that ran the railroads, the mines, and the ranches of the Southwest. The prohibition of Chinese (1882) and Japanese (1907) immigration to the United States left Mexico as the most convenient source of unskilled workers for the rapidly developing economy of the Southwest. Since the long boundary between the two countries was difficult to patrol, nativists and Anglo union organizers, who had successfully halted Asian immigration, could not hope to stop the flow from Mexico. U.S. capitalists realized the advantages of the porous boundary and soon learned to use it effectively. By paying wages higher than those in Mexico, North American employers could attract Mexican workers and, by paying them less than Anglos, could increase profits. If Mexicans complained about such discrimination (as they often did), their employers could threaten them with deportation or simply replace them with new arrivals from Mexico.[47]

Mexicans who were citizens of the United States were treated as were the newcomers, as foreigners undeserving of salaries equal to those of Anglos. This was an underlying reason for the Hispanos' desire to distinguish themselves from the recent arrivals. Since both groups were competing for the same jobs, Hispanos resented the newcomers who, by accepting low salaries, depressed the wages of both groups. Whenever strikes were organized by the earlier Mexican residents, employers throughout the Southwest made it common practice to import strikebreakers. The convenience of Mexico as a source of labor became most apparent to Anglo society as a whole with the coming of the depression in 1929. Once Mexicans were no longer needed in an increasingly tight job market, they were deported on a scale unmatched by any other deportation of an ethnic group in recent U.S. history. Rather than support Mexicans who were no longer useful to the economy, local governments found it cheaper to ship thousands back across the conveniently close border. Among those coerced into leaving were many U.S. citizens, including some whose families had been in the Southwest for generations.[48]

Since Mexican labor has always been important to the economy of the Southwest, the history of labor unrest in those industries employing Mexicans stretches at least as far back as 1883. In that year Anglo cowboys and Mexican vaqueros in the Texas Panhandle went on strike and succeeded in getting higher wages. In the mid-1890s the Western Federation of Miners began organizing in an industry heavily dependent on Mexican workers. In 1903 a walkout occurred in the Arizona copper mines when Mexicans refused to accept a pay reduction, but the strike collapsed partly because Anglo miners failed to support it. By 1904 the mine owners were already learning the advantages of the nearby border. When the Western Federation of Miners struck in the coal fields of Colorado, management imported unsuspecting laborers from Mexico to serve as scabs and subsequently broke the strike. This of course led to animosity between Hispanos and newcomers, despite the fact that both groups were members of the same exploited minority. The newcomers, however, were never completely docile, especially after they had had some contact with labor organizers in the United States. As early as 1903, Mexican newcomers building an urban railway struck unsuccessfully in Los Angeles, but despite the failure, the strike showed that the new arrivals could produce leaders and organize against their employers. In fact, even though mine and railroad owners continued to import strikebreakers until the 1920s, before long these same strikebreakers, because conditions were so poor, often joined unions or moved on to other jobs.[49]

Gradually, agriculture began to replace mining and the railroads as the most important employer of Mexicans. Between 1920 and 1930 the number of Mexicans entering the United States rose higher than ever before, and most of them entered the stream of migrant workers that moved from place to place in the Southwest and beyond, harvesting crops of many kinds. Pulled from the soil by the political and economic instability that followed the Mexican Revolution, these newcomers were drawn north by much the same hope that had drawn Anglos west: the desire for a better life. However, when these migrants came to their country's former promising frontier, they found no open land to settle, for by then it was virtually all under the control of Anglo agribusiness. Forced to work for others on farms and ranches that could once have been their own, Mexican migrants moved from one place to another depending on the season and the crop. Lacking year-round residences and often illegally in the United States, migrants had few community ties: they could not vote, live in decent housing, send their children to school, collect welfare, or join unions without serious difficulties. Migrant farm workers were symbolic of what had become of Mexicans in the Southwest: despite the familiar landscapes, the familiar place-names, and the Spanish-speaking barrios throughout the region, Mexicans had become homeless in their own homeland. This became even more true during the depression when thousands of Hispanos were forced to leave their small farms in New Mexico to join more recently arrived Mexicans in their wanderings through the Southwest.[50]

Even though it was very difficult to unionize migrants, Mexican and Japanese sugar-beet workers went on strike as early as 1903 in Ventura, California; in 1913 Mexicans on a hop ranch in Wheatland, California, also struck. Though the resulting improvements were negligible, these strikes indicated that farm workers were dissatisfied with their working conditions. In the late 1920s and in the 1930s, when conditions became even worse, growing dissatisfaction led to constant conflict in agriculture and related industries. A major strike developed in 1928 in the cantaloupe fields of California's Imperial Valley—where 75 percent of the Mexicans were illegal residents. The growers and the authorities used that fact to break the strike; mass arrests were made, and those Mexicans who did not plead guilty and return to work were deported. Once the depression began, Anglos began to compete for agricultural jobs that had once been considered beneath them, and soon Mexicans were being pushed completely out of the job market.[51]

The situation became so serious that in 1936 job-seekers, mostly Hispanos, from New Mexico were prevented from migrating to Colorado. Although *nuevomexicanos* had previously done much of the farm labor in Colorado, jobs had become so scarce that the National Guard was ordered to patrol the Colorado–New Mexico line to keep out migrants. Although this order was declared unconstitutional, it clearly revealed that even Mexicans who were citizens were treated like aliens. Unfortunately, such treatment was common throughout the Southwest. During the unionization of pecan shellers in San Antonio, Texas, in the late 1930s, many Mexicans were threatened with deportation by the U.S. Border Patrol. On one occasion several Mexicans, including U.S. citizens, were herded together and beaten by immigration officers. Such intimidation made scabs of many workers, and even those who were citizens were afraid to assert their rights, since migrants had little power in local communities. By the end of the 1930s, despite a decade of repeated strikes, Mexicans had failed to make any significant gains in agriculture.

Because of the masses of unemployed seeking work during the depression, Mexicans, especially those who caused trouble, could easily be replaced before strikes could succeed.[52]

Between 1929 and 1935 half a million Mexicans were "persuaded" to depart for Mexico, and according to one source, "approximately half of the returnees . . . were American-born." To lighten their welfare rolls, local governments chartered trains and buses, prompting Mexicans to leave by offering free transportation, and threatening to cut welfare payments; of course, forceful deportation was used when possible. If strikers were included on these shipments, repatriation programs were considered all the more successful. That many of the "repatriated" Mexicans were U.S. citizens (mostly children) concerned Anglo-Americans little, since all Mexicans were seen as foreigners. As a result of this attitude, even *nuevomexicano* migrants who happened to be outside New Mexico during the repatriation drives found it necessary and sometimes difficult to prove their citizenship. Mexicans who were repatriated experienced hardships because even though Mexico welcomed its people, it could provide them with little. The government did set up various settlement programs, but by and large the returnees were forced to rely on relatives for support.[53]

Because of such problems, the press in Mexico was frequently critical of North American repatriation policies. How was it, the press asked, that Mexican labor was courted during the good times but deported during the bad? In 1932 the editors of *Excelsior* of Mexico City thought the depression revealed "that anti-Mexican sentiment in the United States has diminished not at all, and . . . we are continuing almost as in those times when their Armies invaded us to the cry of 'Remember the Alamo.' "[54] However, with the threat of World War II, the depression began to subside; deportations gradually ceased, and before long Mexicans were again in demand in the United States. The wartime economy created a shortage of labor in most industries, and of course the military needed soldiers. These needs would lead for a period to an almost complete eclipse of the image of the Southwest as the lost homeland of the Spanish-speaking. With the intense Americanism of World War II, many if not most of the region's Mexicans would come to see themselves as Anglos saw them—as immigrants or the children of immigrants in a new land.

# 6

# The American Southwest

World War II contributed significantly to the eclipse of the Mexicans' image of the Southwest as a lost homeland and of themselves as dispossessed natives. The intense "Americanism" during the war and the postwar period, together with the increased "Americanization" of the region's Spanish-speaking, led to that people's wide acceptance of the Anglo image of the Southwest as a new land, initially populated by Anglo settlers, followed by immigrants, including Mexicans. The eclipse, however, was not total; the traditional image occasionally shone behind the Americanized surface.

By the beginning of the 1940s a sizable new group of Mexicans was taking its place alongside the Hispanos (a term by then usually applied to the earlier Spanish-speaking residents of New Mexico only)[1] and the early twentieth-century newcomers from Mexico. This group was largely composed of the children of those who had arrived during the Mexican Revolution. By the beginning of the war, the members of the second generation, who were usually U.S. citizens by birth, were becoming increasingly Americanized, and their service in the military hastened this process. Having reached draft age by the time of the war, the young men of the second generation entered the armed forces in great numbers, especially since they qualified for few of the deferments available to the upper classes. The intense patriotism in the United States during that period made Mexican-Americans (a term popularized by) the second generation)[2] feel more a part of their country than they ever had before. Those in the military, but also the many civilians who participated in the war effort, felt that by working together with the rest of the nation on this task, they had earned full citizenship. Also, since defense work and the service had allowed Mexican-Americans to see other regions of the United States, and indeed the world, they began to perceive their communities in the Southwest as part of the nation as a whole, rather than primarily an extension of Mexico and Latin America.

Of course, Mexicans had willingly participated in earlier U.S. wars, notably in the conflict with Spain, but World War II was different; it furthered the acculturation of the massive new group that now made up the majority of Mexicans in the United States. Because of their long contact with Anglo culture and also because of their praiseworthy records in earlier wars, Hispanos had previously laid claim to full citizenship, yet the results, as we have seen, had been ambiguous. While Hispanos had come to feel increasingly "American," they were still considered foreigners by their Anglo fellow citizens. Even though it never incorporated them fully into U.S. society, this Americanization had the important effect of separating Hispanos from Mexico. Americanization during World War II had the same effect on the children of the exiles who left Mexico during the revolution. Interestingly, the break that had separated the relatively Anglicized Hispanos from the newcomers for several decades began to close during World War II. As we have already noted, though Hispanos considered themselves more Spanish than the newcomers, what really separated the two groups was the Hispanos' relative Americanization. With the Americanization of the children of the newcomers, Mexicans in the United States were again brought together. After the Second World War, Mexican-Americans found themselves separated from Mexico, unaccepted by the United States, but culturally reunited as an increasingly homogeneous group unique to the Southwest.

After their participation in World War II, the members of the second generation sought their rightful place in U.S. society, sometimes desperately so. Just as the "Spanish-Americans" (Hispanos) had earlier tried to secure a place in that society by renouncing or rewriting their past, many of the second generation tried to forget their unique position in the Southwest and the country as a whole. Wanting desperately to be like other "Americans," ingredients in the mythical melting pot, they came to call themselves Mexican-Americans, a term they hoped might put them on the level with such groups as Irish- or Italian-Americans.[3] The use of the term was unfortunate, however, because with it came attached the myth of "the nation of immigrants," the complex of beliefs that surrounded the idea that the people of the United States had all originated in foreign lands. Despite the fact that the ancestors of Mexicans had been in the Americas and had regarded the Southwest as their homeland for thousands of years, many Mexican-Americans came to accept the belief that their parents were immigrants simply because they had stepped over a line artifically drawn across Mexico.

Thus, what we might call the Mexican-American image of the Southwest became common during and after World War II, and it was not set aside until the coming of the Chicano movement in the late 1960s. The region was increasingly seen as an integral part of the United States, and less as an extension of Mexico; the mental boundary between the Spanish-speaking Southwest and other U.S. regions became lighter, as the boundary with Mexico darkened. In extreme cases, when some Mexican-Americans tried to completely assimilate with Anglos, they refused to see any special tie at all between themselves and the region that had once been northern Mexico. They accepted the idea that the Spanish and the Anglos had settled the land, that the southwestern barrios were simply the equivalents of the immigrant ghettos of the East. The person who could shed his ethnic background, move out of the barrio, even out of the Southwest, was to be regarded as a success. Unfortunately for all Mexican-Americans, those who adopted the new attitude were often those who were most talented and who could have provided badly needed leadership in their communities.

This abandonment was the greatest harm to result from the intense Americanism of World War II. Just as the working class had earlier been deserted by the Hispano elites, it was now surrendered to Anglo exploitation by the successful children of the Mexicans recently settled in the Southwest. Successful Mexican-Americans were often embarrassed by their "foreign" parents and the "alien customs" of their working-class compatriots. Trying to escape the discrimination aimed at their group, these Mexican-Americans disassociated themselves from anything Mexican, at times even boasting of their inability to speak Spanish. Under such circumstances, ideas such as bilingual education or biculturalism were seen as "un-American," an extremism that reached its peak during the McCarthyism and Cold War of the 1950s.

During the 1940s, however, Mexican-Americans had not yet taken their new Americanism to extremes. They were just beginning to enjoy their newly acquired confidence as U.S. citizens and were not yet feeling threatened by reactionary movements. While their participation in the war effort led to their new-found confidence, they also felt encouraged by the gradual change in North American policy toward Mexico and the rest of Latin America, a change that had begun in the late 1920s, gained momentum during the 1930s, and culminated with the military alliance formed by most of the countries of the Western Hemisphere against the Axis powers. After decades of openly aggressive activities toward Latin America, the United States had instituted what came to be known as the Good Neighbor Policy. The salient point of this policy was the decision to reduce North American military interventions in Latin America. Finding that open imperialism only created a poor atmosphere for its political and economic interests, the United States sought, at least in public, to deal with its neighbors as equals rather than inferiors. Also, by showing greater respect for the peoples and cultures of that part of the world, the United States hoped to improve its overall relations with Latin America.[4] These efforts naturally had an important impact on that portion of Spanish

America that penetrated into the southwestern United States because Mexican-Americans, despite their deepening anglicization, to some degree still retained that dimension of their traditional image that depicted the region as an extension of Latin America.

After its victory over Spain at the turn of the century, the United States had become the major imperial power in the Caribbean, exercising that power with little restraint. In 1903 President Theodore Roosevelt instigated a revolution in Colombia, creating the Republic of Panama that in turn allowed the United States to build a canal across its territory. Protecting this right of way then became the rationale for most of the subsequent interventions in countries near the canal site. Although the United States had commendably rejected the temptation to annex Cuba after the Spanish-American War, it made a protectorate of the island and repeatedly sent troops to maintain the peace and North American interests. To prevent European powers from collecting their debts by occupying bankrupt nations uncomfortably close to the Panama Canal, the United States itself occupied those nations and forced them to pay their bills. The Dominican Republic and Nicaragua were two countries that experienced major, lengthy occupations by the military forces of their northern neighbor. That Southwest Mexicans were aware of U.S. activities in places such as Panama, even in 1903, can be seen from the fact that even small community newspapers, such as *El obrero* of Morenci, Arizona, reported these activities regularly.[5]

The United States first intervened in the Dominican Republic in 1905 out of fear of German penetration into the Caribbean. North American troops occupied the republic between 1916 and 1924, and the protectorate did not end until 1941, well after the beginnings of the Good Neighbor Policy. Because Nicaragua provided the best route for a potential rival to the Panama Canal, that country was occupied by Marines almost continuously for two decades. The withdrawal of troops from Nicaragua in 1933 was the first major act of the new policy toward Latin America. In accordance with the new policy, in 1936 the United States also gave up the "right" to intervene in Panama, which had been a protectorate since its separation from Colombia in 1903. Only against this historical background of repeated North American invasions of Hispanic-American lands (not to mention Haiti) can we fully appreciate the impact of the Good Neighbor Policy on Mexican-Americans in the Southwest.[6]

Latin Americans bitterly resented the incursions of the United States; and Mexicans, having the longest history of confrontation with the "colossus of the north," were more bitter than most.[7] Not only had they early lost half of their homeland to the North Americans; during the Wilson administration

they had experienced the occupation of Veracruz and General Pershing's puni-
tive expedition. The 1920s had also been difficult years for relations between
Mexico and the United States. The revolution not yet consolidated, continuing turmoil in Mexico kept the border between the two countries in a state of
unrest, especially along the Texas boundary.

But a more serious difficulty was the conflict arising from the provisions of
the new Mexican constitution that demanded the expropriation of foreign
holdings in Mexico, especially those of oil companies. In the Southwest support for the Mexican position was especially strong in *La prensa,* a Los Angeles newspaper that described itself as constitutionalist. In the early stages of
the disagreement over oil, *La prensa* in issue after issue condemned U.S.
intervention, both military and economic. One article, interestingly enough
by an Anglo-American journalist, John Kenneth Turner, clearly expressed
the Mexican point of view, "from the beginning to the present, [President
Woodrow Wilson] has spoken against [Mexico's] program of nationalization
and land distribution . . . he has opposed all efforts toward an adequate control of . . . large industries, [and] the conservation of natural resources—
especially oil. . . ." Moreover, the article's headline read, "Wall Street Has
Gone Insane in Its Ambition to Despoil Mexico of Its Riches. . . ." This
controversy continued through most of the 1920s and intensified whenever
the Mexican government threatened to enforce the letter of the law. According to historian Thomas A. Bailey, between 1925 and 1927 the situation
became so critical that "a new clamor for war with Mexico arose in the United
States. The oil companies released tons of propaganda, in which they demanded
armed intervention for the protection of their alleged rights." However, in
late 1927, Mexico was persuaded (temporarily) to allow foreign companies
which had begun work before 1917 to retain ownership of their subsoil
properties.[8]

This constant conflict between Mexico and the United States of course did
nothing to improve the situation of Mexicans who arrived in the Southwest
before 1930. With war threatening during the 1920s, Mexicans were not
only considered foreigners but potential enemy aliens. Thus, unlike most other
Latin Americans, Mexicans living in the Southwest faced North American
aggression on a personal level. As a result, they were more than casually concerned with international relations between the Americas, seeing any decline
or improvement in those relations reflecting on their own lives. Of course, a
Mexican national culture that had been anti-American at least since 1836
and emphatically so since the revolution had conditioned them to consider
the United States an enemy. During the oil crisis of the 1920s, for example,
a popular corrido recalled Mexico's oldest grievance against its northern

neighbor, arguing for Mexico to ally itself with an increasingly powerful Japan against the northern colossus:

> Mexico allied with the brave Japanese,
> Will recover the territory lost in the time
>     of Santa Anna;
> Keep harassing her with your complaints,
> And tomorrow you will see what Mexico is worth.[9]

Given this background of hostility and suspicion, Mexican community leaders in the Southwest, especially in the Spanish-language press, carefully followed relations between the two countries. After the oil controversy of the late 1920s, they noticed a mellowing in these relations (despite the deportations of Mexicans then being carried out by the United States). Once Mexico had agreed to allow North American companies to keep their oil holdings, the atmosphere between the two nations cleared somewhat. Furthermore, President Herbert Hoover, finding that open imperialism was increasingly counterproductive, began a public relations campaign in Latin America that eventually developed into the Good Neighbor Policy championed by Franklin D. Roosevelt. As a result, the early 1930s were characterized by a steadily improving climate in the Americas, highlighted in 1933 by the withdrawal of U.S. Marines from Nicaragua. Since Mexico had in the 1920s supported Nicaraguan rebels against the United States, the withdrawal of North American troops greatly improved U.S. relations not only with Latin America in general but with Mexico in particular.[10]

Mexicans in the Southwest were naturally gratified by this turn of events. *La opinión* of Los Angeles reminded its readers that intervention had always been opposed by Mexicans because of their own long history of exploitation at the hands of foreigners: "In our already independent republic, problems confronted us, such as . . . the first war against Texas and the North American invasion of 1847. Then, came the tripartite intervention [by Spain, Britain, and France in the 1860s] in which only France persisted. . . ." The newspaper accurately predicted: "The withdrawal of North American marines from that country [Nicaragua] will contribute greatly, . . . to secure intercontinental concord." During the following decade the United States withdrew troops from other Caribbean lands, giving up its "right" of intervention in such countries as Cuba.[11]

The depression and the election of Franklin D. Roosevelt helped advance the Good Neighbor Policy because North American capitalism was forced into retreat on both domestic and international fronts. Potential investors from the United States had much less money to put into Latin America, and since previous investments had already been lost because of the worldwide depression, these investors had less reason to pressure Washington to intervene south of the border. Moreover, Franklin Roosevelt, elected on an antibusiness platform, saw little advantage in supporting any especially exploitive business adventures, particularly since by 1935 the rise of dictatorships in Europe made neighborliness in the Western Hemisphere increasingly advisable for the security of the United States. Roosevelt's position was severely tested in 1938 when Mexico finally nationalized its entire oil industry. When Mexico refused to compensate North American companies to their satisfaction, they once more clamored for armed intervention, but with the situation in Europe looking more and more grim, Roosevelt decided to acquiesce to Mexico's wishes. This proved to be a wise decision, as Mexico subsequently became an ally during the Second World War rather than the unfriendly neighbor it had been during World War I. As a sign of this new friendship, Mexican school maps that referred to the Southwest as "territory temporarily in the hands of the United States" were in the early 1940s gradually removed from Mexico's classrooms.[12]

While the Good Neighbor Policy and World War II hastened the Americanization of the children of the Mexicans who had arrived in the Southwest during the twentieth century, manifestations of the new, "American" outlook had appeared earlier. In 1929, before the Good Neighbor Policy had gained much momentum, Mexicans in Texas met at Corpus Christi and organized the League of United Latin-American Citizens (LULAC), a coalition of several groups that had formed after World War I.[13] The League's name exhibited the break that its members were trying to make between themselves and Mexico. Since "Latin," like "Spanish," called to mind the members' European rather than Indian ancestry, that term was thought less offensive than "Mexican." In fact LULAC, which soon had chapters throughout the Southwest, was the first major organization dedicated to the assimilation of the Mexican into the "American" melting pot.

According to its constitution, the goal of the League was "to develop within the members of our race the best, purest and most perfect type of a true and loyal citizen of the United States of America." Unlike previous Mexican groups, LULAC abandoned Spanish: "The English language, which is the official language of *our country* [emphasis added] . . ., we declare it to be the official language of this Organization, and we pledge ourselves to learn, and speak and teach same to our children." LULAC also aimed "To assume complete responsibility for the education of our children as to their rights and duties and the . . . *customs of this country* [emphasis added]."[14] The perspective of the Mexican with regard to the Southwest was clearly changing. The founders of LULAC now saw the region as the "American Southwest," an integral part of a country whose language and customs were Anglo, a region that was only theirs insofar as they were true U.S. citizens. This, of course, was the way Anglos saw the region, and the way liberal Anglos thought Mexicans should see it.

Yet, the older Mexican image of the homeland persisted even as LULAC tried to expunge it. Arguing for Americanization, an article in the *Lulac News* (1932) commented:

> We can migrate to the south, leaving *the land of our forefathers* [emphasis added] to our energetic neighbors, and going to a land [Mexico] where our customs are not out of place, thereby holding our own; or we can accept our neighbors' customs, educate our children, and gain their respect. . . . Let us educate our children, enabling them to . . . unquestionably pride themselves citizens of the United States, and owe fealty and allegiance to one flag.

Thus, though Mexicans were not foreign immigrants in the Southwest, the article's author was suggesting they play the part and assimilate as had "all other Americans." Interestingly, the author did not say that Anglo ways were better per se, but that they had to be adopted because

> The gulf [between Anglos and Mexicans] has grown so, in the years, that still you [Mexicans] are a different people, and merely *tolerated* as citizens of a nation in which *you resided even before you joined the union* [emphasis added]. . . . Conditions have reached a point where your neighbors say, "a white man and a Mexican!"

Of course conditions had always been such, but now many Mexicans, becoming Americanized, were more sensitive to racial prejudice. Ironically they felt that more Americanization would solve the problem.[15]

Even though the founders of LULAC declared that they would "maintain a sincere and respectful reverence for our racial origin of which we are proud," they put little or no emphasis on maintaining Mexican culture itself. Individual members were more likely to follow the dictum repeated by one LULAC leader: "If you talk English you will think and act like Americans." This same leader stated: "We tell our people 'if you have not been treated like you should or have not the standard of living it is your own fault. Before asking for your rights you must be prepared.' " In other words, if Mexicans refused to give up the old ways and adopt the new, they themselves were responsible for the racial and economic oppression they experienced. On the other hand, for those who accepted Anglo-American ways, the United States would be the land of opportunity. It should be no surprise that most of LULAC's members were businessmen, professionals, and other U.S.-born, English-speaking members of the middle class. LULAC tried to reach the laboring class, whose un-American ways were often seen as the cause of discrimination against U.S. Mexicans as a whole, but the League's policies had little success because, as LULAC members complained, "100 uneducated Mexicans come in for every one we teach."[16]

The LULAC members' espousal of Americanization met with opposition from the more traditional sectors of Southwest Mexican communities, especially from the first generation:

> The average non-political American of Latin descent calls us [the members of LULAC] "renegades." He says, "you are Mexicans, not Americans." Mexican citizens even in their press attack us. We are called renegades and anti-Mexicans. We call them visitors. They tell us, who are trying to tell them [Mexicans in Texas] to be more loyal to the United States, "But your forefathers are all of Mexican origin and you should continue to be Mexican." We say he is a visitor and it is none of his business.

Despite this division within Mexican communities and despite the League's program of Americanization, LULAC members complained: "We have not been able to convince some people that there is a difference between us. To the average American we are just Mexicans."[17]

The members of LULAC rejected the image of the Southwest as a special place for the Mexican because they believed their people would benefit by conforming to the myth of the "nation of immigrants" and the "land of opportunity." In renouncing their people's traditional image of the Southwest, however, the LULAC members abandoned the old struggle for bilingual/ bicultural education, an issue even the "Spanish-Americans" had never surrendered. Also, in denying the special ties between the Southwest and Mexico (as had Hispanos), the "Latin-Americans" not only minimized their Indian ancestry, they also denied that Mexicans had any special rights of entry into the Southwest. Since continued migration from Mexico increased competition for jobs and hindered LULAC's Americanization efforts, the League sought to restrict further migration from the south. Although LULAC's position on these issues weakened the chances for their people's cultural survival in the Southwest, League members did make a great effort to secure the rights of their people as citizens of the United States.

Although LULAC members believed in the assimilation of U.S. Mexicans into the Anglo world, they were not so busy assimilating themselves as individuals that they forgot their people as a whole. Rather than proceeding on their own, changing their surnames, pretending they were Italian or French in order to melt more easily into the majority, LULAC members insisted on the acceptance of their ethnic group as an equal among other immigrant groups in the United States. With this as an ideological base, the League fought for the civil rights of Mexicans throughout the Southwest and was especially concerned with segregation in the public schools. (Mexicans, they believed, could never become Americanized if they were given separate schooling.) On this front LULAC was strong enough by the 1940s to gain two important victories. In 1945 it brought four southern California school districts to court for *de facto* segregation of Mexican-Americans; the districts were subsequently enjoined from continuing this practice, a decision that was upheld on appeal in 1947. And in Texas the intentional segregation of Mexican-American school children was challenged by LULAC and declared unconstitutional by state courts in 1948.[18] Through such efforts, the League's philosophy of Americanization helped Mexicans rise above their subordinate status, even though that philosophy weakened their culture in the Southwest.

With the implementation of the Good Neighbor Policy and the coming of the Second World War, gradually more Mexican-Americans came to see themselves and the Southwest as did the members of LULAC. With the repatriation of so many Mexicans during the 1930s, Mexico's influence in the southwestern barrios abated somewhat, causing a rise in the general level of Americanization. When the League was founded in the late 1920s, the adult children of the Mexicans who had settled in the Southwest during the twentieth century were a small group, but by the 1940s the second generation, with its increasingly Anglo ways, had become much larger, more influential, and more likely to see its own region as the American Southwest. However, despite its increasing attachment to the United States, this group never completely abandoned the traditional image of the region even at the most patriotic times. In *Among the Valiant* (1966), an account of the Mexican-American military contributions to World War II and the Korean conflict, Raúl Morín has written that, upon hearing the news of Pearl Harbor, two Los Angeles youths jokingly commented on the effects the war might have on Mexican-Americans:

> "*Ya estuvo* (This is it)," said one, "Now we can look for the authorities to round up all the Mexicans and deport them to Mexico—bad security risks."

Another excited character came up with, "They don't have to deport me! I'm going on my own; you're not going to catch me fighting a war for somebody else. I belong to Mexico. *Soy puro mexicano* [I'm 100 percent Mexican]!"[19]

As Morín noted, the first comment was a reference to suggestions, made during World War I, that U.S. Mexicans be considered security risks since Germany had offered Mexico "all [*sic*] the territory that formerly belonged to the southern republic" in return for a victorious alliance against the United States. Both comments indicated that, because of their history as a subjugated and consequently distrusted population in the Southwest, the immediate reaction of Mexican-Americans to Pearl Harbor was a feeling of insecurity and alienation. In spite of this feeling, the very two men who made the comments subsequently served in the army and the Marine Corps in the Pacific Theater. Morín, who himself served in Europe, explained the patriotism of Mexican-Americans:

We felt that this was an opportunity to show the rest of the nation that we *too* were also ready, . . . to fight for our nation. It did not matter whether we were looked upon as Mexicans . . .; the war soon made us all *genuine* Americans, eligible and available immediately . . . to defend our country, the United States of America.[20]

Indeed Mexican-Americans were almost immediately involved in the fighting. Two New Mexico National Guard units, composed mostly of Mexican-Americans, were among the defenders of the Philippines, which were attacked by Japan after Pearl Harbor. At Bataan, they made up a quarter of the combat troops, and after the surrender of Corregidor, they were unfortunately well represented in the infamous Bataan Death March. During the rest of the war, Mexican-Americans did more than their share of the fighting on all fronts. No other ethnic group, according to its percentage of the whole population, had as many men serving in combat divisions. No other ethnic group received as many decorations for valor. Significantly, in addition to the Mexican-Americans who served were many Mexican nationals, residents of the United States, who enlisted with the encouragement of the president of Mexico. Also, after Mexico declared war, many more Mexican citizens crossed the border into the Southwest to volunteer for combat since they knew most of Mexico's own forces would see action only if the hemisphere were invaded.[21]

Despite this overwhelming demonstration of support for the war on the part of Mexicans, they were nonetheless suspected of disloyalty and even treated as enemies on the home front. Anglo xenophobia, intensified by Pearl Harbor, first led to the internment of Japanese-Americans as suspect aliens and soon after made Mexican-Americans targets as well. For much of 1942 the United States was on the defensive in the Pacific, and the general public, fearing an invasion of the West Coast, worried about the possibility of quislings in its midst. With the Japanese-Americans interned, the press in Los Angeles centered the public's attention on the Mexican-American community where it suspected subversive activities among gangs of neighborhood youths. Like other poor urban neighborhoods, the Mexican-American barrios on the east side of Los Angeles suffered from a relatively high crime rate due to the low socioeconomic position of their inhabitants, especially their often unemployed teen-agers. Segregated in schools and denied access to many public places of entertainment because of their race, Mexican-American youths had to rely on each other for social interaction. A small number joined highly cohesive gangs that claimed and defended particular territories against their rivals, a situation that often led to violence. Such domestic violence, in time of war against foreign enemies, seemed nothing short of sedition to the public at large, especially once the press had exaggerated the problem.[22]

From the spring of 1942 until the summer of 1943, the Los Angeles press headlined almost any crime connected with alleged gang members—"zoot-suiters" as they were dubbed after their distinctive and supposedly "un-American" dress. Subsequently, the police, feeling strong pressure from the press and consequently from the public, increased their surveillance of the barrios. This anti-gang campaign reached a climax in late 1942 when twenty-four youngsters were arrested for the apparent murder of a victim of alleged gang violence. The "Sleepy Lagoon Case," sensationalized by the press, became an opportunity for the society at large to express its hostility against zoot-suiters and all Mexicans. Seventeen of the youths were convicted on slight evidence, and though on appeal the convictions were in 1944 unanimously reversed, the trial had damaging effects on cultural relations in Los Angeles and on international relations with Latin America.[23]

During the trial, racist statements concerning the character and loyalty of Mexican-Americans were made in the press and by the police, statements so prejudiced that the federal government feared they would inflame opinion in Latin America against the United States. Shortly after the arrest of the Sleepy Lagoon defendants, the Los Angeles Police Department issued a document purporting to explain the crime wave in East Los Angeles. According to this report, Mexican-Americans were biologically prone to crime and violence, a character inherited from their Indian ancestors, Mongoloid peoples from across the Bering Strait. Mexican-Americans were thus portrayed as biologically linked with the vicious Japanese enemy, deserving treatment little better than that accorded the interned Japanese-Americans. Such anti-Mexican rhetoric became so common during the trial that the Los Angeles County Sheriff (himself, ironically, a *californio*) suggested that before their evacuation Japanese-Americans might have incited Mexican-Americans to violence. With such statements filling the air, it was not surprising that in December 1942 the un-American activities committee of the California assembly began an investigation into possible connections (never substantiated) between gang violence and a group of fifth columnists known as the *sinarquistas*.[24]

The *sinarquistas*, Mexican reactionaries connected with the Falange of Spain, were a threat to the United States because they opposed Mexico's alliance with its northern neighbor and sought the return of the Southwest to Mexico. Feeling that country had always suffered in its dealing with North Americans, *sinarquistas* believed Mexico should have nothing to do with the United States. Also, since they regarded Franco's Spain as a model Christian state, which Mexico should emulate, the *sinarquistas* sympathized with the fascist powers that supported Franco and had, moreover, never harmed Mexico. Though opposed by the Mexican government, *sinarquistas* gained a substantial following south of the border and attempted to do the same north of it. In the spring of 1943, one press report claimed there were 50,000 *sinarquistas* within the Mexican barrios of California alone. Though the actual figure was only 2,000 for the entire United States, the first figure was frightening to a California Anglo population that had already been exposed in the press to an intense anti-Mexican campaign. The *sinarquistas* caused alarmed Anglos to recall Kaiser Wilhelm's courting of Mexico during World War I and the *sedicioso* troubles along the Texas border. Such Anglo fears, however, were no longer realistic because irredentism now had little appeal among Mexican-Americans in the Southwest. The members of the second generation had become so Americanized that they could not see themselves permanently returning to Mexico as individuals, nor could they see their region politically reunited with the motherland.[25]

That Mexican-Americans, on the other hand, were hardly considered "Americans" is evident from events during and after the Sleepy Lagoon Trial. Police stepped up their patrols in the barrios, at one point blockading all the major streets, stopping and searching all cars with Mexican-looking occupants, and arresting over six hundred people on suspicion. Of these, less than a third were ever charged with a crime, let alone convicted. Police harassment of Mexican-Americans continued along with inflammatory newspaper reports throughout the first half of 1943, until anti-Mexican riots erupted in early June of that year. Unfortunately, during that tense period, Los Angeles was filled with servicemen on leave from bases near the city. A number of fights involving servicemen and "zoot-suiters" were reported in the newspapers, which naturally sided with the men in uniform against the "unpatriotic" Mexicans. Incited by these reports, servicemen gathered in the city to get revenge against this "foreign enemy." For about a week of consecutive nights, with the praise of the newspapers and the collaboration of the police, soldiers and sailors conducted raids on the east side, beat and stripped zoot-suiters of their "un-American" garb, and eventually attacked any Mexican or other member of a visible minority who happened to be in their path. Making no attempt to stop these raids, the police would instead appear on the scene of any particular incident just in time to arrest the victims of the crime. In response to all of this, the attitude of the press was best represented by the following headline from the *Los Angeles Times:* "Zoot Suiters Learn Lesson in Fights with Servicemen." The violence finally ceased only after the Mexican government asked the U.S. State Department to intervene. Worried over this threat to the Good Neighbor Policy, Washington then ordered the armed forces to keep their men out of Los Angeles, and the trouble subsided.[26]

The federal government was especially concerned about the racial conflict in Los Angeles because Mexico, as part of its contribution to the war, was sending thousands of its citizens to the Southwest to relieve the labor shortage caused by the draft. Furthermore, the Axis powers were making effective propaganda of the situation in Los Angeles; at one point, after the sentencing of the Sleepy Lagoon defendants, Axis radio broadcast the following to Latin America:

The 360,000 Mexicans of Los Angeles are reported up in arms over this Yankee persecution. The concentration camps of Los Angeles are said to be overflowing with members of this persecuted minority. This is justice for you, as practiced by the "Good Neighbor," Uncle Sam. . . .[27]

Mexico was indeed worried about the fate of its citizens and their descendants in the United States. Mexican newspapers constantly complained about Anglo racism, for attacks on and discrimination against Mexicans occurred in many parts of the United States.[28] Before the disturbances in Los Angeles, there had been outbreaks in Oakland and Venice; during the Los Angeles riots, similar trouble had occurred in Pasadena, Long Beach, and San Diego; Beaumont, Texas, also experienced large-scale riots. Ultimately, the violence spread to several midwestern and eastern cities where other minority groups were included among the victims.[29] However, after the federal government had moved to calm the situation in Los Angeles, the local press, which had incited so much of the trouble, began to reflect Washington's neighborly concern for the victims of the riots: "No friendly government [such as Mexico's] must have just cause for saying that their nationals were mistreated."[30] Sadly, even as the press called for an end to further violence, it refused to admit that most of the victims were U.S. citizens.

Racism at home led some Mexican-Americans to wonder whether their group's high casualties overseas were actually the result of discrimination in combat assignments.[31] If so, Mexican-American servicemen as a whole did not complain. In the armed forces many for the first time experienced what it was like to be the equals of other citizens. After the war, veterans were proud of their new status, proud of their collective military record, and optimistic about the future, especially since many came home with practical skills learned in the service: "We learned new languages and trades and how other people lived, and we learned how Americans lived, too. So we came home with a lot of ideas and plans. . . . The war opened the doors for us."[32] But when these veterans returned, they found things were not as equal at home as in the military. Throughout the Southwest, Mexican-Americans were still refused service in many restaurants, theaters, and other public places; segregated in public schools; discriminated against in hiring; underrepresented in public office and on juries; and as a group still consigned to the lowest levels of society. Unfortunately, many Mexican-American veterans personally experienced such discrimination on their return. Some of the most notorious cases occurred in Texas, where a deceased serviceman was refused burial in his home town and where winners of the Congressional Medal of Honor were denied service in restaurants.[33]

Many Mexican-American veterans found it painful to readjust to southwestern towns that expected them to return to subordinate status. The father of one South Texas veteran said of his son: "After he came home and found that things hadn't changed, he felt that he would rather be just another sailor than the kind of human being the Anglos treated him like."[34] In 1946 a California leader, Ignacio L. López, commented concerning such men:

Every Southwest community has in it young men, formerly "little" Americans but who were able to act as complete Americans for three to four years. They know what it is to be released from the minority burden. They find it a heavy one to be asked to pick up again, on the other side of the tracks in a Southwest city. I am often tempted to say to them, "Go away! Go to another part of the United States!" There are places where there is no prejudice against the Mexican-American, and where they could keep for the rest of their lives the precious feeling of integration and belonging.[35]

Indeed in the East and Midwest Mexican-Americans were more readily accepted as ingredients for the melting pot because in those regions they were
in a truer sense immigrants; in the Southwest, on the other hand, they
remained the impoverished heirs of conquered natives.[36] And, being such,
they could rarely heed López's "advice" to leave their native towns—as one
former corporal put it:

> The rest of the United States isn't like Descanso [a fictitious name for a Califor-
> nia town], I've found out. I'd like to live in the East—I've got a girl there. But
> you couldn't move my mother, and I've got to help her until the kids are
> grown.[37]

Most Mexican-American veterans were unable and unwilling to leave their
southwestern communities, but instead sought to regain their rightful place
in those communities. In doing so, they sometimes proceeded on the basis of
both their new image of themselves as "Americans" *and* their older image of
themselves as dispossessed natives of the Southwest. "How long had we been
missing out on benefits derived as an American citizen?" asked veteran Raúl
Morín. "Oldtimers had told us and we had read in books how the early [Anglo]
settlers had invaded our towns and had shoved us into the 'other side of the
tracks.' "[38] Now, along with other Mexican-Americans who had participated
in the war effort, veterans began to push back into the central life of their
communities. In Edinburg, Texas (and elsewhere), this push met with resistance from the dominant group. For example, the wife of an Anglo veteran
complained in a letter to the *Edinburg Valley Review:* "Edinburg has become
complete Mexican—jobs, houses, everything. . . . let them [Mexicans] go
back over where they were before the war. Give the American [Anglo] boys
. . . a chance; they gave their best to us." Predictably this letter drew angry
responses from Mexican-Americans; one relative of a veteran was especially
upset at the suggestion that Edinburg be given back to the "Americans:"

> Texas was formerly a part of Mexico and Mexico is part of the North Ameri-
> can continent. So anyway you look at it, Mexicans whether U.S.-born or Mex-
> ican-born are Americans.
> So—the Mexicans to Mexico, Germans to Germany, Poles to Poland, etc.
> Let's do give this land back to real Americans—the Indians and the Mexicans.[39]

This exchange revealed that despite the emphasis on Americanism after
World War II, Mexican-Americans had not completely forgotten they were
indigenous to the Southwest, and they were unlikely to abandon the towns

and barrios of the region despite the oppression encountered there. Mario Suárez, one of the first Mexican-Americans to publish short stories in English, described the particular attraction that the barrio (in this case a Tucson community) still had for the returning veteran:

> . . . El Hoyo is something more [than its outward appearance]. It is this something more which brought Felipe Ternero back from the wars. . . . It helped him to marry a fine girl named Julia. It brought Joe Zepeda back without a leg from Luzon and helps him hold more liquor than most men can hold with two. It brought Jorge Casillas . . ., back to compose boleros. Perhaps El Hoyo is the proof that those people exist who, while not being against anything, have as yet failed to observe the more popular [Anglo] modes of human conduct.[40]

The attraction of the southwestern barrio was its culture. There the returning veteran could still establish the kind of family he had always known; there he could feel himself a whole man despite the insults and injuries received in the outer world; there he could recreate his life from within his own cultural traditions. Moreover, from this corner of strength, he could move toward first-class citizenship.

When Mexican-American veterans returned, they helped form a number of organizations whose goals were to eliminate discrimination in public places, in employment, in the legal system, in education, in all those areas where Spanish-speaking citizens received second-class treatment. In California the Unity Leagues and the Community Service Organization (the CSO) were formed soon after the war to help the Mexican-American masses achieve full citizenship through Americanization programs. In Texas, Mexican-American veterans and their families organized the American G. I. Forum to help secure their civil rights. The G. I. Forum appealed largely to the middle class and was in that way similar to the earlier League of United Latin-American Citizens, which also gained strength after the war. Until the election of President Eisenhower, all these organizations relied heavily on the Good Neighbor Policy to influence the general public.[41]

Though Mexican-Americans now stressed their United States citizenship, they also found it advantageous to mention their Latin American heritage. For example, in *Are We Good Neighbors?* (1948), a collection of documents on discrimination against Mexican-Americans, Alonso S. Perales, a diplomat to Latin America and a LULAC leader, argued that people of Latin descent in the Southwest, especially Texas, had to be treated with more dignity if Latin America were ever to take the Good Neighbor Policy seriously. (Interestingly, Perales thus revived the image of his region as a subjugated outpost of Latin

America, even as he argued for the full acceptance of his people into the society of the American Southwest.) As a result of such efforts, in a few years after the war Mexican-Americans succeeded in eliminating some of the more openly racist practices against them, but as the 1950s advanced the postwar changes lost momentum.[42]

During the conservative 1950s, Mexican-Americans went out of their way to be "100 percent Americans," and many chapters of their organizations lost their fervor. LULAC and the G. I. Forum in many cases became nothing more than social clubs, their middle-class members satisfied with their early victories and anxious not to endanger their improved status. Even the CSO, which remained more active than the other groups, turned to red-baiting activities to clear itself of charges that it was communist inspired. This was understandable considering that many Mexican and Mexican-American leaders were harassed and sometimes deported by the federal government, usually for labor activities considered subversive. The Republican administration's deemphasizing of the Good Neighbor Policy also led to greater caution on the part of Mexican-Americans. The Eisenhower administration took a belligerent attitude toward communism in Latin America, in 1954 indirectly intervening to topple a communist-supported government in Guatemala. While this alienated Latin America, Mexican-Americans were either too intimidated or too "patriotic" to protest much. Since the federal government had violated the Good Neighbor Policy abroad, that policy was now certainly of little value to Mexican-Americans in the Southwest.[43]

The Mexican-American emphasis on Americanism during the 1950s left all Mexicans defenseless when confronted by a new assault on their human rights, an assault known as Operation Wetback. Ever since the World War II labor shortage in agriculture, Mexico had been providing the United States with a worker called the bracero (hired hand), whom economist Ernesto Galarza has described as an "indentured alien . . ., an 'input factor' stripped of the political and social attributes that liberal democracy likes to ascribe to all human beings. . . ." Every year a stipulated number of Mexicans were sent to the farms of the Southwest where they were isolated, cheaply housed, fed, and paid while they worked the land. At the end of the season, they were returned to Mexico, thereby relieving the United States of responsibility for their care during the following period of unemployment. In essence the bracero program permitted the United States to obtain the labor it needed while granting the laborers few of the political and social benefits of life in the Southwest. The number of braceros grew year by year as the demands of agriculture increased; however, there never seemed to be enough, and after 1949 huge numbers of "illegal aliens" began to make up for the shortage.[44]

Mexicans entered the United States illegally when the bracero program failed to accept them or because they wished to avoid the bureaucratic difficulties involved; they were hired by employers who were unable to obtain braceros or who wished to avoid the minimum wage and other restrictions imposed under the program. The "problem" with "illegals" was their tendency to remain in the Southwest. Unlike braceros, undocumented workers were more integrated into the Mexican-American communities of the region; they were not merely a source of labor but participants in the life of the Southwest. This increasing "foreign" influence, however, threatened Anglo-Americans who in the 1950s were more fearful of subversive foreigners than usual. As a result, in 1954 the federal government initiated Operation Wetback, a massive deportation program that rivaled the repatriations carried out during the depression. The major reason for the operation was, according to the attorney general of the United States, to rid the country of political subversives. Once again regardless of their place of birth or citizenship, Mexicans were intimidated, separated from their families, and deported as if they were enemy aliens in the Southwest. And, unfortunately, little organized resistance was ever offered. Before the beginning of the operation, Mexican-American organizations had supported restrictions on entrants from Mexico because of the competition given U.S.-born workers and because of the retardation of Americanization efforts. As a result, these organizations could hardly object to Operation Wetback, especially since Mexico, which could only welcome its own people, cooperated with the United States. Thus, satisfied with a bracero program that provided Mexican labor without increasing the local Mexican population, Anglo-Americans once again succeeded in using the artificial international boundary to the detriment of Mexicans on both sides of it.[45]

By the end of 1956 Operation Wetback more or less ceased after well over a million Mexicans had been deported. The deportation of so many Mexicans left the Southwest and its barrios as "American" as they would ever be. It is not surprising that, during the late 1950s and early 1960s, persons who completely denied their ethnic background (a phenomenon never as common among Mexican-Americans as among other groups) became more numerous among the Spanish-speaking. This trend did little to improve the condition of the weakened Mexican-American organizations, since the *vendidos* or "sellouts" (as the defectors were later called) wanted nothing at all to do with their group, not even to Americanize it. Among the defectors, unfortunately, were some of the most talented of Mexican-Americans.[46] One example of this type was a successful doctor respected in the Anglo society of South Texas: "When asked about Mexican-American problems, he bristled. 'How should I know about them?' he countered. 'I don't even speak their language.'" Another example was a businessman who complained, "I wish I could get every drop of Mexican blood out of my veins and change it for something else." To their chagrin, such Mexican-Americans could rarely blend into the Anglo background as easily as could members of European ethnic groups:

> I think like an Anglo and I act like an Anglo but I'll never look like an Anglo. Just looking at me, no one could tell if I am an American or one of those blasted Mexicans from across the river. It's hell to look like a *foreigner in your own country* [emphasis added].[47]

This statement, with its ironic use of so significant a phrase, reflected an extreme change in one aspect of the image the Spanish-speaking had of themselves and the Southwest, and yet that aspect remained somehow the same. In the past Mexicans had been made to seem like foreigners in the country of their ancestors by the invading Anglos; now Mexican-Americans were made to seem like foreigners in the country of their citizenship by incoming Mexican nationals—in both cases Southwest Mexicans were seen as, and consequently felt like aliens. Furthermore, responses to these feelings of alienation had changed. In the past Southwest Mexicans had reacted by strengthening their own culture in the region, but in the 1940s Mexican-Americans began to react to those feelings by trying to adopt Anglo ways. Though some, trying desperately to avoid Anglo prejudice, went to the extreme of denying their race, most Mexican-Americans tried to think of themselves as proud members of one more immigrant group attempting to solve its problem of alienation through Americanization.[48] Their new self-image revealed itself clearly in the first novel about themselves written by one of their own: "If we live in this country," remarked the protagonist of *Pocho* (1959) by José A. Villarreal, "we must live like Americans."[49] Even in New Mexico and Colorado where the myth of the Spanish Southwest persisted, this drive for Americanization began in the 1940s to challenge hispanization as the preferred way of adjusting to the dominant society.[50]

Fortunately for the survival of Southwest Mexican culture, however, many members of the Spanish-speaking population continued to view the region as they traditionally had. At the University of New Mexico in 1942, for example, a Hispano professor recalled the image of the Southwest as a frontier of Latin America, while arguing for bilingual education: "Many believe that English and Spanish should be taught so perfectly to all the citizens of New Mexico, as to equip them to be the bilingual intermediators of the Americas."[51] And in 1958, at the other end of the period of intense Americanization, Mexican-American novelist John Rechy recalled the image of Southwest Mexicans as a conquered people: "The Mexican people of El Paso . . .—are all and always and completely Mexican, and will be. They speak only Spanish to each other and when they say the Capital they mean Mexico DF."[52] Thus, Southwest Mexican nationalism quietly persisted until the radicalized world of the late 1960s roused that pride and channeled it into a forceful political movement demanding the economic, social, and cultural rights of a disinherited people. The image of the lost homeland and its dispossessed native Mexicans would once again come to the fore.

# 7

## Aztlán Rediscovered

During the middle and late 1960s, the political situation in the United States developed into a crisis that permitted a resurgence of the image of the lost land. The myths of the Spanish Southwest and the American Southwest, which the Mexicans of the region had accepted for much of the twentieth century, were suddenly set aside. During that period when so many myths were being reexamined by U.S. society in general, many Mexican-Americans found it possible to challenge the images of themselves and their region that had been imposed by the Anglo majority. The shattering effect that the civil rights and the antiwar movements had on the Anglo self-image led many Mexican-Americans to believe that their attempts to be like Anglos were against their own interests. They began to feel that perhaps they had more in common with blacks and even the Vietnamese than with the dominant Anglo-Americans. Reviewing their own socioeconomic position after two decades of "Americanization," Mexican-Americans found themselves lower even than blacks in income, housing, and education. Though they were not as discriminated against or segregated as blacks, Mexican-Americans realized that they had in no way become the equals of Anglos. In searching for the causes, the view that all "immigrant" groups initially experienced such problems seemed to explain less and less, for by 1960, 81 percent of Mexicans in the Southwest were United States—born. Furthermore, the condition of longtime residents in New Mexico and Texas was no better and often worse than that of other Mexican-Americans.[1]

The nationalist movements of such peoples as the Vietnamese and the Cubans inspired a significant number of Mexican-Americans to reexamine their own condition through history and conclude that they too had been the victims of U.S. imperialism. As a result, the nineteenth- and early twentieth-century image of the Southwest as lost and of themselves as dispossessed reemerged from the collective unconscious of the region's Mexicans. As we have seen, that image had persisted, largely because of the intense Mexican nationalism that radiated from across the border, but in the 1960s it was reasserted and reshaped under the influence of contemporary ideas. Increasingly after World War II the former colonies of the world gained political independence and established nonwhite rule. Nonwhites sought to reestablish pride in their own racial backgrounds to combat the feelings of inferiority that colonialism had imposed. In the United States this phenomenon manifested itself in calls for black pride and black power, and also in cries for Chicano pride and Chicano power. The use of the term "Chicano," derived from *mexicano* and formerly used disparagingly in referring to lower-class Mexican-Americans, signified a renewed pride in the Indian and mestizo poor who had built so much of the Southwest during the Spanish and Anglo colonizations.[2] While investigating the past of their indigenous ancestors in the Southwest, activist Chicanos rediscovered the myth of Aztlán and adapted it to their own time.

After gaining independence from Spain and again after the revolution of 1910, Mexicans had turned to their ancient Indian past for inspiration. It is no surprise that Chicano activists did the same thing during the radical 1960s, especially given the example of contemporary nationalist movements. In the ancient myth of Aztlán, activists found a tie between their homeland and Mexican culture that antedated the Republic of Mexico, the Spanish exploration of the borderlands, and even Tenochtitlán (Mexico City) itself. As we have seen, ancient Aztec legends, recorded in the chronicles of the sixteenth and seventeenth centuries, recounted that before founding Tenochtitlán the Aztecs had journeyed from a wondrous place to the north called "Aztlán." Since this place of origin, according to some of the chroniclers, was located in what is now the Southwest, Chicano activists reapplied the term to the region, reclaiming the land on the basis of their Indian ancestry. And although the preponderance of evidence indicates that the Aztlán of the Aztecs was actually within present Mexico, the activists' use of the term had merit. While the Aztlán whence the Aztecs departed for Tenochtitlán was probably in the present Mexican state of Nayarit, anthropological studies suggest that the distant ancestors of the Aztecs centuries prior to settling in Nayarit had inhabited and migrated through the Southwest. Thus, on the basis of Indian prehistory, Chicanos had a claim to the region, a claim stronger than any based only on the relatively brief history of Spanish settlement in the borderlands.

Since Aztlán had been the Aztec equivalent of Eden and Utopia, activists converted that ancient idealized landscape into an ideal of a modern homeland where they hoped to help fulfill their people's political, economic, and cultural destiny. Therefore, though "Aztlán" came to refer in a concrete sense to the Southwest, it also applied to any place north of Mexico where Chicanos hoped to fulfill their collective aspirations. These aspirations in the 1960s, it turned out, were more or less the same hopes Southwest Mexicans had had since the Treaty of Guadalupe Hidalgo. Chicanos sought bilingual/bicultural education, just representation in the government, justice in the courts, fair treatment from the police and the military, a decent standard of living, and ultimately that which controlled the possibilities of all their other aspirations— their share of the means of production, for this, intellectuals at least now believed, was what the Anglo conquest had fundamentally denied Southwest Mexicans. The northern homeland had been lost militarily and politically in the 1840s; the economic loss had come in subsequent decades with the usurpation of individually and communally owned lands that produced the wealth of the region. During Mexican rule the wealth of the land had been largely agricultural, but later the land of the Southwest had also given forth gold, silver, copper, coal, oil, uranium, and innumerable other products that enriched the Anglos but left Mexicans impoverished. In this respect, Chicanos increasingly saw a parallel between themselves and the native peoples of other colonized lands: all had been conquered, all had been reduced to menial labor, and all had been used to extract the natural bounty of their own land for the benefit of the conquerers.[3]

The Chicanos' historic loss of the economic power inherent in the land of the Southwest underlay the manifestations of militant nationalism that erupted in the late 1960s: the farmworker strikes in California, the land grant struggle in New Mexico, the revolt of the electorate in Crystal City, Texas, the school walkouts in Denver and Los Angeles, and the other major events of what came to be called the Chicano movement. Though these events exploded with suddenness, they were preceded by calmer yet significant developments in the previous decade that prepared a sizable number of Mexican-Americans for the move away from Americanization. As we have seen, the 1950s and early 1960s had been the nadir in the history of Mexican nationalism in the Southwest. But even though Mexican-American organizations had generally been weakened by the assimilation of potential members into the Anglo world, several new groups had managed to establish themselves during that time. The most important of these were the Mexican-American Political Association (MAPA) founded in California in 1959 and the Political Association of Spanish-Speaking Organizations (PASO or PASSO) founded in Arizona in 1960 and most influential in Texas.[4] These two differed from the League of United Latin American Citizens, the G. I. Forum, and other earlier groups because the new organizations believed in activating the political power of Mexican-Americans for the overall good of Mexican-Americans. Earlier groups, more assimilationist in perspective, preferred a defensive posture, protecting the rights of Mexican-Americans in the name of all U.S. citizens. While the difference may seem subtle, the new emphasis on self-interest rather than universality prepared the way for the rebirth of Chicano nationalism.

It is not surprising that this change occurred in the closing years of the Eisenhower administration when the stress on Americanism was beginning to lose its force. The presidential campaign of John F. Kennedy, with its promise of a return to the principles of the New Deal and the Good Neighbor Policy, galvanized the Mexican-American community into political action. Kennedy's Catholicism, which seemed un-American to so many Anglos, was the critical link that allowed Mexican-Americans to identify with the candidate. Furthermore, Kennedy directly sought their vote with the result that MAPA and PASO members helped form the Viva Kennedy Clubs that won the Mexican-American vote for the Democrats, a vote that proved decisive in bringing victory to their candidate in the crucial state of Texas. With Kennedy's election Mexican-Americans looked forward to improved U.S. relations with Latin America and to better socioeconomic conditions at home.[5]

Even though the Kennedy administration was brief, the expectations of Mexican-Americans were met in several respects. During the Republican years U.S. relations with Latin America had generally been poor, but Mexican-Americans, despite their strong ties with that part of the world and because they did not wish to be considered un-American, had protested little. Given the strong anticommunism of the period, they also thought it unpatriotic to support leftists such as those in Guatemala and Cuba. Mexican-Americans, therefore, welcomed Kennedy's Alliance for Progress, an attempt to improve conditions in Latin America with U.S. foreign aid. They felt that such a cooperative effort would lift Latin America out of poverty, furthering the cause of democracy and free enterprise against Cuban-style communism. The Alliance for Progress, like the Good Neighbor Policy, once again allowed Mexican-Americans to feel more comfortable with their bicultural loyalties. Also, Kennedy's popularity in Mexico itself, resulting from his Catholicism and his demonostrated interest in the Latin American world, naturally pleased Mexican-Americans.

This popularity was evident in the summer of 1962 when Kennedy was well received by the populace of Mexico City during his visit. In his discussions with President Adolfo López Mateos, he agreed to expedite the settlement of a border dispute over a sliver of land known as El Chamizal, a small tract between El Paso and Ciudad Juárez. While only about 630 acres of underdeveloped land were involved, the dispute, caused by a shift in the course of the Rio Grande, had festered for nearly a century. The refusal of the United States to surrender the property, despite its having been awarded to Mexico by an arbitration commission in 1911, caused Mexicans to feel that their neighbor was still as imperialistic as in 1848. El Chamizal had become symbolic of all the land Mexico had lost to the North Americans. President Kennedy's decision to return the property was an intelligent exercise in goodwill because it made Mexicans and Mexican-Americans alike feel that they no longer need fear U.S. aggression. Kennedy's move was especially wise because it made North Americans appear less imperialistic at a time when the United States was carrying out a forceful policy against Fidel Castro's Cuba.[6]

Although Kennedy was able to do little to improve directly the condition of Mexican-Americans, his strong stand for the civil rights of minorities was appreciated. After Kennedy's assassination, Lyndon B. Johnson responded to the civil rights movement by promoting the social legislation that became known as the War on Poverty. Johnson's contact with Mexican-Americans, however, was limited, and they soon felt that their needs were being ignored by an administration which was more concerned with the increasingly volatile black communities. The riots that exploded in the black ghettos in the mid-1960s led the federal government to channel War on Poverty funds into these neighborhoods. Mexican-Americans, who had remained nonviolent despite deplorable conditions in the barrios, protested that the administration should also remember the needs of the quiet Spanish-speaking communities.[7] Shortly after the Watts riot of 1965, the major Mexican-American organizations of California (MAPA, LULAC, the CSO, and the G. I. Forum) sent President Johnson a joint resolution calling for aid to their communities.

This resolution was to be the last major Mexican-American statement couched in the terms of "Americanism." The organizations argued that since Mexican-Americans did not believe in or engage in civil disobedience or violent confrontation, they were good citizens, loyal to the democratic system, and should be included in antipoverty programs. The resolution reminded the President of the excellent military record of Mexican-Americans and of their contributions to the building of the American Southwest. Significantly, in mentioning their historical role in the Southwest, and despite their stress on Americanism, the Mexican-American organizations did not depict their people as immigrants in order to make them seem as "American" as any European ethnic group. The organizations proudly proclaimed their people's early presence in the Southwest, albeit in terms acceptable to the general public in 1965: "Over 150 years ago, Spanish-speaking Mexican-Americans stopped the Russian colonial advance and conquest from Siberia and Alaska, and preserved the Western portion of the United States for our country, which at that time consisted of thirteen colonies struggling for their existence, into which nation we and our predecessors became incorporated as loyal citizens and trustworthy participants in its democratic form of government. . . ."[8]

The Mexican-American organizations were referring to Spain's eighteenth-century efforts in California to prevent any encroachment on New Spain from Czarist Russia, which was advancing from the northwest. Reflecting the anticommunism of the Cold War period, the organizations interpreted the early settlement of the Southwest by the Spanish-speaking as historically significant because it prevented a potential Soviet presence on territory that would later become part of the United States. Though this interpretation was Americanist in that it portrayed the region as manifestly destined for democracy and the Union, it also revealed that some Mexican-Americans by then not only refused to see themselves as immigrants but declined to call themselves Spanish. Within a short while Chicano activists were to radicalize this image as they adopted the militant beliefs and tactics that the message to President Johnson had decried. Militants quickly learned the apparent lesson: if a minority group showed no signs of violence, it could expect little attention from U.S. society. Before long they also concluded that the War on Poverty, like the Alliance for Progress, was designed to prevent revolution, not to improve the conditions of the poor.[9]

During the very month that Johnson received the resolution of the California organizations, the quiet Mexican-American minority inaugurated the explosive Chicano movement. On 16 September (Mexican Independence Day) 1965, César Chávez's predominantly Mexican-American National Farm Workers Association (NFWA) voted to join a grape strike initiated in Delano, California, by the Filipino Agricultural Workers Organizing Committee (AWOC). Because of their greater numbers, Mexican-Americans soon dominated the strike and later controlled the United Farm Workers' Organizing Committee (UFWOC), which came into being as a result of the merger of the two original unions.[10] This strike was to lead to the first successful agriculural revolt by one of the poorest groups of Chicanos in the Southwest. Interestingly, this revolt was led by a man who believed in nonviolence, democracy, and religion; who had little faith in government programs; and who distrusted the very Chicano nationalism he inspired.

Chávez, whose grandfather was a "pioneer" in Arizona in the 1880s, was born near Yuma in 1927. "Our family farm was started three years before Arizona became a state," Chávez once remarked. "Yet, sometimes I get crank letters . . . telling me to 'go back' to Mexico!"[11] As a result of the depression the family's land was lost in 1939 because of unpaid taxes, and the Chávezes migrated to California where they became farm workers. After years of such work and a period in the navy, César Chávez joined the Community Service Organization which, though overwhelmingly Mexican-American in membership, stressed the acquisition and exercise of the rights of citizenship by the poor of all ethnic groups. This early influence later helped Chávez gain widespread support for the farm workers, even though it prevented him from becoming a true spokesman for Chicano nationalism. After ten years in the CSO, Chávez in 1962 decided to organize farm workers on his own when the CSO decided the task was beyond its range of activities.[12]

Shortly after the NFWA voted to strike, Chávez appealed to religious and civil rights groups for volunteers. By doing so, he converted a labor dispute into a social movement, and expanded his Mexican-American and Filipino base of support by including all others who wished to help. At the same time he nonetheless acknowledged that race was an issue in the strike. Chávez encouraged nationalism among the farm workers because he knew it could be a cohesive force against the Anglo growers who were accustomed to treating racial minorities as inferiors. Indeed, the Virgin of Guadalupe, the patroness of Mexico, became one of the chief nationalistic symbols used in the movement's demonstrations. Luis Valdez, playwright and propagandist for the farm workers, described her significance:

> The Virgin of Guadalupe was the first hint to farm workers that the pilgrimage [to Sacramento in the spring of 1966] implied social revolution. During the Mexican Revolution, the peasant armies of Emiliano Zapata carried her standard, not only because they sought her divine protection, but because she symbolized the Mexico of the poor and humble. It was a simple Mexican Indian, Juan Diego, who first saw her in a vision at Guadalupe. Beautifully dark and Indian in feature, she was the New World version of the Mother of Christ. Even though some of her worshippers in Mexico still identify her with Tonatzin, an Aztec goddess, she is a Catholic saint of Indian creation—a Mexican. The people's response was immediate and reverent. They joined the march by the thousands, falling in line behind her standard.[13]

Thus, through the Virgin, Chávez and the Chicano workers linked their struggle to their aboriginal Mexican past.

Although the Mexican symbols used by the movement were generally associated with Mexico proper, Chávez was also aware of the Chicano farm workers' indigenous background in the Southwest. He had a personal interest in the history of the California missions and in their treatment of the Indians, the first farm workers. Chávez believed that though the missionaries had indeed used coercion on the Indians, they had saved them from far worse treatment at the hands of the secular authorities and the settlers. They had done this by making the missions sanctuaries where the Indians could work the land communally and by forcing the settlers to treat the Indians as human beings. As

a result, Chávez once commented, "The Spanish began to marry the Indians
. . .: they couldn't destroy them, so instead of wiping out a race, they made
a new one."[14] The relative autonomy of the missions, politically and economically, together with the Franciscans' belief in the equality of all human
souls, permitted the Indians a certain amount of security and even on occasion complete acceptance through intermarriage with the settlers. Like their
Indian predecessors, twentieth-century farm workers, in Chávez's eyes, could
only gain their rightful place in society if they believed in their own racial
equality with other men and established themselves as an independent political and economic force capable of challenging the new owners of the land.

Chávez fully realized what the historic loss of the land had meant to the
Indians and to their Mexican successors. The "Plan of Delano," a Mexican-
style proclamation stating the discontent of the farm workers and the aims of
Chávez and his movement, reminded society of the oppression Southwest Mexicans had endured: "The Mexican race has sacrificed itself for the last hundred
years. Our sweat and our blood have fallen on this land to make other men
rich."[15] Chávez knew that the power of the Anglo growers rested on their
ownership of the land, and he also realized that Chicanos and the other poor
would ultimately achieve full equality only when they had recovered that land:
"While . . . our adversaries . . . are the rich and the powerful and possess
the land, we are not afraid. . . . We know that our cause is just, that history
is a story of social revolution, and that the poor shall inherit the land." Though
Chávez stated this belief publicly, he knew land reform was a distant ideal,
and he was much too practical to make it a goal for his union. Despite this,
the growers claimed that such statements, together with the symbols of Mexican nationalism, revealed Chávez to be communistic and un-American. One
rancher remarked,

> Mr. Cesar Chavez is talking about taking over this state—I don't like that. Too
> much *"Viva Zapata"* and down with the Caucasians, *la raza* [the Latin Ameri-
> can race], and all that. Mister Cesar Chavez is talking about *revolución*. Re-
> member, California once belonged to Mexico, and he's saying, "Look, you dumb
> Mexicans, you lost it, now let's get it back!"[16]

Despite such distortions and in spite of his actual encouragement of nationalism, Chávez feared the divisive effects it could have within the movement. Since the growers were quick to exploit such divisiveness, he would
not allow intolerance to split the ranks of his Chicano, Filipino, and liberal
Anglo supporters. He was especially concerned that Chicanos not let their
incipient nationalism get out of hand: "We oppose some of this La Raza

business. . . . We know what it does. When La Raza means or implies racism, we don't support it. But if it means our struggle, our dignity, or our cultural roots, then we're for it." Because of this guarded attitude, however, Chávez could never become a fully committed advocate of Chicano nationalism. His struggle after all was economic, rather than cultural; his concerns were those of the poor as a whole, rather than more specifically Chicano issues, such as bilingual education. On the other hand, Chávez showed Chicanos that their cultural problems could not be solved by politics alone, since these problems were economic at their source:

> Effective political power is never going to come, particularly to minority groups, unless they have economic power. . . .
> I'm not advocating . . . brown capitalism. . . . What I'm suggesting is a cooperative movement.[17]

Such power lay in numbers and could best be harnessed if minority groups joined together with liberal Anglos in a broad interracial consumer movement.

During the grape strike, Chávez demonstrated how a cooperative movement could generate economic power, enough power to force the capitulation of the growers in 1970. His major weapon was a grape boycott extending beyond the Chicanos' Southwest, throughout the United States, and even into Europe. Since he had made the strike a moral and civil rights movement, many outsiders were willing to cooperate in the boycott. Within the UFWOC itself, as we have seen, Chávez made the workers understand that the struggle was for human equality, not merely for better wages and working conditions. As a result, in practical terms, the UFWOC itself became more a cooperative than a trade union: "It . . . developed for its members a death benefit plan; a coöperative grocery, drug store, and gas station; a credit union; a medical clinic; a social protest theatre group . . .; and a newspaper. . . ." Such cooperative policies together with the nonviolent, mass protest methods of the civil rights movement (methods Mexican-Americans had earlier disdained to use) effectively countered such traditional grower tactics as the employment of strikebreakers from Mexico. After the grape growers agreed to sign contracts with the UFWOC in 1970, the farm-worker movement in the succeeding decades became an ongoing force as the union entered the lettuce fields, fought for the renewal of old contracts, and expanded to other parts of the nation.[18]

"Across the San Joaquin Valley," proclaimed the "Plan of Delano" in 1966, "across California, across the entire Southwest of the United States, wherever there are Mexican people, wherever there are farm workers, our movement is

spreading like flames across a dry plain."[19] Within a short time the farm-worker
front of the Chicano movement had indeed spread to Arizona and Texas, but,
more important, other fronts of the movement had opened independently
throughout the Southwest in other sectors of Chicano life. One of these fronts
was the renewal of the land grant struggle in northern New Mexico. As we
saw earlier, after the Treaty of Guadalupe Hidalgo, Mexicans in the Southwest were gradually deprived of their lands by an Anglo-American legal and
economic system that constantly challenged land grants made under previous
governments. In his investigation of problems resulting from the land grant
issue during the 1960s, Peter Nabokov wrote that in northern New Mexico:

> These ancestral holdings had originally been awarded to single people or to com-
> munities of at least ten village families. A man had his private home and a
> narrow rectangular plot which usually gave him access to river water. But the
> community's grazing and wood-gathering acreage, called *ejido,* was understood
> to be held commonly, and forever, a perpetual trust. A large percentage of the
> New Mexico *ejido* lands had been put in the public domain by the surveyors
> general of the period 1854–1880 because they recognized only claims made on
> behalf of individuals, not communities.[20]

During the twentieth century much of this "public domain" was turned
over to the Forest Service, which in turn was given the authority to lease the
lands to private individuals and companies for the use and development of
natural resources. Unfortunately for the long-settled small farmers of northern New Mexico, large out-of-state corporations, engaged in mining, logging,
and tourism, received preferential treatment in their dealings with the Forest
Service. The impoverished small farmers, on the other hand, were gradually
denied their grazing rights by an agency that was unconcerned with and even
hostile to their needs; in her study of the problem, Patricia Bell Blawis
observed that "while logging firms contracted with the Forest Service for
immense areas on their ancestral land, the grantees were forbidden to cut
stovewood without a permit." Thus, according to Blawis, in the twentieth
century the imperialism of the nineteenth continued surreptitiously: "The
Forest Service is evidence of the colonial policy of the Federal government. . . .
Through this Service, resources of the West are exploited by Washington,
D.C. and its friends."[21] As we have seen, the native Mexicans had in the past
reacted violently to this colonialism: between the 1880s and the late 1920s,
for instance, at least two groups of nightriders, Las Gorras Blancas and La
Mano Negra, had burned buildings, torn down fences, and committed other

such terrorist acts to protest the seizure of their lands.[22] During the late 1960s such violence flared again.

In 1963 the militant Alianza Federal de Mercedes (the Federal Land Grant Alliance—always popularly known as the Alianza, even though the official name changed several times) was incorporated under the direction of a dynamic leader named Reies López Tijerina. Tijerina, whose great-grandfather had been robbed of his land and killed by Anglos, was born in Texas in 1926; he lived and moved throughout the Southwest and beyond as a farm worker and later as a poor itinerant preacher. During these wanderings, he came to believe that the problems of his people had resulted from their loss of the land, for as he later stressed, "the ties of our culture with the land are indivisible."[23] As a consequence, he became interested in the land grant issue, spent a year studying the question in Mexico, and in 1960 settled in New Mexico where he felt there was the best hope of recovering the grants. After organizing many of the heirs into the Alianza, Tijerina unsuccessfully petitioned the U.S. government to investigate the land titles for violations of that portion of the Treaty of Guadalupe Hidalgo that guaranteed the property rights of Mexicans in the Southwest. He had also requested the Mexican government to look into the matter, but Mexico, having gradually become economically dependent on as well as ideologically aligned with the United States since the 1930s, had not and would not support any radical claims made by dissident Chicanos. Rebuffed in his efforts to get consideration through regular legal and political channels, Tijerina turned to civil disobedience.[24]

In October of 1966 Tijerina and other *aliancistas* occupied the Echo Amphitheater, a section of the Carson National Forest that had once been part of the land grant of San Joaquín del Río de Chama. Since the original Spanish and Mexican grants had permitted the villagers a good deal of autonomy, the *aliancistas* declared themselves the Republic of San Joaquín and elected as mayor a direct descendant of the original grantee. When several forest rangers attempted to interfere, they were detained by the "republic," tried for trespassing, and released on suspended sentences. By allowing this, Tijerina hoped to challenge the jurisdiction of the Forest Service over the land, thus forcing the land grant issue into the courts, possibly as far as the Supreme Court. Also, the declaration of autonomy would make public the Chicanos' need for self-determination, their need to escape a whole range of problems caused by their incorporation into U.S. society. Not least of these was the war in Vietnam, which even the traditionally patriotic *nuevomexicanos* were beginning to oppose: "The people," as Tijerina had once remarked, "generally feel that our sons are being sent to Vietnam illegally, because many of these land grants are free city states and are independent." The "liberation" of the Echo Amphitheater had been a dangerous act, but as the increasingly radical Tijerina declared during the occupation: "Fidel Castro has what he has because of his guts. . . . Castro put the gringos off his island and we can do the same." Unfortunately for the Alianza, Tijerina would later serve two years in prison for assault on the rangers at the Echo Amphitheater; furthermore, the courts would refuse to admit discussion of the land grant issue.[25]

During May of 1967, according to Nabokov, "private northern landowners . . . began suffering from the traditional symptoms of unrest—selective cattle rustling, irrigation ditch and fence wreckage, shot-up water tanks, and arson." Although there was no evidence the Alianza had committed these acts, the authorities actually feared that guerrilla warfare might break out in northern New Mexico. When Tijerina revealed that his group planned to have a conference on June 3 at Coyote, a small town near the San Joaquín grant, the authorities anticipated another occupation and prevented the meeting by declaring it an unlawful assembly, blocking the roads to the town, and arresting any *aliancistas* who resisted. This proved to be a mistake, for it brought on the very violence the authorities had feared. Feeling that their right to free assembly had been violated, the *aliancistas* decided to make a citizen's arrest of the district attorney responsible for the police action. On June 5, in the most daring move of the contemporary Chicano movement, Tijerina and about twenty other armed *aliancistas* attacked the courthouse at the county seat at Tierra Amarilla. In the ensuing shoot-out two deputies were wounded, the courthouse was occupied, and the Coyote prisoners were freed. Finding that the district attorney was not present, the *aliancistas* then fled the town with two hostages.[26]

The reaction of the authorities brought the cause of the Alianza to the attention of the entire nation. Imagining "a new Cuba to the north," the state government in Santa Fe sent out four hundred National Guardsmen to join two hundred state troopers in an expedition into northern New Mexico that included the use of helicopters and two tanks.[27] After a few days Tijerina was captured and charged with various crimes connected with the raid, though he was subsequently released on bail. Once in the national spotlight, Tijerina elaborated on the issues and goals of the land grant struggle, issues that were important to Chicanos throughout the Southwest; "Not only the land has been stolen from the good and humble people," he commented, "but also their culture. . . ." And he remarked, "A major point of contention is that we are being deprived of our language. . . ." Tijerina also argued that in addition to property rights, the cultural rights of his people were guaranteed by the Treaty of Guadalupe Hidalgo. Once the guarantees of this treaty were honored and discrimination was ended, Indo-Hispanos, as Tijerina often called his people, would take their rightful place as intermediaries in the pluralistic Southwest:

We have been forced by destiny to adopt two languages; we will be the future ambassadors and envoys to Latin America. At home, I believe that the South-west is breeding a special kind of people that will bridge the color-gap between black and white. . . . [Moreover] We are the people the Indians call their "lost brothers."[28]

While the many charges against him were being handled in the courts, Tijerina continued his activities with the Alianza and also participated in the interracial, antipoverty Poor People's March on Washington in 1968. In 1969, however, the Alianza was deprived of Tijerina's leadership when he was impris-oned for the Echo Amphitheater incident. Suffering from poor health, he was paroled in July 1971, but on condition that he no longer hold office in the Alianza. Deprived of his full leadership and lacking the organized economic power of an institution such as the United Farm Workers, the Alianza lost much of its drive, and not until 1979 was it able to convince the government to give even nominal reconsideration to the land grant issue.[29] Nonetheless, Tijerina and the Alianza did rejuvenate the ethnic pride of a good number of *nuevomexicanos*. Though many Hispanos considered Tijerina an outsider, many others joined his organization, and in doing so reaffirmed their ties to Mexico through reference to the Treaty of Guadalupe Hidalgo, and to their Indian ancestors through acceptance of the facts of *mestizaje* (Indo-Hispano inter-marriage). In New Mexico no longer could "Spanish-Americans" easily deny their background. No longer could Spanish-American politicians, who had generally held a representative number of positions in government, ignore their economically depressed constituents without opposition from Chicano militants around the state—for increasingly among *nuevomexicanos* the image of the Spanish Southwest was giving way to the image of Aztlán.[30]

The person most responsible for the adoption of the term "Aztlán" by the rapidly spreading Chicano movement was Rodolfo "Corky" Gonzales, leader of the Chicano community in Denver, Colorado. In modern times the term was first applied to the Chicano homeland in 1962 by Jack D. Forbes, a Native American professor who argued that Mexicans were more truly an Indian than a mestizo people; his mimeographed manuscript, "The Mexican Heritage of Aztlán (the Southwest) to 1821," was distributed among Mexican-Americans in the Southwest during the early 1960s.[31] The term gained popularity, but was not universally accepted by the Chicano movement until, in the spring of 1969, the first Chicano national conference, in Denver, drafted "El plan espiritual de Aztlán," a document that declared the spiritual independence of the Chicano Southwest from the United States.[32] Paradoxically this sentiment was expressed in a city never legally within the confines of Mexico; however, like arguments for Puerto Rican independence presented in New York, this declaration from Denver signified the desire of a minority group for independence from the colonialism that had subjugated its native land and that continued to affect the individuals of the minority no matter where they resided within the United States.

Born in Denver in 1928, Corky Gonzales was primarily a product of the urban barrios, even though he spent part of his youth working in the fields of southern Colorado. He managed to escape poverty by becoming a successful boxer. As a result of the popularity gained from this career, he became an influential figure in the barrios and was selected to head various antipoverty programs in the early 1960s. By 1965, however, he had become disenchanted with the antipoverty bureaucracy. He concluded earlier than other Chicanos that the War on Poverty was designed to pacify rather than truly help the poor. Had he read it, he would have agreed with a later comment made by a Chicano editor when government and foundation money poured into northern New Mexico in the aftermath of Tierra Amarilla:

> They're trying to create *Vendido* power (sellout power) . . . trying to bring Vietnam to New Mexico and trying to create "leaders" the system can use as tools. But it hasn't worked with the Vietnamese and it's not going to work with Raza here in the United States.

Disgusted with the strings attached to funds from the government and foundations, Gonzales organized the Crusade for Justice, a community self-help group. Through their own fund-raising efforts, the members established a barrio service center, providing such assistance as child care, legal aid, housing and employment counseling, health care, and other services especially needed in poor urban areas. The Crusade was, moreover, outspoken in its concern for Chicano civil and cultural rights.[33]

More than Chávez and even more than Tijerina, Gonzales felt that nationalism was the force that would get Chicanos to help one another, and that the success of his Crusade exemplified the possibilities of self-determination. Although his participation in the Poor People's March of 1968 revealed his belief in the necessity of interracial cooperation, at heart he felt that Chicanos would have to help themselves and would do so if they became aware of their proud history as a people. Of Chicanos in his state, he once said, "Colorado belongs to our people, was named by our people, discovered by our people and worked by our people. . . . We preach self-respect . . . to reclaim what is ours." Regarding the region as a whole, he commented, "Nationalism exists in the Southwest, but until now it hasn't been formed into an image people can see. Until now it has been a dream. It has been my job to create a reality out of the dream. . . ." The Crusade was part of that reality and so was the Chicano Youth Liberation Conference, called by Gonzales to bring together Chicanos from throughout the nation, but especially from the cities, where 80 percent of all Chicanos lived. In Gonzales urban youth found a leader, unlike Chávez or Tijerina, who had successfully attempted concrete solutions to city problems. Consequently, 1,500 Chicanos from many different organizations attended the conference of this urban nationalist.[34]

As if in exhibit of the problems of urban Chicanos, the week before the conference riots broke out in the Denver barrios, resulting from events that began with a racist remark made by a teacher at a local high school. A student and community protest led to confrontation with police; according to Gonzales, "What took place . . . was a battle between the West Side 'liberation forces' and the 'occupying army.' The West Side won [police suffered some injuries and damage to equipment]."[35] Although Gonzales opposed violence and tried to stop the rioting, he clearly felt the trouble was justified and was proud that Chicanos were capable of defending themselves against the government he believed had made internal colonies of the city's barrios. After the riots, the conference convened in an atmosphere permeated with nationalism and proclaimed the following in "El plan espiritual de Aztlán:"

Conscious . . . of the brutal "Gringo" invasion of our territories, we, the Chicano inhabitants and civilizers of the northern land of Aztlán, from whence came our forefathers, reclaiming the land of their birth. . . . We [who] do not recognize capricious frontiers on the bronze continent. . . . we declare the independence of our mestizo nation.[36]

In that proclamation the Chicano delegates fully revived their people's traditional image of the Southwest and clarified it for their own time: the Southwest was the Chicano homeland, a land paradoxically settled by an indigenous people who were subsequently conquered. Furthermore, these people were now seen as native, not merely because their Spanish ancestors had settled the land hundreds of years before, but because their Indian ancestors had resided on the land thousands of years earlier, tying it permanently to Indian and mestizo Mexico.

With this image of the Southwest, the Chicano delegates established a context for a variety of demands that would gain impetus in the near future.

Before long in the name of Aztlán and its people, activists would demand restitution from the United States for its conquest of the region and for its economic, political, and cultural oppression of the Southwest Mexican population. From the institutions of the United States, Chicanos would reject token representation and poverty programs with strings attached; from state and national institutions they would expect unrestricted compensation; over local institutions they would demand control. With such control, Chicanos hoped to establish bilingual/bicultural education, promote their own arts and customs, tax themselves, hire their own police, select their own juries, sit on their own draft boards, and especially found cooperatives to prevent further economic exploitation. Thus, the separatism at the conference, while expressing itself in the ideal of complete political independence from the United States, more importantly would promote the pragmatic goal of local autonomy. Gonzales' Crusade offered a practical example of how such autonomy might be gained. Another practical means, discussed at the conference, was the creation of a third party independent of Democrats and Republicans, especially in local elections. Many of these ideas found a national forum in the Chicano Youth Liberation Conference. This was Gonzales' major achievement. While his Crusade for Justice continued its work in Denver, as an organization it never spread far beyond that city. However, the delegates to the conference returned to their homes throughout the Southwest inspired by the urban nationalism that the Crusade exemplified.[37]

That the conference had articulated some of the major aspirations of the Chicano movement became evident in 1970 when Chicano activists put their beliefs into practice while seizing political control of Crystal City, Texas. Crystal City, a town of about 10,000 persons, was about 80 percent Mexican-American, but was controlled by the Anglo population, as was the rest of heavily Mexican-American South Texas. Since most of the resident Mexican-Americans were uneducated, often illiterate, semimigrant workers, the Anglos were for decades able to manipulate the elections to ensure all-Anglo city governments. In his *Chicano Revolt in a Texas Town,* John Staples Shockley argued that a colonial situation existed between the two groups, a situation resulting from the gradual Anglo subjugation of the area during the violent times before 1930. In 1963, however, Crystal City's Mexican-Americans, angered by urban renewal projects that were forcing many out of their homes, caught the Anglos by surprise and elected a working-class Mexican-American city government. That government administered the city well, but was unable to institute major reforms because the Anglos controlled the economy and the county tax structure. In a sense the old colonialism was replaced by a neocolonialism that allowed political but not economic independence. By

1965, moreover, the uneducated and inexperienced working-class council-men had quarreled among themselves and were beaten at the polls by a sophis-ticated Anglo coalition that had coopted middle-class Mexican-Americans.[38] Much like the Rhodesian government formed in 1979, the 1965 coalition government in Crystal City was composed of a "native" majority, but served the interests of the Anglo minority.

This form of neocolonialism, according to Shockley, continued in the town until 1969 when José Angel Gutiérrez, a Crystal City native, returned home from college to lead a new assault on Anglo power or, as he put it, "to begin Aztlán!"[39] Holding a master's degree in political science and thoroughly versed in the ideas and organizing methods of radical college movements, Gutiérrez converted an incident of discrimination in the schools into another electoral revolt. After organizing a third party called La Raza Unida, Gutiérrez's activ-ists and working-class Chicanos seized the school board and city council from the Anglo and Mexican-American coalition. Better equipped to govern than the leaders of the first revolt, La Raza Unida from the beginning used its new political power to the fullest to counteract continuing Anglo economic domi-nance. For example, the school system, which was one of the largest employ-ers in the county, soon helped relieve Mexican-American unemployment by dramatically increasing the number of the schools' nonprofessional positions. Also, the city government launched efforts to annex and tax a neighboring fruit-packing plant, while La Raza Unida ran candidates for county offices that could be used to increase taxes on Anglo-owned agricultural lands and oil properties, the area's chief means of production. Outside of government, the community organized cooperatives, Chicano businesses, and boycotts against hostile merchants. On the economic front, however, La Raza Unida was not nearly so successful as it was in instituting relevant educational programs, better police-community relations, improved public works, hous-ing assistance, community health and legal services, and other projects directly affected by government.[40]

As the successes of Castro's Cuba promised to spread his revolution to the rest of Latin America, Anglos feared the successes of Crystal City would spread similar revolts throughout the Southwest. In fact, in the early 1970s La Raza Unida party was organized and fielded candidates throughout the region; but like Castro's revolution, Gutiérrez's movement was contained. Although La Raza Unida won victories in other South Texas cities, in those cities it rarely achieved the firm position it won in Crystal City, and in areas outside Texas its successes were minimal despite much early enthusiasm. The reason for this was that the cohesive Chicano majority that existed in rural Crystal City was unique even in heavily Chicano South Texas. In the urban Southwest,

where most Chicanos lived, they were rarely majorities in their gerryman-
dered districts, and they were too numerous and divided to be readily organized electorates, especially once the Anglos intensified their co-optation tactics
to counter the third-party threat.[41]

Just as its outward expansion was halted by the manipulative structures of
U.S. politics, La Raza Unida's revolution within Crystal City was restricted
by similar local structures designed to defend the economic status quo. In
spite of his attacks on big business, Gutiérrez's power was too limited to
implement thoroughly the socialism he believed was necessary.[42] What Crystal City showed Chicanos was that while they could gain a measure of local
autonomy by their own nationalistic political efforts, they could not gain true
self-determination without control of the local economy that provided their
livelihoods. Since that economy was in the hands of businesses that operated
on a national scale, only a national multiethnic movement to capture the federal government could ever secure true self-determination for individual
minorities. This point was not lost on Chicano intellectuals, who were becoming increasingly radical, sometimes Marxist, as the Chicano movement progressed. In his *Occupied America* (1972), for example, Rodolfo Acuña wrote:

> The only way the Chicanos of South Texas (or, for that matter, the United States)
> are going to realize self-determination is for the federal government to inter-
> vene and expropriate the land and means of production and give it to the people
> living in the *barrios* and *colonias*. The same principle must be applied internally
> that is applied when U.S. business is expropriated abroad.[43]

Chicano intellectuals had found Gutiérrez's activities especially significant
because he, being the most educated of the major Chicano leaders, had been
the first to try putting radical "academic" theories into practice. The impact
of a college graduate like Gutiérrez on the Chicano movement was also significant because he symbolized the importance to the movement of Chicano intellectuals and students generally. Indeed, in urban areas, students from high
school through graduate school had been the major force behind the Chicano
movement at least since 1968. In the spring of that year Chicanos in five East
Los Angeles high schools walked out of classes to protest conditions in the
schools that resulted in extremely high drop-out rates. This led, over the
next few years, to a series of walk-outs in one city after another, as Chicano
students and instructors throughout the Southwest demanded new schools,
more sensitive teachers, and bilingual/bicultural education. Although Chicano student groups had been organized before 1968, the activism of that
year put those groups into the forefront of the urban movement. In the col-

leges and universities of the Southwest, these groups successfully demanded Chicano studies and affirmative action programs, programs that would help produce the first group of Chicano college graduates committed to the cultural survival of their people. Even before they had graduated, these students became involved in off-campus groups to organize the poor and uneducated in the barrios and rural towns. These were the college people Gutiérrez symbolized.[44]

As time passed, campus groups that in 1967 had given themselves names such as the United Mexican American Students and the Mexican American Student Confederation became more militant. After many walk-outs and after Corky Gonzales's Chicano Youth Liberation Conference in 1969, most campus groups changed their names to El Movimiento Estudiantil Chicano de Aztlán (MECHA—The Chicano Student Movement of Aztlán), revealing their increasingly radical nationalism. At the Second Annual Chicano Youth Conference in the spring of 1970, representatives of student and other youth groups, reflecting their disenchantment with the United States, declared their opposition to the war in Vietnam. Many Chicanos were no longer proud of the fact that they, as a people, were once again dying in a U.S. war in disproportionately high numbers; moreover, they opposed dying in a war fought against a people they believed were victims of the same colonialism they themselves were experiencing. To demonstrate their opposition, a national Chicano antiwar rally was planned for August 1970 to be held in East Los Angeles, the barrio with the largest concentration of Mexican-Americans in the nation. Unfortunately, the rally became a riot when the police attempted to break up the demonstration and only succeeded in provoking the participants into the worst mass violence in East LA since 1943. For months thereafter violent protests erupted periodically, and the number of police on the streets of East LA visibly increased. Rarely had the colonial status of Chicanos seemed so evident.[45]

After 1970 the open confrontations of the previous five years became less frequent as the Chicano movement entered a period of consolidation. Having had many of its hopes and grievances dramatized, the Chicano community was gradually able to take advantage of the advances the movement had attained, especially in education and self-awareness. With a renewed pride in their culture, Chicano intellectuals set out to express a world view that had long been suppressed. That their image of the Southwest as Aztlán was an important part of that world view was clear from the titles of many of the publications that appeared as Chicano culture experienced a renewal in literature, art, and social thought. A scholarly quarterly entitled *Aztlán: Chicano Journal of the Social Sciences and the Arts* was first issued in 1970 by Aztlán

Publications at the University of California, Los Angeles. A bibliography by Ernie Barrios published in 1971 bore the title *Bibliografía de* Aztlán. In 1973 Luis Valdez and Stan Steiner edited a work called *Aztlán: An Anthology of Mexican American Literature*. Two novels, *Peregrinos de Aztlán* (1974) by Miguel Méndez M. and *Heart of Aztlan* (1976) by Rudolfo A. Anaya, also carried the ancient name of the Southwest. As if to secure that name for posterity, *Aztlan: The Southwest and Its People,* a history for juveniles by Luis F. Hernández, was published in 1975.[46] Many other works with less obvious titles also reflected the rediscovered Chicano image of the Southwest. Among the most important was the already mentioned *Occupied America* (1972) by Rodolfo Acuña. In this history of Chicanos, Acuña interpreted the tradition of the lost northern homeland according to the modern theory of colonialism, a theory that made the image of Aztlán more meaningful to contemporary Chicanos.

Needless to say, not all Mexican-Americans accepted the image of Aztlán. Among the masses the images of the Spanish Southwest and the American Southwest continued to predominate during the 1970s, and into the 1980s, largely because these were still promoted by the educational system and the mass media. Through bicultural and Chicano studies programs, Chicano intellectuals worked to change this situation. However, a small group of Mexican-Americans conversant with the affairs of their ethnic group refused to abandon borrowed images of the Southwest, usually because their lives had been formed within those images or because those views continued to help them accommodate themselves to the standards of Anglo society. Congressman Henry B. González of San Antonio, Texas, for example, had built his political career around the integrationist civil rights movement of the 1950s and early 1960s; as a result the nationalism of the Chicano movement struck him as nothing less than reverse racism. Since González accepted the integrationist melting pot ideal, he also perceived his region as the American Southwest, to which his parents, like European arrivals on the East Coast, had come to join the "nation of immigrants." Thus, in an address to Congress in 1969, he remarked:

> As it happens my parents were born in Mexico and came to this country seeking safety. . . . It follows that I, and many other residents of my part of Texas and other Southwestern States—happen to be what is commonly referred to as a Mexican-American.

Since his background only "happened" to be Mexican, González could see little importance in notions such as Aztlán and vigorously opposed Chicano militancy.[47]

Another knowledgeable individual who rejected the image of Aztlán was the Franciscan man of letters Fray Angelico Chavez, a descendant of some of the original *nuevomexicano* settlers. Fray Angelico had spent more than twenty years writing poetry, essays, and history on the subject of New Mexico, always with the image of the Spanish Southwest in mind. Although he was too well informed to believe that *nuevomexicanos* were of pure Spanish descent, he nevertheless convinced himself that they were more Spanish than people south of the border and that Indian genes within the *nuevomexicano* population were largely confined to certain sections of the lower class.[48] Fray Angelico believed it was these lower-class people

> who join the agrarian and urban Mexicans or Mexican-Americans in their social protests, and consequently like to be called "Chicanos" along with them.
> The true Spanish New Mexican *castizo* [pure-blood] does not. . . .[49]

He made this comment in an informal history of his state called *My Penitente Land: Reflections on Spanish New Mexico* (1974), a work that revealed his complete fealty to the image of the Spanish Southwest.

Even though borrowed images of the Chicanos' place in the Southwest persisted, by the late 1970s some of the new group of educated Chicanos were in positions where they could reveal the image of Aztlán to the general public. For example, Tony Castro, a graduate of Baylor University, spent several years writing for various major newspapers around the country and was then hired in the late 1970s as a regular columnist for the conservative *Los Angeles Herald Examiner*. Devoting most of his columns and later his special reports to Chicano issues, Castro repeatedly exposed the generally conservative readership of that newspaper to the Chicano image of the Southwest:

> The Chicano has been here since the founding of California and the Southwest. His pre-Columbian ancestors wandered here from the north, migrating farther south and establishing the great civilizations of the Maya, the Toltecs, the Aztecs. . . .
> . . . [Yet] Mexican-Americans . . . have been the conquered people, strangers in their own land. . . .[50]

Young professionals like Castro who were willing to argue for their people's rightful place in the Southwest and the United States were the most successful product of the 1960s movement. As we have seen, educational improvement had been a major goal of the movement; consequently during the 1970s education was the area where Chicanos made their greatest strides. With Chicano college enrollment having tripled by 1978 (despite a leveling off of progress by that time), more teachers, social workers, writers, social scientists, and others influenced by the nationalism of the 1960s were echoing that nationalism, albeit with caution, from new positions throughout the Southwest.[51]

Despite the emergence of this educated, nationalistic leadership, the progress of Chicanos as a whole was uneven in the 1970s and stagnant in the early 1980s. They continued to fit the description of a colonized people. In California, for example, where Chicanos were most heavily concentrated and where opportunities were often considered best, "Hispanics" over the age of twenty-five had completed high school at only 56 percent of the rate at which Anglos had gained the same level of schooling. And financially, the median Hispanic family income was only $16,140 or 71 percent of the equivalent white family income (1980 U.S. Census figures). While these figures did indicate some improvement over the 1960s, the gains were threatened by a backlash that persisted into the 1980s. Many of the educational and consequently the income gains of Chicanos had come as a result of affirmative action programs, compensatory programs that gave minorities preferential treatment in schooling and employment. These programs were attacked in the courts as reverse discrimination in case after case by Anglos who, though they failed to destroy the programs, managed to impede their effectiveness. Also, programs in Chicano studies and bilingual/bicultural education, while surviving, constantly met opposition from those who regarded them as contrary to the tradition of the nation of immigrants who learned English and forgot the old country. Given the fact that their educational and income gains were so recent, it is no surprise that Chicanos had accumulated little personal wealth and had made little progress toward recovering the means of production in their southwestern homeland.[52]

This continuing lack of economic power in the 1970s and 1980s caused Chicano gains in the political arena to be inconclusive at best. While U.S. presidents generally appointed an increasing number of Chicanos to positions in their administrations, these appointees usually found themselves beholden to their benefactors and isolated in government with little real power to help their people. Even those Chicanos elected to political office could rarely represent fully the interests of their people, since as politicians they generally owed their elections to the Anglo-controlled coalitions that funded their campaigns. In many cases, of course, the politicians themselves continued to be ideologically traditional. For example, in 1974 Arizona and New Mexico elected as governors conservative Raúl Castro and moderate Jerry Apodaca, the first southwestern governors of Mexican descent since Octaviano Larrazolo fifty years earlier. If traditional electoral politics had been the best way to the improvement of Chicano life, the election of two Mexican-American governors should have brought significant social change for Chicanos in those states, but this did not happen because the ideological frame of mind and the political structures within which the governors worked were developed to protect the status quo. As we have seen, even the radical La Raza Unida party often found the traditional structures impregnable. Without such a radical organizational base, individual Chicano politicians, regardless of any personal nationalism, found themselves coopted by a system that defended the Anglo owners of the means of production. Many newly educated Chicano leaders in other fields found themselves bound by the same strictures. Since their salaries were bestowed on them by the system they often opposed, nationalistic Chicanos could not easily put their more radical beliefs into practice. Thus, though new leaders were more conscious of the forces in control, they were not yet in a position to topple neocolonialism in the Southwest.[53]

This situation, however, failed to prevent Chicano nationalists from voicing their disapproval of the neocolonial practices of the United States. In Latin American affairs, for example, many Chicanos had long since become disillusioned with North American motives; President Johnson's armed intervention in the Dominican Republic in 1965 had shown the United States to be as imperialistic as ever. In 1973 North American cooperation in the overthrow of a democratically elected Marxist government in Chile convinced more Chicanos that the United States was more concerned with its economic interests than it was with democracy or social change in Latin America. In the early 1980s U.S. opposition to the new government of Nicaragua and to the leftist guerrillas of El Salvador caused renewed fears among Chicanos of possible U.S. military intervention in Central America.[54] As we have noted, Mexicans in the United States had always seen their fate as closely tied to that of other Latin Americans, and as a consequence a significant group now believed continuing neocolonialism in Latin America to mean continuing neocolonialism in the Southwest. Quite naturally, Chicanos were most concerned with relations between the United States and Mexico, relations which intellectuals now interpreted as between metropolis and "neocolony."

José Angel Gutiérrez in 1971 remarked concerning Chicanos and Mexico, "the Rio Grande never has separated us and never will."[55] During the 1970s and 1980s the growing dependence of Mexico on the United States would verify Gutiérrez's statement. Although the Mexican Revolution had been fought in part to free the country from foreign, specifically North American, economic domination, by 1978 the United States was once again the major investor in and chief trading partner of Mexico. Similar to the situation during the Díaz dictatorship, the Mexican government was stable, but the economy was erratic—at times superficially prosperous, but ultimately deeply troubled. Unfortunately most of the wealth was once again accruing to foreign investors and to the few Mexicans belonging to the middle and upper classes. The masses, burdened by one of the highest birth rates in the world, continued their struggle with poverty and, as in the past, looked to the north for employment. The most important pattern in Chicano history during the 1970s and 1980s was the renewed migration of Mexicans into the Southwest. Composed almost entirely of undocumented workers, commonly called illegal aliens, this movement was the largest yet from Mexico. Though estimates of their number, based on apprehensions of the undocumented by the Immigration and Naturalization Service (INS), varied tremendously, the actual figure was undoubtedly in the millions.[56]

The arrival of so many undocumented workers presented problems for Chicanos; nevertheless, it could be argued that the migration was beneficial. As in previous migratory waves, the new arrivals competed with U.S. Mexicans for low-paying jobs and low-cost housing; they seemingly depressed wages and helped cause unemployment; they occasionally served as strikebreakers, and sometimes competed with Chicanos for aid from the government. Since the undocumented generally settled in the southwestern barrios, Chicanos not only bore the brunt of competition from the newcomers, but were also exposed to renewed Anglo-American xenophobia. With the appearance of so many un-Americanized newcomers, the Anglo notion that all people in the barrios were foreigners once again seemed plausible. As a result, harassment of Chicanos by INS agents increased, and some employers became more cautious about hiring anyone who looked Mexican since that person might be an undocumented worker. During the 1970s and 1980s, the illegal alien question, of all issues concerning Chicanos, was by far the most commonly discussed in the Anglo communications media. Though the undocumented were usually discussed in terms of a social problem, for example as an alleged tax burden on the citizenry, these terms usually hid a very real Anglo fear that the Southwest was being culturally and racially reconquered by Mexicans—a fear not entirely unfounded.[57]

"There is a distinct possibility," wrote one openly racist Anglo, "if the legal and illegal seepage of Mexican genes across the Rio Grande and the high Mexican-American birthrate continue at present levels, that Mexican-Americans will regain their lost territories of Alta California and Texas . . .—not by violence or minority politics but simply by exercising squatters' rights."[58] In October of 1977, this fear of Mexican invasion was so aroused by the media that the Ku Klux Klan announced it would conduct its own armed surveillance of the boundary to assist the undermanned Border Patrol in arresting illegal aliens. With the tacit approval of certain officials in the INS and of the San Diego (California) police, some Klan patrols were planned, but this activity ceased after strenuous protests from Chicano and other minority groups. Their nationalism having been revived during the 1960s, most U.S. Mexicans no longer disassociated themselves from their fellows across the border; they were no longer willing to stand by, as they had in the 1930s and 1950s, and watch Mexicans mistreated simply for lacking proper documents. Even though undocumented workers competed directly with Mexican-Americans, most Chicanos now felt their common national heritage outweighed their practical differences. Indeed, this feeling was strong enough that Chicano activists threatened to form their own armed patrols to counter the Klan's.[59]

That Chicanos had to some extent readopted their Mexican imagination was evident from the similarity of their image of the Southwest to the image of the region perceived by the undocumented. "Undocumented workers," reported Grace Halsell, author of *The Illegals*, "do not feel they commit a crime in traveling north from Mexico. They call it going to *el norte*. As far as the Southwest is concerned, 'we are the legals, the Anglos the illegals,' one Mexican said."[60] In spite of the artificial international boundary, many Chicanos now realized more than ever that both they and Mexicans belonged in the Southwest, and that the fate of Chicanos in that region would always be influenced by people from Mexico. Because of this, as long as Mexico existed in a neocolonial relationship with the United States, the Chicano barrios and hamlets in the Southwest would continue to be internal colonies of the United States. Deprived of a living by a Mexican economy profiting North American investors and a domestic elite, undocumented workers would continue to pour into the Southwest to provide capitalists with cheap labor and consumers with lower prices. Since the undocumented would continue to compete with Chicanos at the bottom of the economic ladder, Chicanos would continue to have a difficult time climbing out of poverty, especially given the cooptation, discrimination, and other forms of subjugation traditionally used in the Southwest to keep the Spanish-speaking colonized.[61]

In the past Mexican-Americans had at times supported efforts to seal the border against their competitors from Mexico, but after the 1960s many concluded that, besides being practically impossible, sealing the border would not eliminate domestic forms of subjugation and would only deprive the Mexican poor of desperately needed income. Many Chicanos concluded it was immoral to deny employment to the undocumented, especially when many were friends and relatives. For this reason, in fact, some Chicanos by 1979 were quietly hoping for a completely open border. Journalist Richard Reeves noted:

> I'm convinced that the real Chicano position on undocumented workers is total amnesty . . ., and a totally open border. . . . No one will say that . . .—but many people said things like this . . .: "We know where the undocumented

workers are—they're sleeping on the couches in our living rooms. . . . They're family and they're just trying to feed their families back home."[62]

Moreover, the undocumented and other recently arrived Mexicans provided Chicanos with the best hope that their culture would survive in the Southwest. Because of the newcomers, Chicanos were forced to maintain their language and culture or suffer a breakdown in barrio communication.

In fact it was the new influx of people from Mexico, together with the emergence of an educated nationalistic leadership, that made Chicano activists in the late 1970s guardedly optimistic about the future, despite the obstacles set up by the dominant society.[63] Of course, they had no illusions that they were about to establish a politically independent Aztlán, nor did they then wish to do so. Several years earlier, this idea had been considered and rejected for obvious reasons. "Would a separate state be viable?" journalist Armando Rendón had asked in 1971. "My guess is that the United States Government would act very quickly to suppress Chicano efforts toward this end." While such a utopian course of action would never be permitted, by the late 1970s Chicano activists were optimistic that more practical social plans would have to be taken seriously by Anglo society, for that society could not continue to ignore the fastest growing minority group in the nation. Given the perpetually high Chicano and Mexican birth rates, Chicano voting strength was growing by the year; if the newly nationalistic leadership ever organized that power, Anglo supremacy throughout the Southwest would be challenged as it had been in Crystal City. Faced with such a possibility, Anglos would have to make concessions because, as columnist Tony Castro commented, "The Mexican-American in the Southwest today is like a Palestinian in the Middle East. An accommodation has to be made."[64]

The analogy with the Palestinians had some merit because, being a dispossessed group, Chicanos continued to have the potential for violent rebellion. That potential became a reality on May 7, 1978, when Houston Chicanos rioted in response to news that city policemen responsible for the death of a young Chicano the previous year had received light sentences for their crime. The Houston riot served as a warning that if Chicano optimism about the 1980s were to become disillusionment that decade could see more violence than had the late 1960s. The analogy with the Palestinians was appropriate in at least one other way—in the mid-1970s the fate of Chicanos began to be influenced by oil. At that time a major oil discovery was made in southern Mexico, and though there was a good deal of controversy concerning its exact size, speculation that the discovery might equal the reserves of Saudi Arabia caused everyone involved to reconsider the relations between the United

States and Mexico, and consequently the relations between Anglo-Americans and persons of Mexican descent.[65]

In the late 1970s some North American businessmen began to consider the advantages of a common market including the United States and Mexico, a common market that, according to Carey McWilliams, would "permit the free movement across their borders not only of all commodities—particularly oil and gas—but also of people." In their need for petroleum, some North Americans were beginning to consider the idea that the boundary between the Southwest and Mexico might indeed be artificial. In return for increased supplies of energy, North Americans were beginning to think about legalizing the seemingly inevitable migration of Mexicans into the Southwest.[66] Such a concession to the Chicano image of the region, while not eliminating the neocolonial status of the Mexican and Chicano masses, would certainly improve their condition by providing economic opportunities for the former, and numerical and cultural strength to the latter. The thought of this is what made Chicano activists optimistic about the future of Aztlán. While such concessions would not end neocolonialism in the Southwest, they would permit Chicanos to entrench themselves until revolutionary changes in the general society of the United States could allow true self-determination.

However, the guarded optimism of the late 1970s decreased as the 1980s proceeded. In the United States the backlash of the former decade increased with the introduction of conservative federal policies on such matters as the enforcement of civil rights laws; moreover, the economic position of minorities suffered during a period of recession and slowed government spending. Declining petroleum prices left Mexico unable to repay huge loans secured with its oil discoveries, and this development stifled idealistic hopes of a common market between the two nations and of swift progress toward equality between Anglos and Chicanos in the Southwest. Significant recovery of control in the region, the myth of Aztlán, seemed as far off as ever. As a result, for the forseeable future, the Chicanos' image of the land as lost, and of themselves as dispossessed, would continue to have credibility.[67]

# Notes

## Introduction

1. See Rupert Norval Richardson and Carl Coke Rister, *The Greater Southwest: The Economic, Social, and Cultural Development of Kansas, Oklahoma, Texas, Utah, Colorado, Nevada, New Mexico, Arizona, and California from the Spanish Conquest to the Twentieth Century* (Glendale, Calif.: Arthur H. Clark Co., 1934), pp. 13–15.

2. Leo Grebler, Joan W. Moore, and Ralph C. Guzmán, *The Mexican-American People: The Nation's Second Largest Minority* (New York: Macmillan Co., Free Press, 1970), p. 15.

3. *The National Atlas of the United States of America*, p. 140; and Richard L. Nostrand, "The Hispanic-American Borderland: Delimitation of an American Culture Region," *Annals of the Association of American Geographers* 60 (December 1970):657.

4. Cf. Henry Nash Smith, *Virgin Land: The American West as Symbol and Myth* (Cambridge: Harvard University Press, 1950), p. 4.

5. Ibid., p. vii.

6. Ibid., p. 3.

7. D[onald] W[illiam] Meinig, *Southwest: Three Peoples in Geographical Change, 1600–1970* (New York: Oxford University Press, 1971), pp. 4–5.

8. Armando B. Rendón, *Chicano Manifesto* (New York: Macmillan Co., 1971), p. 295.

9. Jack D. Forbes, *Aztecas del Norte: The Chicanos of Aztlan* (Greenwich, Conn.: Fawcett Publications, Premier Books, 1973), pp. 13, 183; and Eric R. Wolf, *Sons of the Shaking Earth* (Chicago: University of Chicago Press, Phoenix Books, 1959), p. 32.

10. For general discussions of territoriality and nationalism, see Robert D. Sack, "Human Territoriality: A Theory," *Annals of the Association of American Geographers* 73 (March 1983):55–74; and Hans Kohn, *The Idea of Nationalism: A Study in Its Origins and Background* (New York: Macmillan Co., Paperbacks, 1961), pp. 4–9.

11. Rendón, p. 309.

12. For criticism of the general historical approach and interpretations used in the present work, see Arthur F. Corwin, "Mexican-American History: An Assess-

ment," *Pacific Historical Review* 42 (August 1973):270–73; Bruce Kuklick, "Myth and Symbol in American Studies," *American Quarterly* 24 (October 1972):435–50; and Manuel A. Machado, Jr., *Listen Chicano! An Informal History of the Mexican-American*, with a Foreword by Barry M. Goldwater (Chicago: Nelson Hall, 1978), pp. xii–xvi.

## Chapter 1

1.   Victor Barnouw, *An Introduction to Anthropology*, vol. 1: *Physical Anthropology and Archaeology*, The Dorsey Series in Anthropology, 3rd ed. (Homewood, Ill.: Dorsey Press, 1978), pp. 128, 139, 186; and Richard E. Leakey, *The Making of Mankind* (New York: E.P. Dutton, 1981), pp. 213, 6.

2.   Edward H. Spicer, *Cycles of Conquest: The Impact of Spain, Mexico, and the United States on the Indians of the Southwest, 1533–1960* (Tucson: University of Arizona Press, 1962), pp. 576–77.

3.   Robert F. Berkhofer, Jr., *The White Man's Indian: Images of the American Indian from Columbus to the Present* (New York: Alfred A. Knopf, 1978), p. 3.

4.   Lowell Dunham, trans., Introduction to *The Aztecs: People of the Sun*, by Alfonso Caso, The Civilization of the American Indian Series (Norman: University of Oklahoma Press, 1958), p. xiv.

5.   Barnouw, p. 186; and Lynn I. Perrigo, *Our Spanish Southwest* (Dallas: Banks Upshaw & Co., 1960), p. 1.

6.   Florence Hawley Ellis, "What Utaztecan Ethnology Suggests of Utaztecan Prehistory," in *Utaztekan Prehistory*, ed. Earl H. Swanson, Jr., Occasional Papers of the Idaho State University Museum, no. 22 (Pocatello: Idaho State University, 1968), p. 96.

7.   James A. Goss, "Culture-Historical Inference from Utaztekan Linguistic Evidence," in Swanson, pp. 3, 5, 14; see also Eric R. Wolf, *Sons of the Shaking Earth* (Chicago: University of Chicago Press, Phoenix Books, 1959), pp. 34–41.

8.   C. W. Ceram [Kurt W. Marek], *The First American: A Story of North American Archaeology*, trans. Richard Winston and Clara Winston (New York: Harcourt Brace Jovanovich, 1971), p. 165; Carroll L. Riley, "Early Spanish-Indian Communication in the Greater Southwest," *New Mexico Historical Review* 46 (October 1971): 286–87; and Matt S. Meier and Feliciano Rivera, *The Chicanos: A History of Mexican Americans*, American Century Series (New York: Farrar, Straus & Giroux, Hill & Wang, 1972), pp. 4–5; see also William C. Sturtevant, gen. ed., *Handbook of North American Indians*, 20 vols. (Washington, D.C.: Smithsonian Institution, 1978–    ), vol. 9: *Southwest*, ed. Alfonso Ortiz, pp. 26–30, 48–49, 174.

9.   Wolf, pp. 154–55.

10.   Perrigo, p. 15.

11.   Peter Martyr D'Anghera, *De Orbe Novo: The Eight Decades of Peter Martyr D'Anghera*, trans. Francis Augustus MacNutt, Burt Franklin: Research & Source

Works Series 642, Philosophy Monograph Series 44, 2 vols. (1912; reprint ed., New York: Lenox Hill, Burt Franklin, 1970), 2:350.

12. Hernando Cortés, "Instrucciones dadas . . . a Francisco Cortés . . .," in *Colección de documentos inéditos . . . de Indias,* ed. Joaquín F. Pacheco, Francisco de Cárdenas, and Luis Torres de Mendoza, 42 vols. (1864–84; reprint ed., Vaduz, Liechtenstein: Kraus Reprint, 1964–66), 26:153, my translation.

13. Hernán Cortés, *Hernan Cortes: Letters from Mexico,* trans. and ed. A[nthony] R. Pagden, with an Introduction by J. H. Elliott (New York: Grossman Publishers, Orion Press, 1971), p. 298.

14. Garcí [Rodríguez] Ordóñez de Montalvo, "Las sergas de . . . Esplandián," in *Libros de caballerías,* ed. with a Foreword by Pascual de Gayangos, Biblioteca de Autores Españoles desde la Formación del Lenguaje Hasta Nuestros Días, vol. 40 (Madrid: Ediciones Atlas, 1963), p. 539, my translation; and Carl Ortwin Sauer, *Sixteenth Century North America: The Land and the People as Seen by the Europeans* (Berkeley and Los Angeles: University of California Press, 1971), pp. 152–56.

15. Fray Diego Durán, *The Aztecs: The History of the Indies of New Spain,* trans. with Notes by Doris Heyden and Fernando Horcasitas, with an Introduction by Ignacio Bernal (New York: Orion Press, 1964), p. 134.

16. See *Códice Boturini* and Mapa Sigüenza, best located through Robert Wauchope, gen. ed., *Handbook of Middle American Indians,* 16 vols. (Austin: University of Texas Press, 1964–76), vol. 14: *Guide to Ethnohistorical Sources: Part III,* ed. Howard F. Cline, pp. 100–101, 197–98.

17. Heyden and Horcasitas, Notes to Durán, p. 330, n. 5; and Durán, p. 134.

18. Perrigo, p. 18.

19. Sauer, *Sixteenth Century North America,* pp. 36–46, 108–25.

20. Alvar Nuñez Cabeza de Vaca, *Adventures in the Unknown Interior of America,* trans. Cyclone Covey (New York: Crowell-Collier Publishing Co., Collier Books, 1961; reprint ed., Albuquerque: University of New Mexico Press, 1983), pp. 119, 110.

21. Herbert E. Bolton, *Coronado: Knight of Pueblos and Plains* (New York: McGraw-Hill Book Co., Whittlesey House, 1949; Albuquerque: University of New Mexico Press, 1949), p. 6; T. H. Watkins, *California: An Illustrated History,* The Great West Series (New York: Imprint Society, Weathervane Books, 1973), p. 20; and Carl [Ortwin] Sauer and Donald Brand, *Aztatlán: Prehistoric Mexican Frontier on the Pacific Coast,* Ibero-Americana, no.1 (Berkeley: University of California Press, 1932), p. 42.

22. Bolton, *Coronado,* pp. 18–19.

23. Fray Marcos de Niza, "Relación," in Pacheco, Cárdenas, and Torres de Mendoza, 3:333, my translation.

24. Ibid., pp. 347–48; see also Fray Marcos de Niza, "Report," in *Narratives of the Coronado Expedition, 1540–1542,* ed. George P. Hammond and Agapito Rey (Albuquerque: University of New Mexico Press, 1940; reprint ed., New York: AMS Press, 1977), pp. 66, 77–79; and Sauer, *Sixteenth Century North America,* pp. 127–29.

25. Quoted in Bolton, *Coronado,* p. 128.

26. Francisco Vázquez de Coronado, "Carta . . . al Emperado . . .," in Pacheco, Cárdenas, and Torres de Mendoza, 3:368, my translation.

27. Ibid., pp. 363–69; see also Francisco Vázquez de Coronado, "Letter . . . to the King . . .," in Hammond and Rey, pp. 185–90.

28. *Códice Ramírez, manuscrito del siglo XVI intitulado: Relación del origen de los indios que habitaban esta Nueva Espanña, seqún sus historias,* ed. Manuel Orozco y Berra (Mexico City: Editorial Leyenda, 1944), pp. 17–18, my translation.

29. Heyden and Horcasitas, p. 330, n. 5; and Durán, p. 6.

30. Fernando Alvarado Tezozomoc, *Crónica Mexicayotl,* trans. from Nahuatl to Spanish by Adrián León, Publicaciones del Instituto de Historia, 1st ser., no. 10 (Mexico City: Imprenta Universitaria for the Universidad Nacional Autónoma de México with the Instituto Nacional de Antropología e Historia, 1949), p. 22, my translation from Spanish to English.

31. Fray Antonio Tello, *Crónica miscelánea de la sancta provincia de Xalisco: Libro segundo,* Instituto Jalisciense de Antropología e Historia, Serie de Historia, no. 9, vol. 1 (Guadalajara: Gobierno del Estado de Jalisco for the Universidad de Guadalajara, [1968]), pp. 31, 22, my translation.

32. Herbert E. Bolton, ed., *Spanish Exploration in the Southwest: 1542–1706,* Original Narratives in Early American History ([New York]: Charles Scribner's Sons, 1908; reprint ed., New York: Barnes & Noble, 1969), pp. 199–200, 202.

33. Gaspar Pérez de Villagrá, *A History of New Mexico,* trans. Gilberto Espinosa, Rio Grande Classics ([Los Angeles: Quivira Society], 1933; reprint ed., Chicago: Rio Grande Press, 1962), pp. 58–59.

34. "Description of . . . El Paso . . .," in *Historical Documents Relating to New Mexico . . .,* ed. with an Introduction by Charles Wilson Hackett, 3 vols., Papers of the Division of Historical Research (Washington, D.C.: Carnegie Institution of Washington, 1923–37), 3:506–8.

35. Ibid.; cf. Oakah L. Jones, Jr., *Los Paisanos: Spanish Settlers on the Northern Frontier of New Spain* (Norman: University of Oklahoma Press, 1979), pp. 119–22.

36. Eusebio Francisco Kino, "Report and Relation of the New Conversions . . .," in *Spanish Exploration,* Bolton, p. 457.

37. C[ecil] Alan Hutchinson, *Frontier Settlement in Mexican California: The Híjar-Padrés Colony, and Its Origins, 1769–1835,* Yale Western Americana Series, 21 (New Haven: Yale University Press, 1969), pp. 1–3; and Herbert E. Bolton, *Texas in the Middle Eighteenth Century: Studies in Spanish Colonial History and Administration,* University of California Publications in History, vol. 3 (Berkeley: University of California Press, 1915), pp. 1–2, 375–446.

38. Jack D. Forbes, *Aztecas del Norte: The Chicanos of Aztlan* (Greenwich, Conn.: Fawcett Publications, Premier Books, 1973), pp. 23–29; and Bolton, *Spanish Exploration,* p. 201.

39. Pedro de Castañeda de Nájera, "Narrative of the Expedition to Cíbola, Undertaken in 1540, in Which Are Described All Those Settlements, Ceremonies, and Customs," in Hammond and Rey, p. 272; and Forbes, pp. 70–76.

## Chapter 2

1.  See David J. Weber, *The Mexican Frontier, 1821–1846: The American Southwest under Mexico,* Histories of the American Frontier (Albuquerque: University of New Mexico Press, 1982), pp. 156, 161–62.

2.  Pedro Bautista Pino, Antonio Barreiro, and José Agustín de Escudero, *Three New Mexico Chronicles: The "Exposición" of Don Pedro Bautista Pino, 1812; the "Ojeada" of Lic. Antonio Barreiro, 1832; and the Additions by Don José Agustín de Escudero, 1849,* trans. with an Introduction and Notes by H. Bailey Carroll and J. Villasana Haggard. Quivira Society Publications, vol. ll (Albuquerque: Quivira Society, 1942; reprint ed., New York: Arno Press, 1967).

3.  Ibid., pp. 97–100.

4.  See Max L. Moorhead, *The Presidio: Bastion of the Spanish Borderlands* (Norman: University of Oklahoma Press, 1975), pp. 201–42.

5.  Pino, Barreiro, and Escudero, pp. 84, 56, 51; and Carroll and Haggard, Introduction to Pino, Barreiro, and Escudero, p. xvii.

6.  Pino, Barreiro, and Escudero, pp. 27–28.

7.  Ibid., p. 242, my translation.

8.  Ibid., p. 59.

9.  Ibid., p. 37.

10.  Carroll and Haggard, p. xx.

11.  See C[larence] H. Haring, *The Spanish Empire in America* (New York: Harcourt, Brace & World, Harbinger Books, 1963), pp. 293–313, 323; and Charles Gibson, *Spain in America,* The New American Nation Series (New York: Harper & Row, Harper Torchbooks, University Library, 1966), pp. 168–69, 172, 178.

12.  Weber, p. 157.

13.  Pino, Barreiro, and Escudero, p. 75.

14.  Ibid., pp. 110–11.

15.  Ibid., p. 25.

16.  José María Sánchez, "A Trip to Texas in 1828," trans. Carlos E. Castañeda, *Southwestern Historical Quarterly* 29 (April 1926):283.

17.  Malcolm D. McLean, "Tenoxtitlan: Dream Capital of Texas," *Southwestern Historical Quarterly* 70 (July 1966):23.

18.  Sánchez, pp. 260, 271.

19.  Weber, pp. 161, 184.

20.  McLean, p. 23.

21.  Pino, Barreiro, and Escudero, p. 30.

22.  See Juan Gómez-Quiñones, *Development of the Mexican Working Class North of the Rio Bravo: Work and Culture among Laborers and Artisans, 1600–1900,* Popular Series, no. 2 (Los Angeles: Chicano Studies Research Center Publications, University of California, 1982), pp. 13–18.

23.  D[onald] W[illiam] Meinig, *Imperial Texas: An Interpretive Essay in Cultural Geography,* with an Introduction by Lorrin Kennamer (Austin: University of Texas Press, 1969), p. 28.

24.    Francisco Ruiz to Stephen F. Austin, 26 November 1830, quoted in McLean, p. 27.

25.    Secretary of Foreign Relations to Almonte, 17 January 1834, quoted in Helen Willits Harris, "Almonte's Inspection of Texas in 1834," *Southwestern Historical Quarterly* 41 (January 1938):200.

26.    Michael C. Meyer and William L. Sherman, *The Course of Mexican History*, 2nd ed. (New York: Oxford University Press, 1983), pp. 336–37.

27.    Enrique de la Peña, *With Santa Anna in Texas: A Personal Narrative of the Revolution*, trans. and ed. Carmen Perry, with an Introduction by Llerena Friend (College Station: Texas A&M University Press, 1975), p. 4.

28.    Joseph Martin Dawson, *José Antonio Navarro: Co-creator of Texas* (Waco, Tex.: Baylor University Press, 1969), p. 61.

29.    Cf. Arnoldo de León, *The Tejano Community, 1836–1900*, with a Contribution by Kenneth L. Stewart (Albuquerque: University of New Mexico Press, 1982), p. xvi.

30.    Dawson, p. 31; for an example of local concern over another *tejano's* partiality toward Anglo colonists, see Juan José Hernández, "Alcalde of Goliad to Governor of the State, no. 21, 26 March 1825," in *The Empresario: Don Martín de León*, by A[rthur] B.J. Hammett (Waco, Texas: Texian Press, 1973), pp. 96–97.

31.    Meinig, p. 37.

32.    Eugene C. Barker, *Mexico and Texas, 1821–1835*, University of Texas Research Lectures on the Causes of the Texas Revolution (New York: Russell & Russell, 1928; reprint ed., New York: Russell & Russell, 1965), p. 162.

33.    Peña, pp. 81–82.

34.    Ibid.

35.    Meinig, pp. 39–40.

36.    Joseph Milton Nance, *After San Jacinto: The Texas-Mexican Frontier, 1836–1841* (Austin: University of Texas Press, 1963), p. 115.

37.    *Houston Telegraph and Texas Register*, 25 October 1836, quoted in Nance, p. 21.

38.    Report of "Deaf" Smith to W. S. Fisher, Secretary of War, San Antonio de Béxar, 27 March 1837, quoted in Nance, p. 35.

39.    Seb. S. Wilcox, "Laredo During the Texas Republic," *Southwestern Historical Quarterly* 42 (October 1938):91–103; Dawson, pp. 66–69; and David M. Pletcher, *The Diplomacy of Annexation: Texas, Oregon, and the Mexican War* (Columbia: University of Missouri Press, 1973), p. 69.

40.    Andrew F. Rolle, *California: A History*, 2nd ed. (New York: Thomas Y. Crowell Co., 1969), p. 101.

41.    Weber, pp. 179–83; and Pletcher, pp. 89–93.

42.    Rolle, pp. 164–66.

43.    Ibid., pp. 184–86, 196–202.

44.    Gene M. Brack, *Mexico Views Manifest Destiny, 1821–1846: An Essay on the Origins of the Mexican War* (Albuquerque: University of New Mexico Press, 1975),

pp. 116–17; and Homer Campbell Chaney, Jr., "The Mexican-United States War as Seen by Mexican Intellectuals, 1846–1956" (Ph.D dissertation, Stanford University, 1959), pp. 4–12.

45. Brack, p. 54.

46. Pío Pico to citizens of California, 31 August 1845, MS HM 38235, quoted by permission of the Henry E. Huntington Library, San Marino, Calif., my translation.

47. Brack, p. 181.

48. Ibid., pp. 70–71, 84.

49. See Carlos María de Bustamante, *El nuevo Bernal Díaz del Castillo, o sea historia de la invasión de los anglo-americanos en México,* with an Introduction by Salvador Noriega, Testimonios Mexicanos, Historiadores, 2 (Mexico City: Secretaría de Educación Pública, 1949), p. 12.

50. Daniel Tyler, "Governor Armijo's Moment of Truth," *Journal of the West* 11 (April 1972):312–13; and Howard Roberts Lamar, *The Far Southwest, 1846–1912: A Territorial History,* Yale Western Americana Series, 12 (New Haven: Yale University Press, 1966), pp. 60–70.

51. Leonard Pitt, *The Decline of the Californios: A Social History of the Spanish-Speaking Californians, 1846–1890* (Berkeley and Los Angeles: University of California Press, 1966), pp. 32–35; see also K[arl] Jack Bauer, *The Mexican War, 1846–1848,* The Wars of the United States (New York: Macmillan Co., 1974), pp. 164–200.

52. *El Tratado de Guadalupe Hidalgo, 1848/Treaty of Guadalupe Hidalgo, 1848: A Facsimile Reproduction of the Mexican Instrument of Ratification and Related Documents* (Sacramento, Calif.: Telefact Foundation with California State Department of Education, 1968); see also Pletcher, pp. 522–75.

## Chapter 3

1. See Robert J. Rosenbaum, *Mexicano Resistance in the Southwest: "The Sacred Right of Self-Preservation,"* The Dan Danciger Publication Series (Austin: University of Texas Press, 1981), pp. 25–35.

2. Pablo de la Guerra, Speech to the California Senate, 1856, quoted in David J. Weber, ed., *Foreigners in Their Native Land: Historical Roots of the Mexican Americans,* with a Foreword by Ramón Eduardo Ruiz (Albuquerque: University of New Mexico Press, 1973), p. vi.

3. Pedro Castillo and Albert Camarillo, eds., *Furia y Muerte: Los Bandidos Chicanos,* Aztlán Publications, Monograph no. 4 (Los Angeles: Chicano Studies Center, University of California, 1973), pp. 1–11.

4. *Seventh Census of the United States: 1850,* pp. xxxviii, 972, 976, xxxvii, quoted in Richard Lee Nostrand, "The Hispanic-American Borderland: A Regional, Historical Geography" (Ph.D. dissertation, University of California, Los Angeles, 1968), pp. 147–48.

5. Jay Monaghan, *Chile, Peru, and the California Gold Rush of 1849* (Berkeley and Los Angeles: University of California Press, 1973), p. 250; for higher estimates

of the Spanish-speaking population, see Arthur F. Corwin, "Early Mexican Labor Migration: A Frontier Sketch, 1848–1900," in *Immigrants—and Immigrants: Perspectives on Mexican Labor Migration to the United States,* ed. Arthur F. Corwin, Contributions in Economics and Economic History, no. 17 (Westport, Conn.: Greenwood Press, 1978), p. 25; and Juan Gómez-Quiñones, *Development of the Mexican Working Class North of the Rio Bravo: Work and Culture among Laborers and Artisans, 1600–1900,* Popular Series, no. 2 (Los Angeles: Chicano Studies Research Center Publications, University of California, 1982), p. 16.

6.    Mariano Guadalupe Vallejo, "What the Gold Rush Brought to California," quoted in Myrtle M. McKittrick, *Vallejo: Son of California* (Portland, Ore.: Binfords & Mort, 1944), pp. 286–87.

7.    Donald E. Hargis, "Native Californians in the Constitutional Convention of 1849," *Historical Society of Southern California Quarterly* 36 (March 1954):5, 9–10.

8.    Ibid., pp. 6–8.

9.    Matt S. Meier and Feliciano Rivera, *The Chicanos: A History of Mexican Americans,* American Century Series (New York: Farrar, Straus & Giroux, Hill & Wang, 1972), p. 82.

10.    Hargis, pp. 7–9.

11.    *El clamor público* (Los Angeles), 19 June 1855; all translations from this newspaper are my own.

12.    Ibid., 2 August 1856.

13.    Leonard Pitt, *The Decline of the Californios: A Social History of the Spanish-Speaking Californians, 1846–1890* (Berkeley and Los Angeles: University of California Press, 1966), pp. 48–68 passim; Josiah Royce, *California: From the Conquest in 1846 to the Second Vigilance Committee in San Francisco, a Study of American Character,* with an Introduction by Robert Glass Cleland (New York: Alfred A. Knopf, Borzoi Books, 1948), pp. 282–85; and Rosenbaum, pp. 58–59.

14.    Quoted in Carey McWilliams, *North from Mexico: The Spanish-Speaking People of the United States* (Philadelphia: J. B. Lippincott Co., 1949; reprint ed., New York: Greenwood Press, 1968), pp. 129–30.

15.    Royce, pp. 385–86.

16.    *Joaquin Murieta, the Brigand Chief of California: A Complete History of His Life from the Age of Sixteen to the Time of His Capture and Death in 1853,* with Supplementary Notes by Raymund F. Wood, Americana Reprints, no. 1 (San Francisco: Grabhorn Press, 1932; reprint ed., Fresno, Calif.: Valley Publishers, 1969), pp. 4–5.

17.    "Corrido de Juaquín Murrieta," in *Literatura Chicana: Texto y Contexto/Chicano Literature: Text and Context,* ed. Antonia Castañeda Shular, Tomás Ybarra-Frausto, and Joseph Sommers (Englewood Cliffs, N.J.: Prentice-Hall, 1972), p. 66, my translation.

18.    "Tiburcio Vasquez: An Interview with the Noted Bandit," in *Foreigners,* Weber, p. 227; Rodolfo Acuña, *Occupied America: A History of Chicanos,* 2nd ed. (New York: Harper & Row, 1981), pp. 113–14; and Pitt, p. 257.

19.    *El clamor,* 2 August 1856.

20.    Mario Barrera, *Race and Class in the Southwest: A Theory of Racial Inequality* (Notre Dame, Ind.: University of Notre Dame Press, 1979), pp. 21–22; and W[illiam] W[ilcox] Robinson, *Land in California: The Story of Mission Lands, Ranchos, Squatters, Mining Claims, Railroad Grants, Land Scrip, Homesteads,* Chronicles of California (Berkeley and Los Angeles: University of California Press, 1948), pp. 99–109 passim.

21.    *El clamor,* 19 June 1855; 16 October, 24 July 1858; and 9 February 1856; for further discussion of the repatriation movement, see Richard Griswold del Castillo *The Los Angeles Barrio, 1850–1890: A Social History* (Berkeley and Los Angeles: University of California Press, 1979), pp. 119–24.

22.    *El clamor,* 26 June 1855.

23.    *Monitor republicano* (Mexico City), 27 June 1877, quoted in McKittrick, p. 347.

24.    *El bejareño* (San Antonio), 7 February 1855, my translation.

25.    Ibid.

26.    Juan Nepomuceno Seguín, "Personal Memoirs of John N. Seguín . . .," in *Northern Mexico on the Eve of the United States Invasion: Rare Imprints Concerning California, Arizona, New Mexico and Texas, 1821–1846,* ed. with an Introduction by David J. Weber, The Chicano Heritage (New York: New York Times, Arno Press, 1976), pp. iv, 5–32 passim [of imprint no. 3; pages of each imprint in this volume are numbered separately].

27.    Meier and Rivera, pp. 88–93; C[harles] L[eland] Sonnichsen, *The El Paso Salt War {1877}* (El Paso: Carl Hertzog and the Texas Western Press, 1961), pp. 58–59; and Arnoldo de León, *They Called Them Greasers: Anglo Attitudes toward Mexicans in Texas, 1821–1900* (Austin: University of Texas Press, 1983), pp. 82–83, 55–56.

28.    Juan Nepomuceno Cortina, "Suffer the Death of Martyrs . . .," in *Aztlan: An Anthology of Mexican American Literature,* ed. Luis Valdez and Stan Steiner, Marc Corporation Books (New York: Alfred A. Knopf, 1972), p. 115.

29.    Charles W. Goldfinch, "Juan N. Cortina 1824–1892: A Re-appraisal," in *Juan N. Cortina: Two Interpretations,* The Mexican American (New York: New York Times, Arno Press, 1974), pp. 42–50 [of Goldfinch article; articles in this volume are numbered separately].

30.    Ibid., pp. 51–63.

31.    Meier and Rivera, p. 93; and Arnoldo de León, *The Tejano Community, 1836–1900,* with a Contribution by Kenneth L. Stewart (Albuquerque: University of New Mexico Press, 1982), pp. 48–49, 14, 17, 62, 188–89.

32.    *El horizonte* (Corpus Christi), 8, 19 November 1879, my translation.

33.    Meier and Rivera, p. 97; Richard L. Nostrand, "The Hispano Homeland in 1900," *Annals of the Association of American Geographers* 70 (September 1980):382; and Howard Roberts Lamar, *The Far Southwest, 1846–1912: A Territorial History,* Yale Western Americana Series, 12 (New Haven: Yale University Press, 1966), pp. 82, 420–22.

34.    McWilliams, pp. 119–21; and Rosenbaum, pp. 95, 97.

35.   Meier and Rivera, pp. 104–7; and Rosenbaum, pp. 25–26.

36.   Robert W. Larson, *New Mexico's Quest for Statehood, 1846–1912* (Albuquerque: University of New Mexico Press, 1968), pp. 83–86.

37.   Lamar, pp. 433–35, 421.

38.   Ibid., pp. 219–21.

39.   Ibid., pp. 85–86.

40.   Miguel Antonio Otero, *My Life on the Frontier*, vol. 1: *1864–1882, Incidents and Characters of the Period When Kansas, Colorado, and New Mexico Were Passing through the Last of Their Wild and Romantic Years* (New Mexico: Press of Pioneers, 1935), pp. 280–86.

41.   Ibid., pp. 275–76.

42.   McWilliams, p. 119; and Lamar, p. 166.

43.   Ibid.

44.   Ibid., pp. 186–90; and Miguel Antonio Otero, *My Life on the Frontier*, vol. 2: *1882–1897, Death Knell of a Territory and Birth of a State*, with a Foreword by George P. Hammond (Albuquerque: University of New Mexico Press, 1939), p. 223.

45.   *La crónica de Mora* (N. Mex.), 12 September 1889.

46.   Archbishop Jean Baptiste Lamy, Pastoral Letter, 20 February 1884, MS RI2044, quoted by permission of the Henry E. Huntington Library, San Marino, Calif.; and *El clarín mexicano* (Santa Fe), 10 August 1873, my translation.

47.   Lamar, pp. 198–99; and *Chicago Times-Herald*, 11 June 1897, quoted in Larson, p. 195.

48.   Otero, *1882–1897*, pp. 1–2.

49.   Lamar, p. 199; and Miguel Antonio Otero, *My Nine Years as Governor of the Territory of New Mexico, 1897–1906*, with a Foreword by Marion Dargan (Albuquerque: University of New Mexico Press, 1940), p. 218.

50.   Lamar, pp. 493–94.

51.   Ibid., pp. 495–96; and Meier and Rivera, p. 113.

52.   José Emilio Fernández, *Cuarenta años de legislador, o biografía del senador Casimiro Barela* (Trinidad, Colo.: n.p., 1911; reprint ed., The Chicano Heritage, New York: New York Times, Arno Press, 1976), n. pag., my translation.

53.   Ibid.; and Lamar, pp. 292–93.

## Chapter 4

1.   Matt S. Meier and Feliciano Rivera, *The Chicanos: A History of Mexican Americans*, American Century Series (New York: Farrar, Straus & Giroux, Hill & Wang, 1972), pp. 115–16; and W[illiam] Dirk Raat, *Revoltosos: Mexico's Rebels in the United States, 1903–1923* (College Station: Texas A&M University Press, 1981), pp. xi–xii.

2.   Arthur F. Corwin, "¿Quién Sabe? Mexican Migration Statistics," in *Immi-*

*grants—and Immigrants: Perspectives on Mexican Labor Migration to the United States,* ed. Arthur F. Corwin, Contributions in Economics and Economic History, no. 17 (Westport, Conn.: Greenwood Press, 1978), p. 111; and James Diego Vigil, *From Indians to Chicanos: A Sociocultural History* (St. Louis, Mo.: C. V. Mosby Co., 1980), p. 147.

3.    Arthur F. Corwin, "Early Mexican Labor Migration: A Frontier Sketch, 1848–1900," in *Immigrants,* Corwin, pp. 27–28, 30–31.

4.    See Meier and Rivera, p. 108.

5.    Rodolfo Acuña, *Occupied America: A History of Chicanos,* 2nd ed. (New York: Harper & Row, 1981), pp. 73, 77–78.

6.    Howard Roberts Lamar, *The Far Southwest, 1846–1912: A Territorial History,* Yale Western Americana Series, 12 (New Haven: Yale University Press, 1966), p. 417.

7.    Paul Neff Garber, *The Gadsden Treaty* ([Philadelphia: Press of the University of Pennsylvania, 1924]; reprint ed., Gloucester, Mass.: Peter Smith, 1959), pp. 92–93, 101.

8.    Quoted in Odie B. Faulk, *Too Far North . . . Too Far South,* Great West and Indian Series, 35 (Los Angeles: Westernlore Press, 1967), p. 132.

9.    Ibid., p. 133.

10.    Henry F. Dobyns, *Spanish Colonial Tucson: A Demographic History* (Tucson: University of Arizona Press, 1976), pp. 56–59.

11.    *Las dos repúblicas* (Tucson, Ariz.), 22 July 1877, my translation.

12.    James Colquhoun, "The Early History of the Clifton-Morenci District," in *The Mexican Experience in Arizona,* with an Introduction by Carlos E. Cortés, The Chicano Heritage (New York: New York Times, Arno Press, 1976), pp. 35–37 [of Colquhoun article; articles in this volume are numbered separately].

13.    *El valle del Bravo* (El Paso, Tex.), 17 August 1889.

14.    From *El mercurio de Valparaíso* (Chile), reprinted in *La crónica* (San Francisco), 1 June 1855, my translation.

15.    Frederick Merk, *Manifest Destiny and Mission in American History: A Reinterpretation* (New York: Alfred A. Knopf, Borzoi Books, 1963), pp. 203–7; James Jeffrey Roche, *The Story of the Filibusters: To Which Is Added the Life of Colonel David Crockett,* The Adventure Series (London: T. Fisher Unwin, 1891), pp. 22–28; and Jay J. Wagoner, *Early Arizona: Prehistory to Civil War* (Tucson: University of Arizona Press, 1975), pp. 373–82.

16.    Henry Pickering Walker, "Freighting from Guaymas to Tucson, 1850–1880," *Western Historical Quarterly,* 1 (July 1970):304.

17.    From *La voz de Sonora* (Mexico), reprinted in *El clamor público* (Los Angeles), 16 October 1858, my translation.

18.    From *El eco del Pacífico* (San Francisco), reprinted in *El clamor,* 4 August 1858, my translation.

19.    *La bandera* (Brownsville, Tex.), 4 September 1863, my translation.

20.    Leonard Pitt, "Submergence of the Mexican in California, 1846 to 1890: A

History of Culture Conflict and Acculturation" (Ph.D. dissertation, University of California, Los Angeles, 1958), pp. 378–79.

21. Meier and Rivera, pp. 100–101.

22. Pitt, pp. 394–96.

23. See *La voz de México* (San Francisco), 12 January 1864.

24. *San Francisco Alta Californian,* quoted in *La voz de Chile y el Nuevo Mundo* (San Francisco), 8 July 1867, my translation.

25. Karl M. Schmitt, *Mexico and the United States, 1821–1973: Conflict and Coexistence,* America and the World (New York: John Wiley & Sons, 1974), pp. 81–110.

26. *La república* (San Francisco), 28, 7 October 1882, my translation; *El valle del Bravo,* 25 May 1889; and *El defensor del pueblo* (Albuquerque), 4 July 1891.

27. *La voz del Nuevo Mundo,* 30 December 1882, my translation.

28. *La gaceta* (Santa Barbara, Calif.), 11 October 1879, 1 May 1880; and *Revista hispano-americana* (Los Angeles), 20 October 1894, 17 December 1892.

29. Miguel Antonio Otero, *My Nine Years as Governor of the Territory of New Mexico, 1897–1906,* with a Foreword by Marion Dargan (Albuquerque: University of New Mexico Press, 1940), p. 36; for examples of the same phenomenon in Texas, see Arnoldo de León, *They Called Them Greasers: Anglo Attitudes toward Mexicans in Texas, 1821–1900* (Austin: University of Texas Press, 1983), pp. 61–62.

30. From the *San Francisco Argonaut,* reprinted in *La voz del pueblo* (East Las Vegas, N. Mex.), 2 April 1898; all translations from the latter newspaper are my own; see also Ramón Eduardo Ruiz, *Cuba: The Making of a Revolution,* The Norton Library (New York: W. W. Norton & Co., 1970), pp. 20–25.

31. *La voz del pueblo,* 2 April, 26 March 1898.

32. Ibid., 2, 23 April 1898.

33. Miguel Antonio Otero, "Telegram to *New York World,* 26 February 1898," in *My Nine Years,* Otero, p. 36; and Miguel Antonio Otero, "Telegram to R. A. Alger, Secretary of War," in *My Nine Years,* Otero, p. 38.

34. Quoted in José Emilio Fernández, *Cuarenta años de legislador, o biografía del senador Casimiro Barela* (Trinidad, Colo.: n.p., 1911; reprint ed., The Chicano Heritage, New York: New York Times, Arno Press, 1976). n. pag., my translation.

35. Lamar, pp. 17, 487.

36. Robert W. Larson, *New Mexico's Quest for Statehood, 1846–1912* (Albuquerque: University of New Mexico Press, 1968), pp. 207, 303–4.

37. Corwin, "¿Quién Sabe?" pp. 109–10.

38. See James D. Cockcroft, *Intellectual Precursors of the Mexican Revolution, 1900–1913,* Latin American Monographs, no. 14 (Austin: University of Texas Press, 1976), pp. 117–69.

39. *Regeneración* (Los Angeles), 11 February 1905, my translation.

40. Juan Gómez-Quiñones, *Sembradores, Ricardo Flores Magón y el Partido Liberal Mexicano: A Eulogy and Critique,* Aztlán Publications, Monograph no. 5 (Los Angeles: Chicano Studies Center, University of California, 1973), p. 46; see also Ricardo Flo-

res Magón, "El pueblo mexicano es apto para el comunismo," in Gómez-Quiñones, pp. 118–19.

41.   Acuña, pp. 193–94; Friedrich Katz, *The Secret War in Mexico: Europe, the United States and the Mexican Revolution,* with Portions trans. by Loren Goldner (Chicago: University of Chicago Press, 1981), pp. 29–30, 33; and Raat, pp. 38, 205.

42.   See Howard F. Cline, *The United States and Mexico,* The American Foreign Policy Library (Cambridge: Harvard University Press, 1953), pp. 113–62.

43.   Gómez-Quiñones, pp. 47–48.

44.   *La voz del pueblo,* 7 January, 18, 25 March 1911.

45.   Raat, pp. 57–58; and Katz, pp. 40–42, 112.

46.   Anne Pace, "Mexican Refugees in Arizona, 1910–1911," *Arizona and the West* 16 (Spring 1974):5–18.

47.   Cline, pp. 155–60; and Robert E. Quirk, *An Affair of Honor: Woodrow Wilson and the Occupation of Veracruz,* The Norton Library (New York: W. W. Norton & Co., 1962), pp. 85–103.

48.   D[onald] W[illiam] Meinig, *Imperial Texas: An Interpretive Essay in Cultural Geography,* with an Introduction by Lorrin Kennamer (Austin: University of Texas Press, 1969), p. 40.

49.   See James A. Sandos, "The Plan of San Diego: War and Diplomacy on the Texas Border, 1915–1916," *Arizona and the West* 14 (Spring 1972):5–24.

50.   L. Farrigno et al., "Plan of San Diego, Texas, State of Texas, January 6th, 1915," in *Literatura Chicana: Texto y Contexto/Chicano Literature: Text and Context,* ed. Antonia Castañeda Shular, Tomás Ybarra-Frausto, and Joseph Sommers (Englewood Cliffs, N.J.: Prentice-Hall, 1972), pp. 81–83.

51.   Ibid.

52.   A. S. Garza to Basilio Ramos, 15 January 1915, quoted in William M. Hager, "The Plan of San Diego: Unrest on the Texas Border in 1915," *Arizona and the West* 5 (Winter 1963):331.

53.   Luis de la Rosa and Aniceto Pizaña, "A nuestros compatriotas, los mexicanos en Texas," in *Mexican-American: Movements and Leaders,* by Carlos Larralde (Los Alamitos, Calif.: Hwong Publishing Co., 1976), p. 144; and Raat, p. 264.

54.   Sandos, pp. 5–24; cf. Katz, pp. 339–42.

55.   "Los sediciosos," in *A Texas-Mexican Cancionero: Folksongs of the Lower Border,* ed. Américo Paredes, Music in American Life (Urbana: University of Illinois Press, 1976), pp. 72–73.

56.   Ricardo Flores Magón, "Los levantamientos en Tejas," in Gómez-Quiñones, pp. 132–35, my translation.

57.   See Clarence C. Clendenen, *Blood on the Border: The United States Army and the Mexican Irregulars,* [The Wars of the United States] ([New York]: Macmillan Co., 1969), pp. 196–212.

58.   Cline, pp. 176–81; and Katz, pp. 306–11.

59.   *La voz del pueblo,* 11, 18 March 1916; for further examples of the Southwest

Mexican's precarious position, see Mario T. García, *Desert Immigrants: The Mexicans of El Paso, 1880–1920,* Yale Western Americana Series, 32 (New Haven: Yale University Press, 1981), pp. 184–96; and Ricardo Romo, *East Los Angeles: History of a Barrio* (Austin: University of Texas Press, 1983), pp. 95–102.

60. "Pancho Villa," in *Literary Folklore of the Hispanic Southwest,* comp. Aurora Lucero-White Lea (San Antonio: Naylor Co., 1953), p. 135, my translation.

61. Cline, p. 185; see also Katz, pp. 350–78, 514–15.

62. Quoted in Merle E. Simmons, *The Mexican Corrido as a Source for Interpretive Study of Modern Mexico (1870–1950),* Indiana University Publications, Humanities Series, no. 38 (Bloomington: Indiana University Press, 1957; reprint ed., New York: Kraus Reprint Co., 1969), p. 423, my translation.

63. Meier and Rivera, p. 132.

64. Cecilio Chávez, "The Emigrant's Farewell," in *Puro Mexicano,* ed. J. Frank Dobie, Texas Folklore Society Publications, no. 12 (Dallas, Tex.: Southern Methodist University Press, 1935), p. 224.

65. Meier and Rivera, pp. 113–14.

## Chapter 5

1. Nancie L. González, *The Spanish-Americans of New Mexico: A Heritage of Pride,* rev. and enl. ed. (Albuquerque: University of New Mexico Press, 1969), pp. 80–81; and Albert Camarillo, *Chicanos in a Changing Society: From Mexican Pueblos to American Barrios in Santa Barbara and Southern California, 1848–1930* (Cambridge: Harvard University Press, 1979), p. 183.

2. Arthur L. Campa, *Hispanic Culture in the Southwest* (Norman: University of Oklahoma Press, 1979), pp. 3–4; Carey McWilliams, *North from Mexico: The Spanish-Speaking People of the United States* (Philadelphia: J. B. Lippincott Co., 1949; reprint ed., New York: Greenwood Press, 1968), pp. 39, 43–44; and Leonard Pitt, *The Decline of the Californios: A Social History of the Spanish-Speaking Californians, 1846–1890* (Berkeley and Los Angeles: University of California Press, 1966), p. 267.

3. McWilliams, pp. 60–61.

4. Harry Clark, "Their Pride, Their Manners, and Their Voices: Sources of the Traditional Portrait of the Early Californians," *California Historical Quarterly* 53 (Spring 1974):71–72; and Pitt, pp. 284–91.

5. Arthur G. Pettit, *Images of the Mexican American in Fiction and Film,* ed. with an Afterword by Dennis E. Showalter (College Station: Texas A&M University Press, 1980), pp. 22–24, 85, 88–89.

6. Hubert Howe Bancroft, *The Works of Hubert Howe Bancroft,* vol. 34: *California Pastoral,* 1769–1848 (San Francisco: History Co., 1888), pp. 260–61, 276–77.

7. Ibid., p. 611.

8. Cecil Robinson, *Mexico and the Hispanic Southwest in American Literature*, rev. from *With the Ears of Strangers* (Tucson: University of Arizona Press, 1977), pp. 137–39.

9. Helen [Hunt] Jackson, *Ramona: A Story* (n.p.: Roberts Bros., 1884; reprint ed., Boston: Little, Brown, & Co., 1919), chaps. 1–2.

10. Raymund Arthur Paredes, "The Image of the Mexican in American Literature" (Ph.D. dissertation, University of Texas at Austin, 1973), pp. 235–36, 213–14.

11. Bret Harte, "The Devotion of Enríquez," in *The Chicano: From Caricature to Self-portrait*, ed. with an Introduction by Edward Simmen (New York: New American Library, Mentor Books, 1971), pp. 51, 62.

12. Pitt, pp. 280–81; see also Angustias de la Guerra Ord, *Occurrences in Hispanic California*, trans. and ed. Francis Price and William H. Ellison (Washington, D.C.: Academy of American Franciscan History, 1956); and Pío Pico, *Don Pío Pico's Historical Narrative*, trans. Arthur P. Botello, ed. with an Introduction by Martin Cole and Henry Welcome (Glendale, Calif.: Arthur H. Clark Co., 1973).

13. Pitt, pp. 289–90.

14. See, for example, "First Census of Los Angeles," in *Foreigners in Their Native Land: Historical Roots of the Mexican Americans*, ed. David J. Weber, with a Foreword by Ramón Eduardo Ruiz (Albuquerque: University of New Mexico Press, 1973), pp. 33–35; and C[ecil] Alan Hutchinson, *Frontier Settlement in Mexican California: The Híjar-Padrés Colony, and Its Origins, 1769–1835*, Yale Western Americana Series, 21 (New Haven: Yale University Press, 1969), p. 61.

15. Paredes, pp. 210–11.

16. Cf. Campa, *Hispanic Culture*, p. 5.

17. Guadalupe Vallejo, "Ranch and Mission Days in Alta California," *Century Magazine*, December 1890, pp. 183–92 passim, 184, 183, 191.

18. Charles F. Lummis, *The Land of Poco Tiempo* (New York: Charles Scribner's Sons, 1893; reprint ed., Albuquerque: University of New Mexico Press, 1952), pp. 2–3.

19. McGregor [pseud.?], "Our Spanish-American Fellow Citizens," *Harper's Weekly*, 20 June 1914, p. 7.

20. Ernest Peixotto, *Our Hispanic Southwest* (New York: Charles Scribner's Sons, 1916), p. 180; for further comment on this building, see Trent Elwood Sanford, *The Architecture of the Southwest: Indian, Spanish, American* (New York: W. W. Norton & Co., 1950), pp. 90–91.

21. McGregor, p. 6.

22. Enrique Hank López, "Back to Bachimba: A Hyphenated American Discovers That He Can't Go Home Again," *Horizon*, Winter 1967, p. 80.

23. Oliver La Farge, *Behind the Mountains* (Boston: Houghton Mifflin Co., Riverside Press, 1956), pp. 173–74.

24. See immigration figures in Lawrence A. Cardoso, *Mexican Emigration to the*

*United States, 1897–1931: Socio-Economic Patterns* (Tucson: University of Arizona Press, 1980), pp. 53, 94–95.

25.   Manuel Gamio, comp., *The Life Story of the Mexican Immigrant: Autobiographic Documents Collected by Manuel Gamio,* with a new Introduction by Paul S. Taylor (Chicago: University of Chicago Press, 1931; reprint ed., New York: Dover Publications, 1971), p. iv.

26.   Ibid., pp. 271–75.

27.   Ibid., pp. 275–78.

28.   Herbert E. Bolton, *The Spanish Borderlands: A Chronicle of Old Florida and the Southwest,* The Chronicles of America Series, vol. 23, Abraham Lincoln Edition (New Haven: Yale University Press, 1921), p. 294; and Nellie Van de Grift Sánchez, *Spanish Arcadia,* California (Los Angeles: Powell Publishing Co., 1929), n. pag.

29.   Alfonso Yorba, "Old San Juan: Last Stronghold of Spanish California," *Historical Society of Southern California Quarterly* 17 (March 1935):7.

30.   Adelina Otero Warren, "The Spell of New Mexico," in *A Documentary History of the Mexican Americans,* ed. Wayne Moquin with Charles Van Doren, with an Introduction by Feliciano Rivera (New York: Praeger Publishers, 1971), p. 284.

31.   Ibid., pp. 285, 288.

32.   Nina Otero-Warren, *Old Spain in Our Southwest* (New York: Harcourt, Brace & Co., 1936; reprint ed., Chicago: Rio Grande Press, 1962), p. 64.

33.   Warren, "The Spell," p. 283.

34.   Aurelio M. Espinosa, *España en Nuevo Méjico: Lecturas elementales sobre la historia de Nuevo Méjico y su tradición española* (Boston: Allyn & Bacon, Norwood Press, 1937), pp. v–vi, 42 (my translation), 69 (my translation).

35.   Ibid., pp. 39–40.

36.   Aurelio M. Espinosa, New Mexican Spanish Folk-Lore," *Journal of American Folk-Lore* 29 (October–December 1916):520; see also Aurelio M. Espinosa, "Folk-Lore from Spain: The *Fiesta del Gallo* in Barbadillo," *Modern Philology* 20 (May 1923):432.

37.   Aurelio M. Espinosa, "The Tar-Baby Story," *Journal of American Folk-Lore* 43 (April–June 1930):131.

38.   Espinosa, *España en Nuevo Méjico,* pp. 70–73, my translation.

39.   Arthur L. Campa, "The Spanish Folksong in the Southwest," p. 13, and "Spanish Religious Folktheatre in the Southwest," pp. 6–7 [pages of articles in this volume are numbered separately], in *Hispanic Folklore Studies of Arthur L. Campa,* with an Introduction by Carlos E. Cortés, The Chicano Heritage (New York: New York Times, Arno Press, 1976).

40.   Arthur L. Campa, "Spanish Folk-Poetry in New Mexico," pp. 6–7, 14, in *Hispanic Folklore.*

41.   Ibid., pp. 15–16.

42.   Francisca López de Belderrain, "The Awakening of Paredon Blanco under a California Sun," *Historical Society of Southern California Annual* 14 (1928):65–79; and

George I. Sánchez, *Forgotten People: A Study of New Mexicans* (Albuquerque: University of New Mexico Press, 1940), pp. vii, 3–4.

43. Antonio López de Santa-Anna et al., *The Mexican Side of the Texan Revolution, 1836: By the Chief Mexican Participants,* trans. with Notes by Carlos E. Castañeda (Dallas: P. L. Turner Co., 1928; reprint ed., The Chicano Heritage, New York: New York Times, Arno Press, 1976); Felix D. Almarez, Jr., "Carlos Eduardo Castañeda, Mexican-American Historian: The Formative Years, 1896–1927," *Pacific Historical Review* 42 (August 1973): 319–34.; Josephina Niggli, *Mexican Folk Plays,* ed. with an Introduction by Frederick H. Koch (Chapel Hill: University of North Carolina Press, 1938; reprint ed., The Chicano Heritage, New York: New York Times, Arno Press, 1976), pp. 53–114, 151–78.

44. *La opinión* (Los Angeles), 18 September 1926, my translation.

45. Maurilio E. Vigil, *Los Patrones: Profiles of Hispanic Political Leaders in New Mexico History* (Washington, D.C.: University Press of America, 1980), pp. 122–23; and *Santa Fe New Mexican,* 21 December 1910, 31 August 1911, quoted in Alfred C. Córdova and Charles B. Judah, *Octaviano Larrazolo: A Political Portrait,* Publications of the Division of Government Research, no. 32 (Albuquerque: Division of Research, Department of Government, University of New Mexico, 1952), pp. 12, 8, 1–21 passim.

46. Carlos Larralde, *Mexican-American: Movements and Leaders* (Los Alamitos, Calif.: Hwong Publishing Co., 1976), pp. 148, 147–51 passim; Córdova and Judah, pp. 23, 25, 30; and Vigil, pp. 124–25.

47. Matt S. Meier and Feliciano Rivera, *The Chicanos: A History of Mexican Americans,* American Century Series (New York: Farrar, Straus & Giroux, Hill & Wang, 1972), pp. 125–26; and Mario Barrera, *Race and Class in the Southwest: A Theory of Racial Inequality* (Notre Dame, Ind.: University of Notre Dame Press, 1979), pp. 70–71.

48. Abraham Hoffman, *Unwanted Mexican Americans in the Great Depression: Repatriation Pressures, 1929–1939,* with a Foreword by Julián Nava (Tucson: University of Arizona Press, 1974), p. 126; and Frances Leon Swadesh, *Los Primeros Pobladores: Hispanic Americans of the Ute Frontier* (Notre Dame, Ind.: University of Notre Dame Press, 1974), pp. 205–6.

49. Meier and Rivera, pp. 169–70; and Charles Wollenberg, "Working on *El Traque:* The Pacific Electric Strike of 1903," *Pacific Historical Review* 42 (August 1973):359.

50. Barrera, p. 129; and Roxanne Dunbar Ortiz, *Roots of Resistance: Land Tenure in New Mexico, 1680–1980,* [Monograph no. 10] (Los Angeles: Chicano Studies Research Center Publications and American Indian Studies Center, University of California, 1980), pp. 110, 112.

51. Meier and Rivera, pp. 170–75; and Rodolfo Acuña, *Occupied America: The Chicano's Struggle toward Liberation* (San Francisco: Harper & Row, Canfield Press, 1972), p. 158.

52. Meier and Rivera, p. 152; and Larralde, p. 164.
53. Hoffman, p. 126; and Meier and Rivera, pp. 160–64.
54. *Excelsior* (Mexico City), 2 June 1932, quoted in Hoffman, p. 134.

## Chapter 6

1. For further discussion of this term, see Niles Hansen, "Commentary: The Hispano Homeland in 1900," *Annals of the Association of American Geographers* 71 (June 1981):280–81; and Richard L. Nostrand, "Comment in Reply," *Annals of the Association of American Geographers* 71 (June 1981):282–83.

2. Idem, *Los chicanos: Geografía histórica regional,* trans. from English to Spanish by Roberto Gómez Ciriza (Mexico City: Sep/setentas, 1976), p. 141.

3. Paul Schuster Taylor, *An American-Mexican Frontier: Nueces County, Texas* ([Chapel Hill]: University of North Carolina Press, 1934; reprint ed., New York: Atheneum Publishers, Russell & Russell, 1971), p. 241.

4. Bryce Wood, *The Making of the Good Neighbor Policy* (New York: Columbia University Press, 1961), pp. 7–8.

5. Samuel Flagg Bemis, *A Diplomatic History of the United States,* 4th ed. (New York: Henry Holt & Co., 1955), pp. 514–15; Thomas A. Bailey, *A Diplomatic History of the American People,* 7th ed. (New York: Meredith Publishing Co., Appleton-Century-Crofts, 1964), pp. 499–501, 504–7; and *El obrero* (Morenci, Ariz.), 21, 28 November 1903.

6. Bemis, pp. 526–29, 539, 518; see also Martin C. Needler, *The United States and the Latin American Revolution,* UCLA Latin American Studies, vol. 38, rev. ed. (Los Angeles: UCLA Latin American Center Publications, University of California, 1977), pp. 17–19.

7. John T. Reid, *Spanish American Images of the United States, 1790–1960,* A University of Florida Book (Gainesville: University Presses of Florida, 1977), pp. 153–62; however, for an example of Southwest Mexican support for U.S. intervention in one case, see *El obrero,* 4 July 1903.

8. *La prensa* (Los Angeles), 3, 17, 24 January, 7, 14, 21, 28 February, 6, 13 March 1920, my translation; and Bailey, pp. 679–80.

9. "Los ambiciosos patones," quoted in Merle E. Simmons, *The Mexican Corrido as a Source for Interpretive Study of Modern Mexico (1870–1950),* Indiana University Publications, Humanities Series, no. 38 (Bloomington: Indiana University Press, 1957; reprint ed., New York: Kraus Reprint Co., 1969), pp. 450–51, my translation.

10. Francisco E. Balderrama, *In Defense of La Raza: The Los Angleles Mexican Consulate and the Mexican Community, 1929 to 1936* (Tucson: University of Arizona Press, 1982), p. 15; and Bailey, pp. 680–82.

11. *La opinión* (Los Angeles), 7 January 1933, my translation; and Bailey, p. 683.

12. Bailey, pp. 684–85; J[ohn] Lloyd Mecham, *The United States and Inter-*

*American Security, 1889–1960* (Austin: University of Texas Press for the Institute of Latin American Studies, 1961), p. 122; and Carey McWilliams, *North from Mexico: The Spanish-Speaking People of the United States* (Philadelphia: J. B. Lippincott Co., 1949; reprint ed., New York: Greenwood Press, 1968), p. 103.

13.   Pauline R. Kibbe, *Latin Americans in Texas,* Inter-Americana Studies 3 (Albuquerque: University of New Mexico Press for the School of Inter-American Affairs, 1946), p. 263.

14.   "Constitution of the League of United Latin-American Citizens, 1929, Article 11," in Taylor, pp. 243–44.

15.   *Lulac News* (San Antonio), September 1932, quoted in Edgar Greer Shelton, Jr., "Political Conditions among Texas Mexicans along the Rio Grande" (Master's thesis, University of Texas, 1946), pp. 114, 111.

16.   Quoted in Taylor, pp. 343, 316, 315.

17.   Ibid., p. 315.

18.   Matt S. Meier and Feliciano Rivera, *The Chicanos: A History of Mexican Americans,* American Century Series (New York: Farrar, Straus & Giroux, Hill & Wang, 1972), p. 242; see also Balderrama, pp. 58–60.

19.   Quoted in Raúl Morín, *Among the Valiant: Mexican-Americans in WW II and Korea,* with an Introduction by Lyndon B. Johnson (Alhambra, Calif.: Borden Publishing Co., 1966), p. 15.

20.   Ibid., pp. 15, 24.

21.   Meier and Rivera, pp. 186–87; Rodolfo Acuña, *Occupied America: A History of Chicanos,* 2nd ed. (New York: Harper & Row, 1981), p. 323; and Morín, pp. 25–27.

22.   McWilliams, pp. 239–41; cf. Joan W. Moore with others, *Homeboys: Gangs, Drugs, and Prison in the Barrios of Los Angeles* (Philadelphia: Temple University Press, 1978), pp. 43, 52–54.

23.   McWilliams, pp. 227–29; and Acuña, pp. 328–29.

24.   Acuña, pp. 324–25; McWilliams, p. 234; and *Eastside Journal* (East Los Angeles), 16 December 1942, 15 March 1944.

25.   Félix Díaz Escobar, "The Spread of *Sinarquismo,*" *Nation,* 3 April 1943, p. 487; and Betty Kirk, "Mexico's 'Social Justice' Party," *Nation,* 12 June 1943, pp. 827–31.

26.   *Los Angeles Times,* 7 June 1943; McWilliams, p. 236; and Acuña, pp. 326–29.

27.   Axis broadcast, 13 January 1943, quoted in McWilliams, p. 238.

28.   See Curtis Vinson, "Race Issue Arouses Ire of Mexicans," in *Are We Good Neighbors?* by Alonso S. Perales (San Antonio: Artes Graficas, 1948; reprint ed., The Mexican American, New York: New York Times, Arno Press, 1974), pp. 269–70.

29.   McWilliams, p. 256; Acuña, p. 326; and Meier and Rivera, p. 194.

30.   *Belvedere Citizen* (East Los Angeles), 18 June 1943.

31.   See Perales, pp. 277, 283.

32.   Quoted in Beatrice Griffith, *American Me* (Boston: Houghton Mifflin Co., 1948; reprint ed., Westport, Conn.: Williamhouse-Regency, Greenwood Press, 1973), p. 299.

33.   Meier and Rivera, p. 190; and Griffith, p. 266.

34.   Quoted in Ozzie G. Simmons, "Anglo Americans and Mexican Americans in South Texas: A Study in Dominant-Subordinate Group Relations," 2 vols. (Ph.D. dissertation, Harvard University, 1952), 2:549.

35.   Ignacio L. López, Foreword to *Not with the Fist: Mexican-Americans in a Southwest City,* by Ruth D. Tuck (New York: Harcourt, Brace & Co., 1946), p. ix.

36.   See McWilliams, pp. 221–23.

37.   Quoted in Tuck, p. 221.

38.   Morín, pp. 277–78.

39.   Mrs. Charles Keller, "Veteran's Wife Returning to Edinburg Wants Town Returned to Americans," in Perales, p. 251; and Robert Rodríquez, *"Letter to Edinburg* (Tex.) *Valley Review,"* in Perales, p. 257.

40.   Mario Suárez, "El Hoyo," *Arizona Quarterly* 3 (Summer 1947):114.

41.   Acuña, pp. 331–32.

42.   Perales, p. 7.

43.   Kaye Lynn Briegel, "The History of Political Organizations among Mexican-Americans in Los Angeles Since the Second World War" (Master's thesis, University of Southern California, 1967), p. 78; Acuña, p. 158; and Needler, p. 20.

44.   Ernesto Galarza, *Merchants of Labor: The Mexican Bracero Story, an Account of the Managed Migration of Mexican Farm Workers in California, 1942–1960,* with a Preface by Ernest Gruening (Charlotte, N.C.: McNally & Loftin, 1964), p. 16; see also Juan Ramón García, *Operation Wetback: The Mass Deportation of Mexican Undocumented Workers in 1954,* Contributions in Ethnic Studies, no. 2 (Westport, Conn.: Greenwood Press, 1980), pp. 18–61.

45.   Meier and Rivera, pp. 220–21, 227; and García, pp. 183–221 passim.

46.   Galarza, p. 70; Tuck, p. 134; Briegel, pp. 76–77; and Griffith, pp. 235–36.

47.   Quoted in William Madsen, *Mexican-Americans of South Texas,* Case Studies in Cultural Anthropology (New York: Holt, Rinehart & Winston, 1964), pp. 110, 43, 8.

48.   See Ignacio Reyes, "A Survey of the Problems Involved in the Americanization of the Mexican-American" (Master's thesis, University of Southern California, 1957).

49.   José Antonio Villarreal, *Pocho* (Garden City, N.Y.: Doubleday & Co., Anchor Books, 1970), p. 133.

50.   See Julián Samora, "Minority Leadership in a Bicultural Community" (Ph.D. dissertation, Washington University, 1953), pp. 62–65, 76.

51.   Joaquín Ortega, *New Mexico's Opportunity: A Message to My Fellow New Mexicans* (Albuquerque: University of New Mexico Press, 1942), p. 12.

52.   John Rechy, "El Paso del Norte," *Evergreen Review* 2 (Autumn 1958):127.

## Chapter 7

1.   Leo Grebler, Joan W. Moore, and Ralph C. Guzmán, *The Mexican-American People: The Nation's Second Largest Minority* (New York: Macmillan Co., Free Press, 1970), pp. 29, 143, 185, 251.

2.   Edward Murguía, *Assimilation, Colonialism and the Mexican American People,* Mexican American Monograph Series, no. 1 (Austin: Center for Mexican American Studies, University of Texas, 1975), pp. 1, 62; Frantz Fanon, *Black Skin, White Masks,* trans. Charles Lam Markmann (New York: Grove Press, Evergreen Black Cat, 1968), pp. 223–32 passim; Albert Memmi, *The Colonizer and the Colonized,* trans. Howard Greenfeld, with an Introduction by Jean-Paul Sartre (Boston: Beacon Press, 1967), pp. 145–53 passim; and Fernando Peñalosa, *Chicano Sociolinguistics: A Brief Introduction,* Series in Sociolinguistics (Rowley, Mass.: Newbury House Publishers, 1980), pp. 2–3.

3.   Gilberto López y Rivas, *Los chicanos: Una minoría nacional explotada,* Temas de Actualidad, 3rd ed. (Mexico City: Editorial Nuestro Tiempo, 1979), pp. 107–14, 148; and Mario Barrera, *Race and Class in the Southwest: A Theory of Racial Inequality* (Notre Dame, Ind.: University of Notre Dame Press, 1979), pp. 218–19.

4.   Matt S. Meier and Feliciano Rivera, *The Chicanos: A History of Mexican Americans,* American Century Series (New York: Farrar, Straus & Giroux, Hill & Wang, 1972), pp. 247–50.

5.   Ibid.

6.   Gladys Gregory, "The Chamizal Settlement: A View from El Paso," *Southwestern Studies* 1 (Summer 1963):4–5; and Sheldon B. Liss, *A Century of Disagreement: The Chamizal Conflict, 1864–1964* (Washington, D.C.: University Press and Latin American Institute, 1965), pp. 104–7.

7.   Rodolfo Acuña, *Occupied America: The Chicano's Struggle toward Liberation* (San Francisco: Harper & Row, Canfield Press, 1972), pp. 225–26.

8.   Eduardo Quevedo et al., "Open Resolution Directed to the President of the United States and Executive Departments and Agencies, by National Hispanic and Mexican-American Organizations on Civil Disobedience and Riot Investigations," in "The History of Political Organizations among Mexican-Americans in Los Angeles Since the Second World War," by Kaye Lynn Briegel (Master's thesis, University of Southern California, 1967), p. 64.

9.   Acuña, p. 225.

10.   Meier and Rivera, pp. 260–61.

11.   Quoted in Jacques E. Levy, *Cesar Chavez: Autobiography of La Causa* (New York: W. W. Norton & Co., 1975), p. 8.

12.   Ibid., pp. 42, 84, 98, 144–45.

13.   Quoted in Peter Matthiessen, *Sal Si Puedes: Cesar Chavez and the New American Revolution,* rev. ed. (New York: Random House, 1973), pp. 128–29; see also Levy, pp. 196–98.

14.   Quoted in Matthiessen, p. 300.

15. [Luis Valdez], "The Plan of Delano," in *Aztlan: An Anthology of Mexican American Literature,* ed. Luis Valdez and Stan Steiner, Marc Corporation Books (New York: Alfred A. Knopf, 1972), p. 198.

16. Quoted in Matthiessen, pp. 347, 73.

17. Quoted in Levy, pp. 123, 537; see also Matthiessen, pp. 108–10, 143–45, 179.

18. Meier and Rivera, pp. 261–62, 269; see also *Albuquerque Journal,* 7 June 1980.

19. Valdez, "The Plan," p. 201.

20. Peter Nabokov, *Tijerina and the Courthouse Raid* (Albuquerque: University of New Mexico Press, 1969), p. 27; cf. Roxanne Dunbar Ortiz, *Roots of Resistance: Land Tenure in New Mexico, 1680–1980,* [Monograph no. 10] (Los Angeles: Chicano Studies Research Center Publications and American Indian Studies Center, University of California, 1980), pp. 45–47, 96–97.

21. Patricia Bell Blawis, *Tijerina and the Land Grants: Mexican Americans in Struggle for Their Heritage* (New York: International Publishers Co., New World Paperbacks, 1971), pp. 41, 43.

22. Nancie L. González, *The Spanish-Americans of New Mexico: A Heritage of Pride,* rev. and enl. ed. (Albuquerque: University of New Mexico Press, 1969), p. 90, and Robert J. Rosenbaum, *Mexicano Resistance in the Southwest: "The Sacred Right of Self-Preservation,"* The Dan Danciger Publication Series (Austin: University of Texas Press, 1981), pp. 118–24, 139.

23. Quoted in Blawis, p. 26.

24. Nabokov, pp. 194, 204, 211.

25. Quoted in Nabokov, pp. 19, 227; see Blawis, pp. 56–60.

26. Nabokov, pp. 28, 66, 74, 82–88; and Reies López Tijerina, *Mi lucha por la tierra,* with a Prologue by Jorge A. Bustamante, Vida y Pensamiento de México (Mexico City: Fondo de Cultura Económica, 1978), pp. 152–56.

27. Alfonso Sánchez, quoted in Nabokov, p. 185; and Meier and Rivera, p. 271.

28. Quoted in Blawis, pp. 146, 139–40. For further comment on the relationship between Chicanos and Native Americans, see Rudolph O. de la Garza, Z. Anthony Kruszewski, and Tomás A. Arciniega, comps., *Chicanos and Native Americans: The Territorial Minorities* (Englewood Cliffs, N.J.: Prentice-Hall, Spectrum Books, 1973), p. 4; Jack D. Forbes, *Aztecas del Norte: The Chicanos of Aztlán* (Greenwich, Conn.: Fawcett Publications, Premier Books, 1973), pp. 178–205; and Armando B. Rendón, *Chicano Manifesto* (New York: Macmillan Co., 1971), pp. 294–95, 297.

29. Meier and Rivera, pp. 273–74; *Albuquerque Journal,* 16 March 1979.

30. F. Chris García, "Manitos and Chicanos in New Mexico Politics," in *La Causa Política: A Chicano Politics Reader,* ed. F. Chris García (Notre Dame, Ind.: University of Notre Dame Press, 1974), pp. 271–80.

31. Forbes, p. 17.

32. "The Spiritual Manifesto of Aztlán," in *Literatura Chicana: Texto y Contexto/*

*Chicano Literature: Text and Context,* ed. Antonia Castañeda Shular, Tomás Ybarra-Frausto, and Joseph Sommers (Englewood Cliffs, N.J.: Prentice Hall, 1972), p. 84.

33. *El Papel* (Albuquerque), April 1970, quoted in Blawis, p. 175; Stan Steiner, "The Poet in the Boxing Ring," in García, *La Causa Política,* pp. 323–25; and Meier and Rivera, pp. 274–75.

34. Quoted in Steiner, p. 326; see also Mario Barrera, Carlos Muñoz, and Charles Ornelas, "The Barrio as an Internal Colony," in García, *La Causa Política,* p. 282; and Meier and Rivera, p. 276.

35. Quoted in Steiner, p. 329.

36. "The Spiritual Manifesto," p. 84.

37. See Richard Santillán, *La Raza Unida,* Chicano Politics (Los Angeles: Tlaquilo Publications, 1973), pp. 19–24; and *Denver Post,* 11 September 1977.

38. John Staples Shockley, *Chicano Revolt in a Texas Town* (Notre Dame, Ind.: University of Notre Dame Press, 1974), pp. 3–4, 79.

39. José Angel Gutiérrez, "Aztlan: Chicano Revolt in the Winter Garden," *La Raza* 1, no. 4 [1971], n. pag.

40. Shockley, pp. 162, 200–205.

41. Santillán, p. 16; Tony Castro, *Chicano Power: The Emergence of Mexican America* (New York: Saturday Review Press/E. P. Dutton & Co., 1974), pp. 181–82; Shockley, pp. 214–16, 225; and *San Antonio Express,* 3 October 1980.

42. Ibid., 9 March 1975.

43. Acuña, p. 236.

44. Ibid., pp. 227–29; and Meier and Rivera, p. 252.

45. Acuña, pp. 229, 258–60.

46. Ernie Barrios, *Bibliografía de Aztlán: An Annotated Chicano Bibliography* (San Diego, Calif.: Centro de Estudios Chicanos Publications, San Diego State College, 1971); Luis Valdez and Stan Steiner, eds., *Aztlan: An Anthology of Mexican American Literature,* Marc Corporation Books (New York: Alfred A. Knopf, 1972); Miguel Méndez M., *Peregrinos de Aztlán: Literatura chicana (novela)* (Tucson, Ariz.: Editorial Peregrinos, 1974); Rudolfo A. Anaya, *Heart of Aztlan* (Berkeley, Calif.: Editorial Justa Publications, 1976); and Luis F. Hernández, *Aztlan: The Southwest and Its Peoples* (Rochelle Park, N.J.: Hayden Book Co., 1975).

47. Henry B. González, "An Attack on Chicano Militants," in *A Documentary History of the Mexican Americans,* ed. Wayne Moquin with Charles Van Doren, with an Introduction by Feliciano Rivera (New York: Praeger Publishers, 1971), pp. 358–59; see also Richard Rodríguez, *Hunger of Memory: The Education of Richard Rodriguez, an Autobiography,* Bantam Windstone Books (New York: Bantam Books, 1983), pp. 157–60.

48. Fray Angélico Chávez, *My Penitente Land: Reflections on Spanish New Mexico* (Albuquerque: University of New Mexico Press, 1974), pp. 223, 200–202; cf. González, *The Spanish-Americans,* pp. 26–27.

49. Chávez, p. 270.

50. *Los Angeles Herald Examiner,* 8 October 1978, 24 July 1983.

51. Lorenzo Middleton, "Colleges Urged to Alter Tests, Grading for Benefit of Minority Group Students: A Ford Foundation Commission Endorses a System to Admit Students Based on Potential," *Chronicle of Higher Education* 23 (3 February 1982):1,10.

52. *La Red/The Net* (Ann Arbor, Mich.), June 1982; see also *Los Angeles Times,* 1 August 1983; and Tom Mathews with Diane Camper, "The Hard Cases Coming," *Newsweek,* 10 July 1978, p. 32.

53. *Arizona Republic* (Phoenix), 5 January 1975; and Shockley, pp. 218–19.

54. *La opinión* (Los Angeles), 21 August 1983; and *Los Angeles Times,* 24 July 1983; also resolutions against the violence and intervention in Central America were issued by the Association of Mexican American Educators (14 November 1981), the California Association for Bilingual Education (12 March 1982), and the National Association for Chicano Studies (25–27 March 1982).

55. Quoted in Shockley, p. 226.

56. *Arizona Republic,* 25 July 1978; Grace Halsell, *The Illegals,* John L. Hochmann Books (New York: Stein & Day, 1978), pp. 211–12; and George W. Grayson, *The Politics of Mexican Oil,* Pitt Latin American Series (Pittsburgh, Pa.: University of Pittsburgh Press, 1980), p. 161.

57. See Griffin Smith, Jr., "The Mexican Americans: A People on the Move," *National Geographic,* June 1980, pp. 794–96; and Kurt Anderson, "'The New Ellis Island': Immigrants from All Over Change the Beat, Bop and Character of Los Angeles," *Time,* 13 June 1983, pp. 22–24.

58. Wilmot Robertson, *The Dispossessed Majority,* 2nd rev. ed. (Cape Canaveral, Fla.: Howard Allen, 1976), p. 196; cf. letters to the editor in *Herald Examiner,* 19 September 1977, and in *UCLA Monthly,* March–April 1979.

59. *Herald Examiner,* 21–22 October 1977.

60. Grace Halsell, "Who Are the Real Illegals in California?" *Herald Examiner,* 26 July 1978; see also *Los Angeles Times,* 19 August 1979.

61. Shockley, p. 226; and Barrera, pp. 128, 103, 197.

62. Richard Reeves, "Mexican America: Frito Bandito Is Dead— Mexico's Oil Is Giving Chicanos New Power," *Esquire,* 2–16 January 1979, pp. 8, 10.

63. See Jonathan Kirsch, "Chicano Power: There Is One Inevitable Fact—by 1990 California Will Become America's First Third World State," *New West,* 11 September 1978, pp. 35–40.

64. Rendón, p. 309; and *Herald Examiner,* 20 May 1979.

65. *Young Socialist* (New York), July–August 1978; *Los Angeles Times,* 18 May 1979; and Grayson, p. 225.

66. Carey McWilliams, "A Way Out of the Energy Squeeze?" *Los Angeles Times,* 8 April 1979; cf. Grayson, p. 230.

67. Cheryl M. Fields, "Administration Moves to Ease Federal Anti-bias Regulations: Critics Charge That White House Efforts Will Weaken Affirmative Action," *Chronicle of Higher Education* 23 (2 September 1981):1, 21; and B. Nissen, "Mexico: Hard Times for an Oil Giant," *Newsweek,* 12 July 1982, p. 51.

# Bibliography

## Books

Acuña, Rodolfo. *Occupied America: A History of Chicanos.* 2nd ed. New York: Harper & Row, 1981.

――――. *Occupied America: The Chicano's Struggle toward Liberation.* San Francisco: Harper & Row, Canfield Press, 1972.

Alvarado Tezozomoc, Fernando. *Crónica Mexicayotl.* Translated from Nahuatl to Spanish by Adrián León. Publicaciones del Instituto de Historia, 1st ser., no. 10. Mexico City: Imprenta Universitaria for the Universidad Nacional Autónoma de México with the Instituto Nacional de Antropología e Historia, 1949.

Anaya, Rudolfo A. *Heart of Aztlan.* Berkeley, Calif.: Editorial Justa Publications, 1976.

Bailey, Thomas A. *A Diplomatic History of the American People.* 7th ed. New York: Meredith Publishing Co., Appleton-Century-Crofts, 1964.

Balderrama, Francisco E. *In Defense of La Raza: The Los Angeles Mexican Consulate and the Mexican Community, 1929 to 1936.* Tucson: University of Arizona Press, 1982.

Bancroft, Hubert Howe. *The Works of Hubert Howe Bancroft.* Vol. 34: *California Pastoral, 1769–1848.* San Francisco: History Co., 1888.

Barker, Eugene C. *Mexico and Texas, 1821–1835.* University of Texas Research Lectures on the Causes of the Texas Revolution. New York: Russell & Russell, 1928; reprint ed., New York: Russell & Russell, 1965.

Barnouw, Victor. *An Introduction to Anthropology.* Vol. 1: *Physical Anthropology and Archaeology.* The Dorsey Series in Anthropology. 3rd ed. Homewood, Ill.: Dorsey Press, 1978.

Barrera, Mario. *Race and Class in the Southwest: A Theory of Racial Inequality.* Notre Dame, Ind.: University of Notre Dame Press, 1979.

Barrios, Ernie. *Bibliografía de Aztlán: An Annotated Chicano Bibliography.* San Diego, Calif.: Centro de Estudios Chicanos Publications, San Diego State College, 1971.

Bauer, K[arl] Jack. *The Mexican War, 1846–1848.* The Wars of the United States. New York: Macmillan Co., 1974.

Bemis, Samuel Flagg. *A Diplomatic History of the United States.* 4th ed. New York: Henry Holt & Co., 1955.

181

Berkhofer, Robert F., Jr. *The White Man's Indian: Images of the American Indian from Columbus to the Present.* New York: Alfred A. Knopf, 1978.

Blawis, Patricia Bell. *Tijerina and the Land Grants: Mexican Americans in Struggle for Their Heritage.* New York: International Publishers Co., New World Paperbacks, 1971.

Bolton, Herbert E. *Coronado: Knight of Pueblos and Plains.* New York: McGraw-Hill Book Co., Whittlesey House, 1949; Albuquerque: University of New Mexico Press, 1949.

————. *The Spanish Borderlands: A Chronicle of Old Florida and the Southwest.* The Chronicles of America Series, vol. 23. Abraham Lincoln Edition. New Haven: Yale University Press, 1921.

————, ed. *Spanish Exploration in the Southwest: 1542–1706.* Original Narratives of Early American History. [New York]: Charles Scribner's Sons, 1908; reprint ed., New York: Barnes & Noble, 1969.

————. *Texas in the Middle Eighteenth Century: Studies in Spanish Colonial History and Administration.* University of California Publications in History, vol. 3. Berkeley: University of California Press, 1915.

Brack, Gene M. *Mexico Views Manifest Destiny, 1821–1846: An Essay on the Origins of the Mexican War.* Albuquerque: University of New Mexico Press, 1975.

Bustamante, Carlos María de. *El nuevo Bernal Díaz del Castillo, o sea historia de la invasión de los anglo-americanos en México.* Introduction by Salvador Noriega. Testimonios Mexicanos, Historiadores, no. 2. Mexico City: Secretaría de Educación Pública, 1949.

Camarillo, Albert. *Chicanos in a Changing Society: From Mexican Pueblos to American Barrios in Santa Barbara and Southern California, 1848–1930.* Cambridge: Harvard University Press, 1979.

Campa, Arthur L. *Hispanic Culture in the Southwest.* Norman: University of Oklahoma Press, 1979.

Cardoso, Lawrence A. *Mexican Emigration to the United States, 1897–1931: Socio-Economic Patterns.* Tucson: University of Arizona Press, 1980.

Castillo, Pedro, and Camarillo, Albert, eds. *Furia y Muerte: Los Bandidos Chicanos.* Aztlán Publications, Monograph no. 4. Los Angeles: Aztlán Publications, Chicano Studies Center, University of California, 1973.

Castro, Tony. *Chicano Power: The Emergence of Mexican America.* New York: Saturday Review Press/E. P. Dutton & Co., 1974.

Ceram, C. W. [Marek, Kurt W.]. *The First American: A Story of North American Archaeology.* Translated by Richard Winston and Clara Winston. New York: Harcourt Brace Jovanovich, 1971.

Chávez, Angélico, Fray. *My Penitente Land: Reflections on Spanish New Mexico.* Albuquerque: University of New Mexico Press, 1974.

Clendenen, Clarence C. *Blood on the Border: The United States Army and the Mexican Irregulars* [The Wars of the United States]. [New York]: Macmillan Co., 1969.

Cline, Howard F. *The United States and Mexico.* The American Foreign Policy Library. Cambridge: Harvard University Press, 1953.

Cockcroft, James D. *Intellectual Precursors of the Mexican Revolution, 1900–1913.* Latin American Monographs, no. 14. Austin: University of Texas Press, 1976.

*Códice Ramírez, manuscrito del siglo XVI intitulado: Relación del origen de los indios que habitaban esta Nueva España, según sus historias.* Edited by Manuel Orozco y Berra. Mexico City: Editorial Leyenda, 1944.

Córdova, Alfred C., and Judah, Charles B. *Octaviano Larrazolo: A Political Portrait.* Publications of the Division of Government Research, no. 32. Albuquerque: Division of Research, Department of Government, University of New Mexico, 1952.

Cortés, Hernán. *Hernan Cortes: Letters from Mexico.* Translated and edited by A[nthony] R. Pagden. Introduction by J. H. Elliott. New York: Grossman Publishers, Orion Press, 1971.

D'Anghera, Peter Martyr. *De Orbe Novo: The Eight Decades of Peter Martyr D'Anghera.* Translated by Francis Augustus MacNutt. Burt Franklin: Research & Source Works Series 642, Philosophy Monograph Series 44. 2 vols. 1912; reprint ed., New York: Lenox Hill, Burt Franklin, 1970.

Dawson, Joseph Martin. *Jose Antonio Navarro: Co-creator of Texas.* Waco, Tex.: Baylor University Press, 1969.

De la Garza, Rudolph O., Kruszewski, Z. Anthony, and Arciniega, Tomás A., comps. *Chicanos and Native Americans: The Territorial Minorities.* Englewood Cliffs, N.J.: Prentice-Hall, Spectrum Books, 1973.

De León, Arnoldo. *The Tejano Community, 1836–1900.* Contribution by Kenneth L. Stewart. Albuquerque: University of New Mexico Press, 1982.

———. *They Called Them Greasers: Anglo Attitudes toward Mexicans in Texas, 1821– 1900.* Austin: University of Texas Press, 1983.

Dobyns, Henry F. *Spanish Colonial Tucson: A Demographic History.* Tucson: University of Arizona Press, 1976.

Durán, Diego, Fray. *The Aztecs: The History of the Indies of New Spain.* Translated with Notes by Doris Heyden and Fernando Horcasitas. Introduction by Ignacio Bernal. New York: Orion Press, 1964.

Espinosa, Aurelio M. *España en Nuevo Méjico: Lecturas elementales sobre la historia de Nuevo Méjico y su tradición española.* Boston: Allyn & Bacon, Norwood Press, 1937.

Fanon, Frantz. *Black Skin, White Masks.* Translated by Charles Lam Markmann. New York: Grove Press, Evergreen Black Cat, 1968.

Faulk, Odie B. *Too Far North . . . Too Far South.* Great West and Indian Series, 35. Los Angeles: Westernlore Press, 1967.

Fernández, José Emilio. *Cuarenta años de legislador, o biografía del senador Casimiro Barela.* Trinidad, Colo.: n.p., 1911; reprint ed., The Chicano Heritage, New York: New York Times, Arno Press, 1976.

Forbes, Jack D. *Aztecas del Norte: The Chicanos of Aztlan*. Greenwich, Conn.: Fawcett Publications, Premier Books, 1973.

Galarza, Ernesto. *Merchants of Labor: The Mexican Bracero Story, an Account of the Managed Migration of Mexican Farm Workers in California, 1942–1960*. Preface by Ernest Gruening. Charlotte, N.C.: McNally & Loftin, 1964.

Gamio, Manuel, comp. *The Life Story of the Mexican Immigrant: Autobiographic Documents Collected by Manuel Gamio*. A new Introduction by Paul S. Taylor. Chicago: University of Chicago Press, 1931; reprint ed., New York: Dover Publications, 1971.

Garber, Paul Neff. *The Gadsden Treaty*. [Philadelphia: Press of the University of Pennsylvania, 1924]; reprint ed., Gloucester, Mass.: Peter Smith, 1959.

García, Juan Ramón. *Operation Wetback: The Mass Deportation of Mexican Undocumented Workers in 1954*. Contributions in Ethnic Studies, no. 2. Westport, Conn.: Greenwood Press, 1980.

García, Mario T. *Desert Immigrants: The Mexicans of El Paso, 1880–1920*. Yale Western Americana Series, 32. New Haven: Yale University Press, 1981.

Gibson, Charles. *Spain in America*. The New American Nation Series. New York: Harper & Row, Harper Torchbooks, University Library, 1966.

Gómez-Quiñones, Juan. *Development of the Mexican Working Class North of the Rio Bravo: Work and Culture among Laborers and Artisans, 1600–1900*. Popular Series, no. 2. Los Angeles: Chicano Studies Research Center Publications, University of California, 1982.

————. *Sembradores, Ricardo Flores Magón y el Partido Liberal Mexicano: A Eulogy and Critique*. Aztlán Publications, Monograph no. 5. Los Angeles: Aztlán Publications, Chicano Studies Center, University of California, 1973.

González, Nancie L. *The Spanish-Americans of New Mexico: A Heritage of Pride*. Rev. and enl. ed. Albuquerque: University of New Mexico Press, 1969.

Grayson, George W. *The Politics of Mexican Oil*. Pitt Latin American Series. Pittsburgh, Pa.: University of Pittsburgh Press, 1980.

Grebler, Leo, Moore, Joan W., and Guzmán, Ralph C. *The Mexican-American People: The Nation's Second Largest Minority*. New York: Macmillan Co., Free Press, 1970.

Griffith, Beatrice. *American Me*. Boston: Houghton Mifflin Co., 1948; reprint ed., Westport, Conn.: Williamhouse-Regency, Greenwood Press, 1973.

Griswold del Castillo, Richard. *The Los Angeles Barrio, 1850–1890: A Social History*. Berkeley and Los Angeles: University of California Press, 1979.

Halsell, Grace. *The Illegals*. John L. Hochmann Books. New York: Stein & Day, 1978.

Haring, C[larence] H. *The Spanish Empire in America*. New York: Harcourt, Brace & World, Harbinger Books, 1963.

Hernández, Luis F. *Aztlan: The Southwest and Its People*. Rochelle Park, N.J.: Hayden Book Co., 1975.

Hoffman, Abraham. *Unwanted Mexican Americans in the Great Depression: Repatriation*

*Pressures, 1929–1939.* Foreword by Julián Nava. Tucson: University of Arizona Press, 1974.

Hutchinson, C[ecil] Alan. *Frontier Settlement in Mexican California: The Híjar-Padrés Colony, and Its Origins, 1769–1835.* Yale Western Americana Series, 21. New Haven: Yale University Press, 1969.

Jackson, Helen [Hunt]. *Ramona: A Story.* N.p.: Roberts Bros., 1884; reprint ed., Boston: Little, Brown, & Co., 1919.

*Joaquin Murieta, the Brigand Chief of California: A Complete History of His Life from the Age of Sixteen to the Time of His Capture and Death in 1853.* Supplementary Notes by Raymond F. Wood. Americana Reprints, no. 1. San Francisco: Grabhorn Press, 1932; reprint ed., Fresno, Calif.: Valley Publishers, 1969.

Jones, Oakah L., Jr. *Los Paisanos: Spanish Settlers on the Northern Frontier of New Spain.* Norman: University of Oklahoma Press, 1979.

Katz, Friedrich. *The Secret War in Mexico: Europe, the United States and the Mexican Revolution.* Portions translated by Loren Goldner. Chicago: University of Chicago Press, 1981.

Kibbe, Pauline R. *Latin Americans in Texas.* Inter-Americana Studies 3. Albuquerque: University of New Mexico Press for the School of Inter-American Affairs, 1946.

Kohn, Hans. *The Idea of Nationalism: A Study in Its Origins and Background.* New York: Macmillan Co., Paperbacks, 1961.

La Farge, Oliver. *Behind the Mountains.* Boston: Houghton Mifflin Co., Riverside Press, 1956.

Lamar, Howard Roberts. *The Far Southwest, 1846–1912: A Territorial History.* Yale Western Americana Series, 12. New Haven: Yale University Press, 1966.

Larralde, Carlos. *Mexican-American: Movements and Leaders.* Los Alamitos, Calif.: Hwong Publishing Co., 1976.

Larson, Robert W. *New Mexico's Quest for Statehood, 1846–1912.* Albuquerque: University of New Mexico Press, 1968.

Leakey, Richard E. *The Making of Mankind.* New York: E. P. Dutton, 1981.

Levy, Jacques E. *Cesar Chavez: Autobiography of La Causa.* New York: W. W. Norton & Co., 1975.

Liss, Sheldon B. *A Century of Disagreement: The Chamizal Conflict, 1864–1964.* Washington, D.C.: University Press and Latin American Institute, 1965.

López y Rivas, Gilberto. *Los chicanos: Una minoría nacional explotada.* Temas de Actualidad. 3rd ed. Mexico City: Editorial Nuestro Tiempo, 1979.

Lummis, Charles F. *The Land of Poco Tiempo.* [New York]: Charles Scribner's Sons, 1893; reprint ed., Albuquerque: University of New Mexico Press, 1952.

Machado, Manuel A., Jr. *Listen Chicano! An Informal History of the Mexican-American.* Foreword by Barry M. Goldwater. Chicago: Nelson Hall, 1978.

McKittrick, Myrtle M. *Vallejo: Son of California.* Portland, Ore.: Binfords & Mort, 1944.

McWilliams, Carey. *North from Mexico: The Spanish-Speaking People of the United States.*

Philadelphia: J. B. Lippincott Co., 1949; reprint ed., New York: Greenwood Press, 1968.

Madsen, William. *Mexican-Americans of South Texas*. Case Studies in Cultural Anthropology. New York: Holt Rinehart & Winston, 1964.

Matthiessen, Peter. *Sal Si Puedes: Cesar Chavez and the New American Revolution*. Rev. ed. New York: Random House, 1973.

Mecham, J[ohn] Lloyd. *The United States and Inter-American Security, 1889–1960*. Austin: University of Texas Press for the Institute of Latin American Studies, 1961.

Meier, Matt S., and Rivera, Feliciano. *The Chicanos: A History of Mexican Americans*. American Century Series. New York: Farrar, Straus & Giroux, Hill & Wang, 1972.

Meinig, D[onald] W[illiam]. *Imperial Texas: An Interpretive Essay in Cultural Geography*. Introduction by Lorrin Kennamer. Austin: University of Texas Press, 1969.

———. *Southwest: Three Peoples in Geographical Change, 1600–1970*. New York: Oxford University Press, 1971.

Memmi, Albert. *The Colonizer and the Colonized*. Translated by Howard Greenfeld. Introduction by Jean-Paul Sartre. Boston: Beacon Press, 1967.

Méndez M., Miguel. *Peregrinos de Aztlán: Literatura chicana (novela)*. Tucson, Ariz.: Editorial Peregrinos, 1974.

Merk, Frederick. *Manifest Destiny and Mission in American History: A Reinterpretation*. New York: Alfred A. Knopf, Borzoi Books, 1963.

Meyer, Michael C., and Sherman, William L. *The Course of Mexican History*. 2nd ed. New York: Oxford University Press, 1983.

Monaghan, Jay. *Chile, Peru, and the California Gold Rush of 1849*. Berkeley and Los Angeles: University of California Press, 1973.

Moore, Joan W.; with García, Robert; García, Carlos; Cerda, Luis; and Valencia, Frank. *Homeboys: Gangs, Drugs, and Prison in the Barrios of Los Angeles*. Philadelphia: Temple University Press, 1978.

Moorhead, Max L. *The Presidio: Bastion of the Spanish Borderlands*. Norman: University of Oklahoma Press, 1975.

Morín, Raúl. *Among the Valiant: Mexican-Americans in WW II and Korea*. Introduction by Lyndon B. Johnson. Alhambra, Calif.: Borden Publishing Co., 1966.

Murguía, Edward. *Assimilation, Colonialism and the Mexican American People*. Mexican American Monograph Series, no. 1. Austin: Center for Mexican American Studies, University of Texas, 1975.

Nabokov, Peter. *Tijerina and the Courthouse Raid*. Albuquerque: University of New Mexico Press, 1969.

Nance, Joseph Milton. *After San Jacinto: The Texas-Mexican Frontier, 1836–1841*. Austin: University of Texas Press, 1963.

Needler, Martin C. *The United States and the Latin American Revolution*. UCLA Latin American Studies, vol. 38. Rev. ed. Los Angeles: UCLA Latin American Center Publications, University of California, 1977.

Niggli, Josephina. *Mexican Folk Plays*. Edited with an Introduction by Frederick H. Koch. Chapel Hill: University of North Carolina Press, 1938; reprint ed., The Chicano Heritage, New York: New York Times, Arno Press, 1976.

Nostrand, Richard L. *Los chicanos: Geografía histórica regional*. Translated from English to Spanish by Roberto Gómez Ciriza. Mexico City: Sep/setentas, 1976.

Núñez Cabeza de Vaca, Alvar. *Adventures in the Unknown Interior of America*. Translated by Cyclone Covey. New York: Crowell-Collier Publishing Co., Collier Books, 1961; reprint ed., Albuquerque: University of New Mexico Press, 1983.

Ord, Angustias de la Guerra. *Occurrences in Hispanic California*. Translated and edited by Francis Price and William H. Ellison. Washington, D.C.: Academy of American Franciscan History, 1956.

Ortega, Joaquín. *New Mexico's Opportunity: A Message to My Fellow New Mexicans*. Albuquerque: University of New Mexico Press, 1942.

Ortiz, Roxanne Dunbar. *Roots of Resistance: Land Tenure in New Mexico, 1680–1980*. [Monograph no. 10]. Los Angeles: Chicano Studies Research Center Publications and American Indian Studies Center, University of California, 1980.

Otero, Miguel Antonio. *My Life on the Frontier*. Vol. 1: *1864–1882, Incidents and Characters of the Period When Kansas, Colorado, and New Mexico Were Passing through the Last of Their Wild and Romantic Years*. New York: Press of the Pioneers, 1935.

———. *My Life on the Frontier*. Vol. 2: *1882–1897, Death Knell of a Territory and Birth of a State*. Foreword by George P. Hammond. Albuquerque: University of New Mexico Press, 1939.

———. *My Nine Years as Governor of the Territory of New Mexico, 1897–1906*. Foreword by Marion Dargan. Albuquerque: University of New Mexico Press, 1940.

Otero-Warren, Nina. See Warren, Nina Otero-.

Peixotto, Ernest. *Our Hispanic Southwest*. New York: Charles Scribner's Sons, 1916.

Peña, Enrique de la. *With Santa Anna in Texas: A Personal Narrative of the Revolution*. Translated and edited by Carmen Perry. Introduction by Llerena Friend. College Station: Texas A&M University Press, 1975.

Peñalosa, Fernando. *Chicano Sociolinguistics: A Brief Introduction*. Series in Sociolinguistics. Rowley, Mass.: Newbury House Publishers, 1980.

Perales, Alonso S. *Are We Good Neighbors?* San Antonio: Artes Graficas, 1948; reprint ed., The Mexican American, New York: New York Times, Arno Press, 1974.

Pérez de Villagrá, Gaspar. *A History of New Mexico*. Translated by Gilberto Espinosa. Rio Grande Classics. [Los Angeles: Quivira Society], 1933; reprint ed., Chicago: Rio Grande Press, 1962.

Perrigo, Lynn I. *Our Spanish Southwest*. Dallas: Banks Upshaw & Co., 1960.

Pettit, Arthur G. *Images of the Mexican American in Fiction and Film*. Edited with an Afterword by Dennis E. Showalter. College Station: Texas A&M University Press, 1980.

Pico, Pío. *Don Pío Pico's Historical Narrative*. Translated by Arthur P. Botello, Edited with an Introduction by Martin Cole and Henry Welcome. Glendale, Calif.: Arthur H. Clark Co., 1973.

Pino, Pedro Bautista, Barreiro, Antonio, and Escudero, José Agustín de. *Three New Mexico Chronicles: The "Exposición" of Don Pedro Bautista Pino, 1812; the "Ojeada" of Lic. Antonio Barreiro, 1832; and the Additions by Don José Agustín de Escudero, 1849.* Translated with an Introduction and Notes by H. Bailey Carroll and J. Villasana Haggard. Quivira Society Publications, vol. ll. Albuquerque: Quivira Society, 1942; reprint ed., New York: Arno Press, 1967.

Pitt, Leonard. *The Decline of the Californios: A Social History of the Spanish-Speaking Californians, 1846–1890.* Berkeley and Los Angeles: University of California Press, 1966.

Pletcher, David M. *The Diplomacy of Annexation: Texas, Oregon, and the Mexican War.* Columbia: University of Missouri Press, 1973.

Quirk, Robert E. *An Affair of Honor: Woodrow Wilson and the Occupation of Veracruz.* The Norton Library. New York: W. W. Norton & Co., 1962.

Raat, W[illiam] Dirk. *Revoltosos: Mexico's Rebels in the United States, 1903–1923.* College Station: Texas A&M University Press, 1981.

Reid, John T. *Spanish American Images of the United States, 1790–1960.* A University of Florida Book. Gainesville: University Presses of Florida, 1977.

Rendón, Armando B. *Chicano Manifesto.* New York: Macmillan Co., 1971.

Richardson, Rupert Norval, and Rister, Carl Coke. *The Greater Southwest: The Economic, Social, and Cultural Development of Kansas, Oklahoma, Texas, Utah, Colorado, Nevada, New Mexico, Arizona, and California from the Spanish Conquest to the Twentieth Century.* Glendale, Calif.: Arthur H. Clark Co., 1934.

Robertson, Wilmot. *The Dispossessed Majority.* 2nd rev. ed. Cape Canaveral, Fla.: Howard Allen, 1976.

Robinson, Cecil. *Mexico and the Hispanic Southwest in American Literature.* Rev. from *With the Ears of Strangers.* Tucson: University of Arizona Press, 1977.

Robinson, W[illiam] W[ilcox]. *Land in California: The Story of Mission Lands, Ranchos, Squatters, Mining Claims, Railroad Grants, Land Scrip, Homesteads.* Chronicles of California. Berkeley and Los Angeles: University of California Press, 1948.

Roche, James Jeffrey. *The Story of the Filibusters: To Which Is Added the Life of Colonel David Crockett.* The Adventure Series. London: T. Fisher Unwin, 1891.

Rodríguez, Richard. *Hunger of Memory: The Education of Richard Rodriguez, an Autobiography.* Bantam Windstone Books. New York: Bantam Books, 1983.

Rolle, Andrew F. *California: A History.* 2nd ed. New York: Thomas Y. Crowell Co., 1969.

Romo, Ricardo. *East Los Angeles: History of a Barrio.* Austin: University of Texas Press, 1983.

Rosenbaum, Robert J. *Mexicano Resistance in the Southwest: "The Sacred Right of Self-Preservation."* The Dan Danciger Publication Series. Austin: University of Texas Press, 1981.

Royce, Josiah. *California: From the Conquest in 1846 to the Second Vigilance Committee in*

*San Francisco, a Study of American Character*. Introduction by Robert Glass Cleland. Western Americana. New York: Alfred A. Knopf, Borzoi Books, 1948.

Ruiz, Ramón Eduardo. *Cuba: The Making of a Revolution*. The Norton Library. New York: W. W. Norton & Co., 1970.

Sánchez, George I. *Forgotten People: A Study of New Mexicans*. Albuquerque: University of New Mexico Press, 1940.

Sánchez, Nellie Van de Grift. *Spanish Arcadia*. California. Los Angeles: Powell Publishing Co., 1929.

Sanford, Trent Elwood. *The Architecture of the Southwest: Indian, Spanish, American*. New York: W. W. Norton & Co., 1950.

Santa-Anna, Antonio López de; Martínez Caro, Ramón; Filisola, Vicente; Urrea, José; and Tornel, José María. *The Mexican Side of the Texan Revolution, 1836: By the Chief Mexican Participants*. Translated with Notes by Carlos E. Castañeda. Dallas: P. L. Turner Co., 1928; reprint ed., The Chicano Heritage, New York: New York Times, Arno Press, 1976.

Santillán, Richard. *La Raza Unida*. Chicano Politics. Los Angeles: Tlaquilo Publications, 1973.

Sauer, Carl [Ortwin], and Brand, Donald. *Aztatlán: Prehistoric Mexican Frontier on the Pacific Coast*. Ibero-Americana, no. 1. Berkeley: University of California Press, 1932.

Sauer, Carl Ortwin. *Sixteenth Century North America: The Land and the People as Seen by the Europeans*. Berkeley and Los Angeles: University of California Press, 1971.

Schmitt, Karl M. *Mexico and the United States, 1821–1973: Conflict and Coexistence*. America and the World. New York: John Wiley & Sons, 1974.

Shockley, John Staples. *Chicano Revolt in a Texas Town*. Notre Dame, Ind.: University of Notre Dame Press, 1974.

Simmons, Merle E. *The Mexican Corrido as a Source for Interpretive Study of Modern Mexico (1870–1950)*. Indiana University Publications, Humanities Series, no. 38. Bloomington: Indiana University Press, 1957; reprint ed., New York: Kraus Reprint Co., 1969.

Smith, Henry Nash. *Virgin Land: The American West as Symbol and Myth*. Cambridge: Harvard University Press, 1950.

Sonnichsen, C[harles] L[eland]. *The El Paso Salt War {1877}*. El Paso: Carl Hertzog and the Texas Western Press, 1961.

Spicer, Edward H. *Cycles of Conquest: The Impact of Spain, Mexico, and the United States on the Indians of the Southwest, 1533–1960*. Tucson: University of Arizona Press, 1962.

Sturtevant, William C., gen. ed. *Handbook of North American Indians*. 20 vols. Washington, D.C.: Smithsonian Institution, 1978–     Vol. 9: *Southwest*. Edited by Alfonso Ortiz.

Swadesh, Frances Leon. *Los Primeros Pobladores: Hispanic Americans of the Ute Frontier*. Notre Dame, Ind.: University of Notre Dame Press, 1974.

Taylor, Paul Schuster. *An American-Mexican Frontier: Nueces County, Texas*. [Chapel

Hill]: University of North Carolina Press, 1934; reprint ed., New York: Atheneum Publishers, Russell & Russell, 1971.

Tello, Antonio, Fray. *Crónica miscelánea de la sancta provincia de Xalisco: Libro segundo.* Instituto Jalisciense de Antropología e Historia, Serie de Historia, no. 9, vol. 1. Guadalajara: Gobierno del Estado de Jalisco for the Universidad de Guadalajara, [1968].

Tijerina, Reies López. *Mi lucha por la tierra.* Prologue by Jorge A. Bustamante. Vida y Pensamiento de México. Mexico City: Fondo de Cultura Económica, 1978.

*El Tratado de Guadalupe Hidalgo, 1848/Treaty of Guadalupe Hidalgo, 1848: A Facsimile Reproduction of the Mexican Instrument of Ratification and Related Documents.* Sacramento, Calif.: Telefact Foundation with California State Department of Education, 1968.

Tuck, Ruth D. *Not with the Fist: Mexican-Americans in a Southwest City.* Foreword by Ignacio L. López. New York: Harcourt, Brace & Co., 1946.

Valdez, Luis, and Steiner, Stan, eds. *Aztlan: An Anthology of Mexican American Literature.* Marc Corporation Books. New York: Alfred A. Knopf, 1972.

Vigil, James Diego. *From Indians to Chicanos: A Sociocultural History.* St. Louis, Mo.: C. V. Mosby Co., 1980.

Vigil, Maurilio E. *Los Patrones: Profiles of Hispanic Political Leaders in New Mexico History.* Washington, D.C.: University Press of America, 1980.

Villarreal, José Antonio. *Pocho.* Garden City, N.Y.: Doubleday & Co., Anchor Books, 1970.

Wagoner, Jay J. *Early Arizona: Prehistory to Civil War.* Tucson: University of Arizona Press, 1975.

Warren, Nina Otero-. *Old Spain in Our Southwest.* New York: Harcourt, Brace & Co., 1936; reprint ed., Chicago: Rio Grande Press, 1962.

Watkins, T. H. *California: An Illustrated History.* The Great West Series. New York: Imprint Society, Weathervane Books, 1973.

Wauchope, Robert, gen. ed. *Handbook of Middle American Indians.* 16 vols. Austin: University of Texas Press, 1964–76. Vol. 14: *Guide to Ethnohistorical Sources: Part III.* Edited by Howard F. Cline.

Weber, David J., ed. *Foreigners in Their Native Land: Historical Roots of the Mexican Americans.* Foreword by Ramón Eduardo Ruíz. Albuquerque: University of New Mexico Press, 1973.

————. *The Mexican Frontier, 1821–1846: The American Southwest under Mexico.* Histories of the American Frontier. Albuquerque: University of New Mexico Press, 1982.

Wolf, Eric R. *Sons of the Shaking Earth.* Chicago: University of Chicago Press, Phoenix Books, 1959.

Wood, Bryce. *The Making of the Good Neighbor Policy.* New York: Columbia University Press, 1961.

## Selections from Larger Works

Barrera, Mario, Muñoz, Carlos, and Ornelas, Charles. "The Barrio as an Internal Colony." In *La Causa Política: A Chicano Politics Reader,* pp. 281–301. Edited by F. Chris García. Notre Dame, Ind.: University of Notre Dame Press, 1974.

Campa, Arthur L. "Spanish Folk-Poetry in New Mexico." In *Hispanic Folklore Studies of Arthur L. Campa.* Introduction by Carlos E. Cortés. The Chicano Heritage. New York: New York Times, Arno Press, 1976.

———. "The Spanish Folksong in the Southwest." In *Hispanic Folklore Studies of Arthur L. Campa.* Introduction by Carlos E. Cortés. The Chicano Heritage. New York : New York Times, Arno Press, 1976.

———. "Spanish Religious Folktheatre in the Southwest." In *Hispanic Folklore Studies of Arthur L. Campa.* Introduction by Carlos E. Cortés. The Chicano Heritage. New York: New York Times, Arno Press, 1976.

Carroll, Bailey, and Haggard, J. Villasana, trans. Introduction to *Three New Mexico Chronicles: The "Exposición" of Don Pedro Bautista Pino, 1812; the "Ojeada" of Lic. Antonio Barreiro, 1832; and the Additions by Don José Agustín de Escudero, 1849.* Quivira Society Publications, vol. ll. Albuquerque: Quivira Society, 1942; reprint ed., New York: Arno Press, 1967.

Castañeda de Nájera, Pedro de. "Narrative of the Expedition to Cibola, Undertaken in 1540, in Which Are Described All Those Settlements, Ceremonies, and Customs." In *Narratives of the Coronado Expedition, 1540–42,* pp. 191–283. Edited by George P. Hammond and Agapito Rey. Albuquerque: University of New Mexico Press, 1940; reprint ed., New York: AMS Press, 1977.

Chávez, Cecilio. "The Emigrant's Farewell." In *Puro Mexicano,* pp. 222–24. Edited by J. Frank Dobie. Texas Folklore Society Publications, no. 12. Dallas: Southern Methodist University Press, 1935.

Colquhoun, James. "The Early History of the Clifton-Morenci District." In *The Mexican Experience in Arizona.* Introduction by Carlos E. Cortés. The Chicano Heritage. New York: New York Times, Arno Press, 1976.

"Constitution of the League of United Latin-American Citizens, 1929, Article II." In *An American-Mexican Frontier: Nueces County, Texas,* pp. 243–44. By Paul Schuster Taylor. [Chapel Hill]: University of North Carolina Press, 1934; reprint ed., New York: Atheneum Publishers, Russell & Russell, 1971.

"Corrido de Juaquín Murrieta." In *Literatura Chicana: Texto y Contexto/Chicano Literature: Text and Context,* pp. 65–67. Edited by Antonia Castañeda Shular, Tomás Ybarra-Frausto, and Joseph Sommers, Englewood Cliffs, N.J.: Prentice-Hall, 1972.

Cortés, Hernando. "Instrucciones dadas por Hernando Cortés a Francisco Cortés su lugartiniente en la Villa de Colima." In *Colección de documentos inéditos relativos al descubrimiento, conquista y organización de las antiguas posesiones españolas de América y Oceanía sacados de los archivos del reino y muy especialmente del de Indias.* 42 vols.,

26:149–59. Edited by Joaquín F. Pacheco, Francisco de Cárdenas and Luis Torres de Mendoza. 1864–84; reprint ed., Vaduz, Liechtenstein: Kraus Reprint, 1964–66.

Cortina, Juan Nepomuceno. "Suffer the Death of Martyrs: Proclamation of Juan Nepomuceno Cortina." In *Aztlan: An Anthology of Mexican American Literature*, pp. 111–16. Edited by Luis Valdez and Stan Steiner. Marc Corporation Books. New York: Alfred A. Knopf, 1972.

"Description of the Most Notable Characteristics of the Settlement of El Paso del Río del Norte, as Given by One of Its Citizens, after Seven Years' Residence There." In *Historical Documents Relating to New Mexico, Nueva Vizcaya, and Approaches Thereto, to 1773.* 3 vols., 3:506–9. Edited with an Introduction by Charles Wilson Hackett. Papers of the Division of Historical Research. Washington, D.C.: Carnegie Institution of Washington, 1923–37.

Corwin, Arthur F. "Early Mexican Labor Migration: A Frontier Sketch, 1848–1900." In *Immigrants—and Immigrants: Perspectives on Mexican Labor Migration to the United States*, pp. 25–37. Edited by Arthur F. Corwin. Contributions in Economics and Economic History, no. 17. Westport, Conn.: Greenwood Press, 1978.

————. "¿Quién Sabe? Mexican Migration Statistics." In *Immigrants—and Immigrants: Perspectives on Mexican Labor Migration to the United States*, pp. 108–35. Edited by Arthur F. Corwin. Contributions in Economics and Economic History, no. 17. Westport, Conn.: Greenwood Press, 1978.

Dunham, Lowell, trans. Introduction to *The Aztecs: People of the Sun*, by Alfonso Caso. The Civilization of the American Indian Series. Norman: University of Oklahoma Press, 1958.

Ellis, Florence Hawley. "What Utaztecan [*sic*] Ethnology Suggests of Utaztecan Prehistory." In *Utaztekan Prehistory*, pp. 53–105. Edited by Earl H. Swanson, Jr. Occasional Papers of the Idaho State University Museum, no. 22. Pocatello: Idaho State University, 1968.

Farrigno, L.; Garza, Augustín S.; Flores, Manuel; Ramos, B., Jr.; Gonzales, A.; Saenz, A. A.; Cisneros, E.; and Alamraz, A. C. "Plan of San Diego, Texas, State of Texas, January 6th, 1915." In *Literatura Chicana: Texto y Contexto/ Chicano Literature: Text and Context*, pp. 81–83. Edited by Antonia Castañeda Shular, Tomás Ybarra-Frausto, and Joseph Sommers. Englewood Cliffs, N.J.: Prentice-Hall, 1972.

"First Census of Los Angeles, Peninsula of California." In *Foreigners in Their Native Land: Historical Roots of the Mexican Americans*, pp. 33–35. Edited by David J. Weber. Foreword by Ramón Eduardo Ruíz. Albuquerque: University of New Mexico Press, 1973.

Flores Magón, Ricardo. "Los levantamientos en Tejas." In *Sembradores, Ricardo Flores Magón y el Partido Liberal Mexicano: A Eulogy and Critique*, pp. 132–35. By Juan Gómez-Quiñones. Aztlán Publications, Monograph no. 5. Los Angeles: Aztlán Publications, Chicano Studies Center, University of California, 1973.

————. "El pueblo mexicano es apto para el comunismo." In *Sembradores, Ricardo*

*Flores Magón y el Partido Liberal Mexicano: A Eulogy and Critique,* pp. 118–19.
By Juan Gómez-Quiñones. Aztlán Publications, Monograph no. 5. Los Angeles:
Aztlán Publications, Chicano Studies Center, University of California, 1973.

García, F. Chris. "Manitos and Chicanos in New Mexico Politics." In *La Causa
Política: A Chicano Politics Reader,* pp. 271–80. Edited by F. Chris García. Notre
Dame, Ind.: University of Notre Dame Press, 1974.

Goldfinch, Charles W. "Juan N. Cortina 1824–1892: A Re-appraisal." In *Juan N.
Cortina: Two Interpretations.* The Mexican American. New York: New York
Times, Arno Press, 1974.

González, Henry B. "An Attack on Chicano Militants." In *A Documentary History of
the Mexican Americans,* pp. 358–62. Edited by Wayne Moquin with Charles
Van Doren. Introduction by Feliciano Rivera. New York: Praeger Publishers,
1971.

Goss, James A. "Culture-Historical Influence from Utaztekan Linguistic Evidence."
In *Utaztekan Prehistory,* pp. 1–42. Edited by Earl H. Swanson, Jr. Occasional
Papers of the Idaho State University Museum, no. 22. Pocatello: Idaho State
University, 1968.

Harte, Bret. "The Devotion of Enríquez." In *The Chicano: From Caricature to Self-
Portrait,* pp. 48–71. Edited with an Introduction by Edward Simmen. New
York: New American Library, Mentor Books, 1971.

Hernández, Juan José. "Alcalde of Goliad to Governor of the State, no. 21, 26 March
1825." In *The Empresario: Don Martín de León,* pp. 96–97. By A[rthur] B. J.
Hammett. Waco, Tex.: Texian Press, 1973.

Keller, Mrs. Charles. "Veteran's Wife Returning to Edinburg Wants Town Returned
to American." In *Are We Good Neighbors?,* pp. 250–51. By Alonso S. Perales.
San Antonio: Artes Graficas, 1948; reprint ed., the Mexican American, New
York: New York Times, Arno Press, 1974.

Kino, Eusebio Francisco. "Report and Relation of the New Conversions, by Eusebio
Francisco Kino, 1710." In *Spanish Exploration in the Southwest: 1542–1706,* pp.
433–63. Edited by Herbert E. Bolton. Original Narratives of Early American
History. [New York]: Charles Scribner's Sons, 1908; reprint ed., New York:
Barnes & Noble, 1969.

López, Ignacio L. Foreword to *Not with the Fist: Mexican-Americans in a Southwest City,*
by Ruth D. Tuck. New York: Harcourt, Brace & Co., 1946.

Niza, Marcos de, Fray. "Relación. In *Colección de documentos inéditos relativos al descubrimiento, conquista y colonización de las posesiones españolas en América y Oceania
sacados en su major parte del Real Archivo de Indias.* 42 vols., 3:329–50. Edited by
Joaquín F. Pacheco, Francisco de Cárdenas, and Luis Torres de Mendoza. 1864–
84; reprint ed., Vaduz, Liechtenstein: Kraus Reprint, 1964–66.

———. "Report." In *Narratives of the Coronado Expedition, 1540–1542,* pp. 63–82.
Edited by George P. Hammond and Agapito Rey. Albuquerque: University of
New Mexico Press, 1940; reprint ed., New York: AMS Press, 1977.

Otero, Miguel Antonio. "Telegram to *New York World,* 26 February 1898." In *My*

*Nine Years as Governor of the Territory of New Mexico, 1897–1906,* p. 36. By Miguel Antonio Otero. Foreword by Marion Dargan. Albuquerque: University of New Mexico Press, 1940.

————."Telegram to R. A. Alger, Secretary of War." In *My Nine Years as Governor of the Territory of New Mexico, 1897–1906,* p. 38. By Miguel Antonio Otero. Foreword by Marion Dargan. Albuquerque: University of New Mexico Press, 1940.

"Pancho Villa." In *Literary Folklore of the Hispanic Southwest,* pp. 135–36. Compiled by Aurora Lucero-White Lea. San Antonio: Naylor Co., 1953.

Quevedo, Eduardo; Campos, Dan; Villa, Pete; Barraza, Louis; Ornelos, John; and Ruiz, Manuel. "Open Resolution Directed to the President of the United States and Executive Departments and Agencies, by National Hispanic and Mexican-American Organizations on Civil Disobedience and Riot Investigations." In "The History of Political Organizations among Mexican-Americans in Los Angeles Since the Second World War," pp. 63–65. By Kaye Lynn Briegel. Master's thesis, University of Southern California, 1967.

Rodríguez, Robert. "Letter to *Edinburg* (Tex.) *Valley Review.*" In *Are We Good Neighbors?,* p. 257. By Alonso S. Perales. San Antonio: Artes Graficas, 1948; reprint ed., The Mexican American, New York: New York Times, Arno Press, 1974.

[Rodríguez] Ordóñez de Montalvo, Garcí. "El ramo que de los cuatro libros de Amadís de Gaula sale llamado las sergas del muy esforzado caballero Esplandián, hijo del excelente rey Amadís de Gaula." In *Libros de caballerías,* pp. 403–561. Edited with a Foreword by Pascual de Gayangos. Biblioteca de Autores Españoles desde la Formación del Lenguaje Hasta Nuestros Días, vol. 40. Madrid: Ediciones Atlas, 1963.

Rosa, Luis de la, and Pizaña, Aniceto. "A nuestros compatriotas, los mexicanos en Texas." In *Mexican-American: Movements and Leaders,* p. 144. By Carlos Larralde. Los Alamitos, Calif.: Hwong Publishing Co., 1976.

"Los sediciosos." In *A Texas-Mexican Cancionero: Folksongs of the Lower Border,* pp. 71–73. Edited by Américo Paredes. Music in American Life. Urbana: University of Illinois Press, 1976.

Seguín, Juan Nepomuceno. "Personal Memoirs of John N. Seguín: From the Year 1834 to the Retreat of General Woll from the City of San Antonio, 1842." In *Northern Mexico on the Eve of the United States Invasion: Rare Imprints Concerning California, Arizona, New Mexico, and Texas, 1821–1846,* imprint no. 3. Edited with an Introduction by David J. Weber. The Chicano Heritage. New York: New York Times, Arno Press, 1976.

"The Spiritual Manifesto of Aztlán." In *Literatura Chicana: Texto y Contexto/Chicano Literature: Text and Context,* p. 84. Edited by Antonia Castañeda Shular, Tomás Ybarra-Frausto, and Joseph Sommers. Englewood Cliffs, N.J.: Prentice-Hall, 1972.

Steiner, Stan. "The Poet in the Boxing Ring." In *La Causa Política: A Chicano Politics*

*Reader,* pp. 322–30. Edited by F. Chris García. Notre Dame, Ind.: University of Notre Dame Press, 1974.

"Tiburcio Vasquez: An Interview with the Noted Bandit." In *Foreigners in Their Native Land: Historical Roots of the Mexican Americans,* pp. 227–28. Edited by David J. Weber. Foreword by Ramón Eduardo Ruiz. Albuquerque: University of New Mexico Press, 1973.

[Valdez, Luis.] "The Plan of Delano." In *Aztlan: An Anthology of Mexican American Literature,* pp. 197–201. Edited by Luis Valdez and Stan Steiner. Marc Corporation Books. New York: Alfred A. Knopf, 1972.

Vázquez de Coronado, Francisco. "Carta de Francisco Vázquez Coronado al Emperador, dándole cuenta de la espedición a la provincia de Quivira, y de la inexactitud de lo referido a Fr. Marcos de Niza, acerca de aquel país." In *Colección de documentos inéditos relativos al descubrimiento, conquista y colonización de las posesiones españolas en América y Oceanía sacados en su mayor parte del Real Archivo de Indias.* 42 vols., 3: 363–69. Edited by Joaquín F. Pacheco, Francisco de Cárdenas, and Luis Torres de Mendoza. 1864–84; reprint ed., Vaduz, Liechtenstein: Kraus Reprint, 1964–66.

———. "Letter of Coronado to the King, from the Province of Tiguex." In *Narratives of the Coronado Expedition, 1540–1542,* pp. 185–90. Edited by George P. Hammond and Agapito Rey. Albuquerque: University of New Mexico Press, 1940; reprint ed., New York: AMS Press, 1977.

Vinson, Curtis. "Race Issue Arouses Ire of Mexicans." In *Are We Good Neighbors?,* pp. 269–70. By Alonso S. Perales. San Antonio: Artes Graficas, 1948; reprint ed., The Mexican American, New York: New York Times, Arno Press, 1974.

Warren, Adelina Otero. "The Spell of New Mexico." In *A Documentary History of the Mexican Americans,* pp. 282–88. Edited by Wayne Moquin with Charles Van Doren. Introduction by Feliciano Rivera. New York: Praeger Publishers, 1971.

## Articles from Journals and Magazines

Almaraz, Felix D., Jr. "Carlos Eduardo Castañeda, Mexican-American Historian: The Formative Years, 1896–1927." *Pacific Historical Review* 42 (August 1973): 319–34.

Anderson, Kurt. "'The New Ellis Island': Immigrants from All Over Change the Beat, Bop and Character of Los Angeles." *Time,* 13 June 1983, pp. 18–25.

Belderrain, Francisca López de. "The Awakening of Paredon Blanco under a California Sun." *Historical Society of Southern California Annual* 14 (1928):65–79.

Clark, Harry. "Their Pride, Their Manners, and Their Voices: Sources of the Traditional Portrait of the Early Californians." *California Historical Quarterly* 53 (Spring 1974):71–82.

Corwin, Arthur F. "Mexican-American History: An Assessment." *Pacific Historical Review* 42 (August 1973):269–308.

Díaz Escobar, Félix. "The Spread of *Sinarquismo.*" *Nation,* 3 April 1943, p. 487.

Espinosa, Aurelio M. "Folk-Lore from Spain: The *Fiesta del Gallo* in Barbadillo." *Modern Philology* 20 (May 1923):425–34.

———. "New Mexican Spanish Folk-Lore." *Journal of American Folk-Lore* 29 (October–December 1916):505–46.

———. "The Tar-Baby Story." *Journal of American Folk-Lore* 43 (April–June 1930): 129–209.

Fields, Cheryl M. "Administration Moves to Ease Federal Anti-bias Regulations: Critics Charge That White House Efforts Will Weaken Affirmative Action." *Chronicle of Higher Education* 23 (2 September 1981):1, 21.

Gregory, Gladys. "The Chamizal Settlement: A View from El Paso." *Southwestern Studies* 1 (Summer 1963):3–52.

Gutiérrez, José Angel. "Aztlan: Chicano Revolt in the Winter Garden." *La Raza* 1, no. 4 [1971], n. pag.

Hager, William M. "The Plan of San Diego: Unrest on the Texas Border in 1915." *Arizona and the West* 5 (Winter 1963):327–36.

Hansen, Niles. "Commentary: The Hispano Homeland in 1900." *Annals of the Association of American Geographers* 71 (June 1981):280–81.

Hargis, Donald E. "Native Californians in the Constitutional Convention of 1849." *Historical Society of Southern California Quarterly* 36 (March 1954):3–13.

Harris, Helen Willits. "Almonte's Inspection of Texas in 1834." *Southwestern Historical Quarterly* 41 (January 1938):195–211.

Kirk, Betty. "Mexico's 'Social Justice' Party." *Nation,* 12 June 1943, pp. 827–31.

Kirsch, Jonathan. "Chicano Power: There Is One Inevitable Fact—By 1990 California Will Become America's First Third World State." *New West,* 11 September 1978, pp. 35–40.

Kuklick, Bruce. "Myth and Symbol in American Studies." *American Quarterly* 24 (October 1972):435–50.

López, Enrique Hank. "Back to Bachimba: A Hyphenated American Discovers That He Can't Go Home Again." *Horizon,* Winter 1967, pp. 80–83.

McGregor [pseud.?]. "Our Spanish-American Fellow Citizens." *Harper's Weekly,* 20 June 1914, pp. 6–8.

McLean, Malcolm D. "Tenoxtitlan: Dream Capital of Texas." *Southwestern Historical Quarterly* 70 (July 1966):23–43.

Mathews, Tom, with Camper, Diane. "The Hard Cases Coming." *Newsweek,* 10 July 1978, p. 32.

Middleton, Lorenzo. "Colleges Urged to Alter Tests, Grading for Benefit of Minority Group Students: A Ford Foundation Commission Endorses a System to Admit Students Based on Potential." *Chronicle of Higher Education* 23 (3 February 1982):1, 10.

Nissen, B. "Mexico: Hard Times for an Oil Giant." *Newsweek,* 12 July 1982, pp. 51–53.

Nostrand, Richard L. "Comment in Reply." *Annals of the Association of American Geographers* 71 (June 1981):282–83.

————. "The Hispanic-American Borderland: Delimitation of an American Culture Region." *Annals of the Association of American Geographers* 60 (December 1970): 638–61.

————. "The Hispano Homeland in 1900." *Annals of the Association of American Geographers* 70 (September 1980):382–96.

Pace, Anne. "Mexican Refugees in Arizona, 1910–1911." *Arizona and the West* 16 (Spring 1974):5–18.

Rechy, John. "El Paso del Norte." *Evergreen Review* 2 (Autumn 1958):127–40.

Reeves, Richard. "Mexican America: Frito Bandito Is Dead—Mexico's Oil Is Giving Chicanos New Power." *Esquire,* 2–16 January 1979, pp. 8, 10.

Riley, Carroll L. "Early Spanish-Indian Communication in the Greater Southwest." *New Mexico Historical Review* 46 (October 1971):285–314.

Sack, Robert D. "Human Territoriality: A Theory." *Annals of the Association of American Geographers* 73 (March 1983):55–74.

Sánchez, José María. "A Trip to Texas in 1828." Translated by Carlos E. Castañeda. *Southwestern Historical Quarterly* 29 (April 1926):249–88.

Sandos, James A. "The Plan of San Diego: War and Diplomacy on the Texas Border, 1915–1916." *Arizona and the West* 14 (Spring 1972):5–24.

Smith, Griffin, Jr. "The Mexican Americans: A People on the Move." *National Geographic,* June 1980, pp. 780–809.

Suárez, Mario. "El Hoyo." *Arizona Quarterly* 3 (Summer 1947): 112–15.

Tyler, Daniel. "Governor Armijo's Moment of Truth." *Journal of the West* 11 (April 1972):307–16.

Vallejo, Guadalupe. "Ranch and Mission Days in Alta California." *Century Magazine,* December 1890, pp. 183–92.

Walker, Henry Pickering. "Freighting from Guaymas to Tucson, 1850–1880." *Western Historical Quarterly* 1 (July 1970):291–304.

Wilcox, Seb. S. "Laredo During the Texas Republic." *Southwestern Historical Quarterly* 42 (October 1938):83–107.

Wollenberg, Charles. "Working on *El Traque:* The Pacific Electric Strike of 1903." *Pacific Historical Review* 42 (August 1973):358–69.

Yorba, Alfonso. "Old San Juan: Last Stronghold of Spanish California." *Historical Society of Southern California Quarterly* 17 (March 1935):7–13.

## Newspapers and Newsletters

*Albuquerque Journal,* 16 March 1979; 7 June 1980.

*Arizona Republic* (Phoenix), 5 January 1975; 25 July 1978.

*La bandera* (Brownsville, Tex.), 4 September 1863.

*El bejareño* (San Antonio), 7 February 1855.

*Belvedere Citizen* (East Los Angeles), 18 June 1943.

*El clamor público* (Los Angeles), 19, 26 June 1855; 9 February, 2 August 1956; 24 July, 4 August, 16 October 1858.

*El clarín mejicano* (Santa Fe), 10 August 1873.

*La crónica* (San Francisco), 1 June 1855.

*La crónica de Mora* (N. Mex.), 12 September 1889.

*El defensor del pueblo* (Albuquerque), 4 July 1891.

*Denver Post,* 11 September 1977.

*Las dos repúblicas* (Tucson, Ariz.), 22 July 1877.

*Eastside Journal* (East Los Angeles), 16 December 1942; 15 March 1944.

*La gaceta* (Santa Barbara, Calif.), 11 October 1879; 1 May 1880.

*El horizonte* (Corpus Christi, Tex.), 8, 19 November 1879.

*La Red/The Net* (Ann Arbor, Mich.), June 1982.

*Los Angeles Herald Examiner,* 19 September, 21–22 October 1977; 26 July, 8 October 1978; 20 May 1979; 24 July 1983.

*Los Angeles Times,* 7 June 1943; 8 April, 18 May, 19 August 1979; 24 July, 1 August 1983.

*El obrero* (Morenci, Ariz.), 4 July, 21, 28 November 1903.

*La opinión* (Los Angeles), 18 September 1926; 7 January 1933; 21 August 1983.

*La prensa* (Los Angeles), 3, 17, 24 January, 7, 14, 21, 28 February, 6, 13 March 1920.

*Regeneración* (Los Angeles), 11 February 1905.

*La república* (San Francisco), 7, 28 October 1882.

*Revista hispano-americana* (Los Angeles), 17 December 1892; 20 October 1894.

*San Antonio Express,* 9 March 1975; 3 October 1980.

*UCLA Monthly* (Los Angeles), March–April 1979.

*El valle del Bravo* (El Paso, Tex.), 25 May, 17 August 1889.

*La voz de Chile y el Nuevo Mundo* (San Francisco), 18 July 1867; 30 December 1882.

*La voz del pueblo* (East Las Vegas, N. Mex.), 26 March, 2, 23 April 1898; 7 January, 18, 25 March 1911; 11, 18 March 1916.

*La voz de México* (San Francisco), 12 January 1864.

*Young Socialist* (New York), July–August 1978.

## Theses and Dissertations

Briegel, Kaye Lynn. "The History of Political Organizations among Mexican-Americans in Los Angeles Since the Second World War." Master's thesis, University of Southern California, 1967.

Chaney, Homer Campbell, Jr. "The Mexican–United States War as Seen by Mexican Intellectuals, 1846–1956." Ph.D. dissertation, Stanford University, 1959.

Nostrand, Richard Lee. "The Hispanic-American Borderland: A Regional, Historical Geography." Ph.D. dissertation, University of California, Los Angeles, 1968.

Paredes, Raymund Arthur. "The Image of the Mexican in American Literature."
    Ph.D. dissertation, University of Texas at Austin, 1973.
Pitt, Leonard. "Submergence of the Mexican in California, 1846 to 1890: A History
    of Culture Conflict and Acculturation." Ph.D. dissertation, University of Cali-
    fornia, Los Angeles, 1958.
Reyes, Ignacio. "A Survey of the Problems Involved in the Americanization of the
    Mexican-American." Master's thesis, University of Southern California, 1957.
Samora, Julián. "Minority Leadership in a Bi-cultural Community." Ph.D. disserta-
    tion, Washington University, 1953.
Sheldon, Edgar Greer, Jr. "Political Conditions among Texas Mexicans along the
    Rio Grande." Master's thesis, University of Texas, 1946.
Simmons, Ozzie G. "Anglo Americans and Mexican Americans in South Texas: A
    Study in Dominant-Subordinate Group Relations," 2 vols. Ph.D. dissertation,
    Harvard University, 1952.

## Manuscripts

San Marino, Calif. Henry E. Huntington Library. MS HM 38235. Pío Pico to citi-
    zens of California, 31 August 1845.
San Marino, Calif. Henry E. Huntington Library. MS RI 2044. Archbishop Jean
    Baptiste Lamy, Pastoral Letter, 20 February 1884.

# Index